Founding Documents of America
DOCUMENTS DECODED

Titles in ABC-CLIO's Documents Decoded series

Presidential Campaigns: Documents Decoded
Daniel M. Shea and Brian M. Harward

Women's Rights: Documents Decoded
Aimee D. Shouse

The Death Penalty: Documents Decoded
Joseph A. Melusky and Keith A. Pesto

The Abolitionist Movement: Documents Decoded
Christopher Cameron

The Great Depression and New Deal: Documents Decoded
Mario R. DiNunzio

The Democratic Party: Documents Decoded
Douglas B. Harris and Lonce H. Bailey

The Republican Party: Documents Decoded
Douglas B. Harris and Lonce H. Bailey

1960s Counterculture: Documents Decoded
Jim Willis

The ABC-CLIO series ***Documents Decoded*** guides readers on a hunt for new secrets through an expertly curated selection of primary sources. Each book pairs key documents with in-depth analysis, all in an original and visually engaging side-by-side format. But *Documents Decoded* authors do more than just explain each source's context and significance—they give readers a front-row seat to their own investigation and interpretation of each essential document line-by-line.

Founding Documents of America
DOCUMENTS DECODED

John R. Vile

Documents Decoded

An Imprint of ABC-CLIO, LLC
Santa Barbara, California • Denver, Colorado

Copyright © 2015 by ABC-CLIO, LLC

All rights reserved. No part of this publication may be reproduced, stored in a retrieval system, or transmitted, in any form or by any means, electronic, mechanical, photocopying, recording, or otherwise, except for the inclusion of brief quotations in a review, without prior permission in writing from the publisher.

Library of Congress Cataloging-in-Publication Data

Founding documents of America : documents decoded / John R. Vile.
    pages cm. — (Documents decoded)
    Includes index.
    ISBN 978-1-4408-3928-3 (alk. paper)—ISBN 978-1-4408-3929-0 (ebook)   1. United States—Politics and government—1775–1783—Sources.   2. United States—Politics and government—1783–1809—Sources. 3. United States—Politics and government—To 1775—Sources.   I. Vile, John R., editor.
    E203.F675 2015
    973.3--dc23   2015011139

ISBN: 978-1-4408-3928-3
EISBN: 978-1-4408-3929-0

19 18 17 16 15   1 2 3 4 5

This book is also available on the World Wide Web as an eBook.
Visit www.abc-clio.com for details.

ABC-CLIO
An Imprint of ABC-CLIO, LLC

ABC-CLIO, LLC
130 Cremona Drive, P.O. Box 1911
Santa Barbara, California 93116-1911

This book is printed on acid-free paper ∞
Manufactured in the United States of America

Contents

Introduction, xiii

SECTION I. CONSTITUTIONAL ANTECEDENTS

The Law of the Land, 3
Magna Carta
1215

Against Common Right and Reason, 9
Sir Edward Coke's Dr. Bonham's Case
1610

A Civill Body Politick, 11
The Mayflower Compact
1620

No Man Be Compelled, 13
The Petition of Right
1628

"A Model of Christian Charity," 19
John Winthrop's Sermon
1630

An Orderly and Decent Government, 23
Fundamental Orders of Connecticut
1639

The Free Fruition of Such Liberties, 30
Massachusetts Body of Liberties
1641

The Peace, Safety, and Public Good of the People, 37
John Locke's Second Treatise of Government
1689

The Rights and Liberties of the Subject, 44
English Bill of Rights
1689

There Is No Such Thing as Slavery, 52
Samuel Sewall's *The Selling of Joseph: A Memorial*
1701

Liberty of Conscience, 58
Charter of Privileges Granted to the Inhabitants of Pennsylvania and Territories
October 28, 1701

Proclaim Liberty, 64
Liberty Bell Inscription
1751

Join, or Die, 65
Benjamin Franklin's Sketch
May 9, 1754

Mutual Defence and Security, 66
The Albany Plan of Union
July 10, 1754

SECTION II: THE REVOLUTIONARY AND CONFEDERAL PERIODS

Life, Liberty, and Property, 75
Declaration and Resolves of the First Continental Congress
October 14, 1774

So Void of Common Sense, 81
Washington Forbids Soldiers from Celebrating Guy Fawkes Day
November 5, 1775

'Tis Time to Part, 83
Thomas Paine's *Common Sense*
1776

Contents

Remember the Ladies, 89
Abigail and John Adams, Correspondence on Women's Issues
March–August 1776

Adopt Such Government, 94
Resolution of Second Continental Congress
May 10, 1776

Absolved from All Allegiance, 95
Richard Henry Lee's Resolutions
June 7, 1776

The Basis and Foundation of Government, 96
The Virginia Declaration of Rights
Ratified on June 12, 1776

We Hold These Truths, 100
The Declaration of Independence
July 4, 1776

The Natural Rights of Mankind, 108
A Bill for Establishing Religious Freedom
Introduced June 18, 1779; adopted 1786

Mutual Friendship and Intercourse, 112
Articles of Confederation
Written in 1776; adopted in 1781

E Pluribus Unum, 125
Great Seal of the United States
1782

The Interest of the Community, 127
George Washington's Circular to the States
June 8, 1783

A Firm and Perpetual Peace, 133
Treaty of Paris
September 3, 1783

An Affectionate Farewell, 140
George Washington's Address on Resigning His Commission
December 23, 1783

No Powers but What Were Given, 142
Thomas Jefferson's Notes on the State of Virginia
1785

The Sole and Exclusive Right, 152
Congressional Proposal for Revising the Articles of Confederation
August 7, 1786

SECTION III: CALLING AND CONVENING THE CONSTITUTIONAL CONVENTION

Defects in the System, 157
Annapolis Convention Resolution
1786

As a Mean to Remedy, 162
Congressional Endorsement of Annapolis Convention Resolution
February 21, 1787

An Aggregate View, 164
James Madison Discusses Vices of the Political System of the United States
April 1787

A House to Do Business, 175
Rules for the Constitutional Convention
May 28, 1787

The Infancy of the Science of Constitutions, 180
The Virginia Plan
May 29, 1787

Adequate to the Exigencies of Government, 187
The New Jersey Plan
June 15, 1787

Blessings on Our Deliberations, 191
Debates over State Representation Lead to a Call for Prayer
June 28, 1787

Articles of Compact, 198
Northwest Ordinance
July 13, 1787

This Infernal Trafic, 206
Debates at the Convention over Slavery
August 1787

Contents

Experience Must Be Our Only Guide, 215
John Dickinson Emphasizes the Need for Experience in Governing
August 13, 1787

Cabal and Corruption, 218
Debates over the Presidency
September 4, 1787

Make Manifest Our Unanimity, 226
Benjamin Franklin's Final Speech at the Constitutional Convention
September 17, 1787

We the People, 229
The Constitution of the United States
1787

The Consolidation of Our Union, 250
George Washington Transmits the Constitution to Congress
September 17, 1787

In Conformity to the Resolves, 253
Resolution of Congress Submitting the Constitution to the Several States
September 28, 1787

SECTION IV: DEBATING, RATIFYING, IMPLEMENTING, AND AMENDING THE NEW CONSTITUTION

The Instrument of the Union, 257
James Wilson Comments on Ratifying the Proposed Constitution
October 6, 1787

Our Freedom We've Won, 260
"The Grand Constitution" Song
October 1787

The Destruction of Your Liberties, 263
Brutus Issues His Anti-Federalist Essay
1787

The Mischiefs of Faction, 272
Federalist Papers, No. 10 & No. 51
1787–1788

The Tyranny of Rulers, 290
Patrick Henry's Speech at Virginia's Ratifying Convention
June 5, 1788

The Great National Dome, 301
The Federal Pillars
1788

Ratification and the Bill of Rights, 302
Letters between Madison and Jefferson
1787–1789

Summoned by My Country, 313
George Washington's Inaugural Address
April 30, 1789

To Administer Justice, 318
Judiciary Act of 1789
September 24, 1789

To Bigotry No Sanction, 322
Correspondence between Moses Seixas and President George Washington
1790

Amendments to the Constitution, 326
The Bill of Rights
Proposed by Congress in 1789; ratified in 1791

Timeline of Events, 331

Further Reading, 339

Index, 347

About the Author, 357

Introduction

I am among those scholars who believe that the Declaration of Independence and the U.S. Constitution mark important milestones not only in American history but also in world history, but neither was born in a vacuum. This book is an attempt to situate the American Founding Period within its historical context and to illustrate the progression of this heritage through a series of primary documents, which I have introduced and annotated, or "decoded," throughout the volume.

Section I: Constitutional Antecedents

Whereas a physicist might trace the beginning of the universe and all subsequent historical events to the Big Bang, historians and political scientists look for more proximate causes when they examine forms of government and modern political institutions. The seeds for the rise of Western civilization were planted by Greek philosophers and watered by streams of thought generated by Jewish prophets, Christian apostles, Roman lawgivers, and social contract and Enlightenment thinkers. But the colonies that were to become the United States of America were largely planted by Great Britain. Accordingly, many American conceptions of government had their birth in England. American framers drew deeply from the wells of British thought and practice in which documents like the Magna Carta (1215), Sir Edward Coke's decision in Dr. Bonham's Case (1610), the Petition of Right (1628), and the English Bill of Rights (1689) are prominent. The first section of this book, which covers constitutional antecedents, highlights such legal landmarks.

Not only were they heirs to a great tradition of representative government and respect for human rights, but Americans showed themselves to be cocreators of these traditions. This section of the book thus points to American affirmations of important governmental principles. The Mayflower Compact (1620) shows the tie between American notions of constitutionalism and biblical views of contracts and covenants, while John Winthrop's sermon "A Model of Christian Charity" (1630) demonstrates how American settlers viewed themselves not simply as pilgrims in a wilderness but as a "city on a hill" with a destiny that would either shame its founders or, more hopefully, shine forth to illumine humans everywhere. Although many political rights were initially limited to male church members with property, in time those who lived on the North American continent recognized contradictions between their grand vision and their practices including their treatment of Native Americans and the enslavement of fellow human beings, whom they had brought from Africa. In the meantime, settlers sought to secure the liberties that they and their ancestors had exercised in the home country, or sought in America, by relying on the rights outlined in charters issued by British monarchs, and by creating their own legal codes and representative institutions. Although the colonies were founded individually, in time the colonists began to recognize that the concerns that united them were greater than those that divided them and that continental union would provide greater security against external foes. The Albany Plan of Union (1754), which was largely formulated by Benjamin Franklin, was one manifestation of this desire.

Although Franklin's plan was not adopted, the development of other early American representative institutions was furthered by the distance from the mother country. Historians sometimes refer to the period prior to the French and Indian War (1754–1763) as a period of "salutary neglect" in which the British allowed Americans to make many of their own decisions, while profiting from preferential trade agreements with their colonies. Still, maintaining colonies was expensive, and Britain thought it only fair that the colonists should share in the expenses that were generated by war. Because this book is a complement to another volume in the series that focuses specifically on the Revolutionary War, it does not include deliberations of the Stamp Act Congress of 1765, which reacted to what it considered to be one of Britain's most threatening taxes. But this gathering marked the beginning of systematic colonial resistance to a wide variety of taxes that were enacted by a Parliament to which the colonists did not send representatives and which therefore appeared to violate the principle of "no taxation without representation," which the Magna Carta and other documents had proclaimed.

Section II: The Revolutionary and Confederal Periods

As the colonists proceeded to debate whether they opposed all taxes or only those taxes that were "internal" (thus permitting some duties on imports and exports), and to argue how to claim their rights as Englishmen if they did not profess allegiance to

Introduction

the British Parliament, they sent representatives to two new continental congresses. Although the colonists had clung to the hope that King George III would act on their behalf against parliamentary assertions of authority over them, he rebuffed their petitions. Battles broke out between colonists and British at Lexington and Concord, Massachusetts, and several months later, a recent immigrant named Thomas Paine published *Common Sense*, in which he argued that continuing association with Britain and with the institution of hereditary succession (the method through which the throne was passed from parents to their children, typically sons) was not only foolish and undemocratic but would also involve the colonists in future wars. Recognizing that no people could long survive without some government, Paine urged the people to draw up a constitution and declare that it, rather than a king or parliament, would rule colonial affairs. Even before it declared independence, the Second Continental Congress urged states to draw up new constitutions for their individual governance.

States not only drew up new governments but also began articulating principles, like those in the Virginia Declaration of Rights, which they thought were applicable to all men. Similarly, when Congress adopted the Declaration of Independence, it did not simply list grievances that Americans had with the British (although they composed a large chunk of the document) but also articulated fundamental principles of human equality and liberty, which, as Abigail Adams once hoped, subsequently grew to include women as well as members of racial and other minorities. Even before the outcome of the war with Britain was certain, Jefferson and others were articulating the need not only for political freedoms like speech, press, and peaceable assembly but for freedom of religion (and conscience in general) as well.

In 1777 Congress proposed, and in 1781 the states finally ratified, the Articles of Confederation. It rested chiefly on a unicameral Congress with limited powers in which states were equally represented and in which Congress had to proceed through state governments in raising money and military forces. Key matters required agreement by nine or more states, and amendments required unanimous state consent. This unity became even more difficult once the Treaty of Paris ending the Revolutionary War was signed and the colonists were no longer allied against a common enemy. Despite his concern over congressional fairness to his troops and the disunity he perceived within the nation, George Washington, the nation's greatest military leader, forswore the path of many earlier men in his position by returning his commission to Congress and retiring to private life, thus giving civilian authorities time to formulate solutions to the nation's pressing problems. Congress continued unsuccessfully to press for piecemeal amendments, as thinkers like Adams, Jefferson, and Madison argued for constitutions formulated by, and grounded more securely in the consent of, the people, and better able to protect their rights.

Section III: Calling and Convening the Constitutional Convention

The state of Massachusetts had established a precedent whereby a constitution would be formulated by a special convention and subsequently ratified by the people. As Congress found itself relatively incapable of action, states sought their own solutions. Delegates from Virginia and Maryland formulated an interstate compact to deal with mutual commercial concerns at a meeting at George Washington's home at Mt. Vernon, and used it to call for a wider convention of the states to meet in Annapolis, Maryland, to discuss national commercial matters. Delegates who assembled from five states in turn decided that instead of focusing on the disappointing absence of delegates from other invited states, they would to use the occasion to call for yet another convention. This convention, they asserted, should not only examine commercial relations but also subject the entire governmental system under the Articles of Confederation to review. The call received a fortuitous, albeit disturbing, boost when a taxpayer rebellion known as Shays' Rebellion broke out in Massachusetts during the winter of 1786–1787 and stimulated fears of national anarchy. Congress joined the call for states to send delegates to the new convention.

The following May, delegates began arriving for the grand federal convention that met through September to reformulate the government. Altogether, 55 delegates from 12 states (all but Rhode Island) attended. They included most leading political figures, including George Washington and Benjamin Franklin, many of whom had had experience in formulating and working under state constitutions. After delegates selected George Washington to preside and adopted a set of rules—including secrecy—to facilitate discussion and debate, the Virginia delegates stepped forward with a plan that called not simply for revising the Articles but for devising a new government. It called for creating three branches of government, dividing Congress into two houses in which states would be represented in both according to population, and numerous other reforms. Their ambitious proposals may have caught many delegates, who had anticipated more modest reforms, by surprise.

Initially, the plan seemed to proceed almost too easily through debates. After two weeks, however, William Paterson of New Jersey introduced a rival plan, which would have adhered much more closely to the existing Articles of Confederation. Most significantly—and consistent with New Jersey's own relatively small population—Paterson's plan proposed perpetuating equal state representation within a unicameral Congress; it also favored a plural executive. Although the delegates soon voted to continue with discussion of the Virginia Plan, the New Jersey Plan was a portent of divisions over representation, slavery, the presidency, and other matters that would greatly agitate the delegates. These issues required patient and often complicated compromises before most remaining delegates agreed to support the document that they signed—the U.S. Constitution—on September 17, 1787.

Introduction

I have devoted more readings in this book to the debates at the Constitutional Convention than to any other subject because they demonstrate the wide range of alternatives that were available to the delegates. Although the proceedings were conducted secretly, James Madison, who had learned the difficulty of researching earlier governments, situated himself toward the front of the room and took meticulous notes of the proceedings that, when compared and combined with other contemporary sources (as Max Farrand has brilliantly done),[1] make the debates exceedingly accessible. I have elsewhere argued for the importance of these proceedings as a model for men and women of goodwill who continue to believe that government can be the result of what Alexander Hamilton described in Federalist No. 1 as "establishing good government from reflection and choice" rather than leaving such matters to depend "on accident and force."[2]

The Constitution, consisting of fewer than 5,000 words, outlined three branches of government and emphasized separation of powers and checks and balances among them, in a series of seven articles, most of which were further divided into sections. To cite but two examples, the document entrusted Congress with the power to declare war, but identified the President as commander in chief of the armed forces, and it gave the president the right to appoint ambassadors and negotiate treaties, but required a majority of senators to confirm appointments and a two-thirds majority of the Senate to ratify treaties. Members of the House of Representatives were to be apportioned according to state population and elected to two-year terms while states would be equally represented in the U.S. Senate, whose members would be selected to six-year terms by state legislatures. The Constitution enumerated a variety of congressional powers, including those that deal with "the powers of the purse" and with regulation of interstate and foreign commerce. The President was to be selected to four-year terms by an independent Electoral College, apportioned according to the states' total representation in both houses of Congress. Congress was entrusted with making the laws, but the president had the power to exercise a conditional veto that took two-thirds of both houses to override. The Constitution anticipated a system of federal courts, whose members would be appointed by the president with the advice and consent of the Senate for service "during good behavior." In time, they would exercise the power of judicial review to declare laws unconstitutional, which Sir Edward Coke had advocated centuries earlier in a case presented in an earlier section of this book.

Reflecting the divisions among the three branches of government, the Constitution continued to recognize the powers of the states in a federal system that compromised between the features of a unitary government, like that of England, and the confederal government under the Articles of Confederation. Both the national and state governments were granted power to act on individual citizens, but Article VI of the Constitution proclaimed the supremacy of the national Constitution, and laws and treaties made under its authority, to state constitutions and enactments. The new Constitution provided for what its creators believed would be an easier process of amending the Constitution by two-thirds majorities of Congress and three-fourths of the states (as well as by a still-unused mechanism whereby two-thirds of the state legislatures can request that Congress call a constitutional convention for this purpose). Drawing upon the experience at the state level, the Constitution further provided for adoption by special state conventions called for this purpose rather than by existing state legislatures, which stood to lose power under the new system. Congress in turn approved transmitting the document to the states to elect conventions for the purpose of deciding whether or not to ratify.

Section IV: Debating, Ratifying, Implementing, and Amending the New Constitution

When it emerged from the Convention, the Constitution was merely a proposal. In its favor was widespread recognition that the new government was extremely weak and that it lacked power to resolve pressing issues. Working against it was the widespread fear, expressed by some of the Convention's dissenting delegates in the waning days of the Convention, that its adoption would result in the loss of some of the cherished rights that the nation had secured during the recent Revolution.

The nation subsequently engaged in a debate that was worthy of the seriousness of the proposals that were before it. Federalist supporters of the new document pointed to existing weaknesses under the Articles of Confederation and the advantages to be gained by "a more perfect Union," and sought to allay fears that the new government would take away individual rights. In addition to raising a variety of other objections to individual provisions and institutions created by the document, Anti-Federalists hammered at the omission of a bill of rights plainly outlining the rights that remained with the people and the states. The authors of *The Federalist Papers*, two of whom had attended the Constitutional Convention, brilliantly defended separation of powers and the putative advantages of a representative system of government spread throughout 13 colonies in combatting what James Madison called "factions." Anti-Federalists remained wary. They eventually secured promises from leading Federalists (who had heard similar criticism from those, like Thomas Jefferson, who otherwise supported the document), that they would push for the addition of a bill of rights once the new document was ratified.

Debates in the states were vigorous, and ratification votes in a number of the larger states like New York, Massachusetts, and Virginia, were especially close. When Washington was inaugurated as the nation's first president in 1789 with due expressions of diffidence, North Carolina and Rhode Island had still not joined the new union. Its representatives thus retained an important incentive not only to fill in details of the new government (like the organization of the federal judiciary and who would be responsible for dismissing members of the cabinet), which the Constitution had left sketchy, but also to propose a bill of rights that would induce the remaining states to ratify and secure the support of those who had opposed ratification of the document. With James Madison taking the lead, Congress fairly quickly proposed 12 amendments, 10 of which were adopted as the Bill of Rights, that clearly limited congressional powers over widely accepted individual rights. These rights included freedom to worship, to speak, and to publish; protections against "unreasonable searches and seizures"; and guarantees of a wide variety of procedural rights for individuals who were accused of crimes or on trial for them. Somewhat more ambiguously, the final two amendments pointed to certain unenumerated rights that continued to be reserved for the people and for the states.

The Need for Continuing Study and Understanding

It has been said that "while the people make the Constitution, it also makes the people."[3] Although they labored for what the Preamble of the Constitution called "posterity," one wonders how many of the delegates who met in Philadelphia in 1787 or in the first Congress in 1789 could have imagined that their handiwork, though sometimes amended, would continue to guide the nation for more than 200 years and serve as an inspiration to free peoples throughout the world. Despite such uncertainty, though, the framers acted in a manner that reflected confidence and optimism. In addition to crafting political institutions that they hoped would endure, many framers also founded colleges and universities and recognized the need to convey the sentiments that had motivated them to future generations.

This volume seeks to further that goal by carefully selecting and explaining key documents that are central to our nation's continuing legacy. In 2015, the world celebrated the 800th anniversary of the Magna Carta. If it continues to endure, the United States will celebrate the 250th anniversary of the U.S. Constitution in 2037. I am in no position to predict whether the document will continue in force this long, but I can say with confidence that as long as the ideals of human equality and human liberty prevail, the sentiments that motivated those who wrote and ratified this document will endure.

In addition to my own familiarity with, and genuine love for, the subject matter, one of the reasons that I agreed to write this volume is that I am intrigued by the format, which gathers a variety of primary sources related to America's founding in a single accessible volume that shows both the continuity and progression of American political thought. I provide introductions for each document, highlight key provisions of important documents in bold print, and provide accompanying explanations of important and difficult passages. I think students will find the arrangement of the book to be a welcome contrast to many original documents that they might have otherwise examined.

Students who are new to the series should begin by scanning the Table of Contents to see what documents it includes and how they are organized. The volume includes a timeline that will further situate these documents in relation to others, as well as an index through which readers can look up key events and participants and a bibliography that provides additional sources for students interested in pursuing their understanding of this time period still further. The volume should be suitable both for those who are interested in examining one or more of the documents that this book covers as well as for those who would like to trace the evolution of the Constitution through the Founding Period. Readers should realize that I had to choose among hundreds of documents in composing this work and that the documents that I have highlighted are designed to carry readers through the major currents of early American thought.

Acknowledgments

I am pleased to recognize the continuing support of the administration at Middle Tennessee State University and of members of the Honors College who helped me to download and edit documents. I owe thanks to the editors at ABC-CLIO, and especially to Kevin Hillstrom and Robin Tutt. I would also like to thank Nicholle Lutz at BookComp and Silverander Communications for the cover design.

John R. Vile, Middle Tennessee State University

Notes

[1] Max Farrand, ed., *The Records of the Federal Convention of 1787*, 1937 rev. ed., 4 vols. (New Haven, CT: Yale University Press, 1966). Also see James H. Hutson, ed., *Supplement to Max Farrand's The Records of the Federal Convention of 1787* (New Haven, CT: Yale University Press, 1987).

[2] John R. Vile, *The Writing and Ratification of the U.S. Constitution: Practical Virtue in Action* (Lanham, MD: Rowman & Littlefield, 2012). The quotation is from Alexander Hamilton, James Madison, and John Jay, *The Federalist Papers*, intro. by Clinton Rossiter (New York: New American Library, 1961), p. 33.

[3] Peter W. Schramm and Christopher Flannery, eds., *A Constitutional Conversation: The Complete Letters from an Ohio Farmer* (Ashland, OH: Ashbrook Center, 2012), p. 191.

Founding Documents of America
DOCUMENTS DECODED

Section I: Constitutional Antecedents

The Law of the Land
Magna Carta
1215

INTRODUCTION

Although the Magna Carta was a British document originally written in Latin (*Magna Carta* means "Great Charter") that predated the U.S. Constitution by more than 500 years, the two documents are often linked. American colonists proclaimed the principle of "no taxation without representation," which they attributed to the Magna Carta, during disputes that led to the American Revolution in 1776. Moreover, a copy of the Magna Carta purchased by Ross Perot was part of an exhibit that visited each of the original 13 states during the bicentennial celebrations of the U.S. Constitution in 1987. In 2015, the New York Public Library loaned a copy of the Declaration of Independence in Thomas Jefferson's handwriting and the U.S. National Archives loaned one of 14 original copies of the U.S. Bill of Rights for a display by the British Library, which was also displaying one of the original copies of the Magna Carta in conjunction with the celebration of its 800th anniversary.

The document was an agreement between King John of England and his noblemen, many with grievances against him. It was signed at Runnymede, England, about 20 miles west of London. The document was reaffirmed by a number of subsequent kings. It has served as the foundation for many of the fundamental principles not only of the English government, but also for the American system. As citizenship was widened to include ordinary citizens, they too claimed the rights that were once reserved only for the upper class.

The original document contained 63 sections, not all of which were reaffirmed in subsequent documents (those marked with an asterisk were missing, for example, from the document of 1225). This selection includes those provisions that have been particularly important in U.S. history.

JOHN, by the grace of God King of England, Lord of Ireland, Duke of Normandy and Aquitaine, and Count of Anjou, to his archbishops, bishops, abbots, earls, barons, justices, foresters, sheriffs, stewards, servants, and to all his officials and loyal subjects, Greeting.

KNOW THAT . . .

(1) FIRST, THAT WE HAVE GRANTED TO GOD, and by this present charter have confirmed for us and our heirs in perpetuity, that the English Church shall be free, and shall have its rights undiminished, and its liberties unimpaired. That we wish this so to be observed, appears from the fact that of our own free will, before the outbreak of the present dispute between us and our barons, we granted and confirmed by charter the freedom of the Church's elections—a right reckoned to be of the greatest necessity and importance to it—and caused this to be confirmed by Pope Innocent III. This freedom we shall observe ourselves, and desire to be observed in good faith by our heirs in perpetuity.

TO ALL FREE MEN OF OUR KINGDOM we have also granted, for us and our heirs for ever, all the liberties written out below, to have and to keep for them and their heirs, of us and our heirs:

(14) To obtain the general consent of the realm for the assessment of an 'aid'—except in the three cases specified above—or a 'scutage', we will cause the archbishops, bishops, abbots, earls, and greater barons to be summoned individually by letter. To those who hold lands directly of us we will cause a general summons to be issued, through the sheriffs and other officials, to come together on a fixed day (of which at least forty days notice shall be given) and at a fixed place. In all letters of summons, the cause of the summons will be stated. When a summons has been issued, the business appointed for the day shall go forward in accordance with the resolution of those present, even if not all those who were summoned have appeared.

> This document was written at a time when the Roman Catholic Church and various secular governments often exercised overlapping responsibilities. This statement guaranteed the right of the Church to choose its own leaders. During the reign of Henry VIII, the English, or Anglican, Church would later split from the Roman Catholic Church, and the former would become the official Church of England headed by the reigning monarch. Although some U.S. states initially formed established churches, the U.S. government repudiated the idea of a national church, most notably in the First Amendment to the U.S. Constitution, which prohibits the "establishment" of religion.

> This section is the foundation of the notion of "no taxation without representation." The term "scutage" refers to a tax on land for those who held it by virtue of their service as knights.

(17) Ordinary lawsuits shall not follow the royal court around, but shall be held in a fixed place.

At the time of this document, there were local courts and royal courts. This provision indicates that the latter would not usurp the former. An inquest was conducted by a group similar to modern grand juries. An inquest of novel disseisin involved an action to recover land that had been taken by another, the inquest of mort d'ancestor was brought by an heir who believed he had been illegally disposed of an inheritance, and the inquest of darrein provided title to patronage from a religious body.

(18) Inquests of novel disseisin, mort d'ancestor, and darrein presentment shall be taken only in their proper county court. We ourselves, or in our absence abroad our chief justice, will send two justices to each county four times a year, and these justices, with four knights of the county elected by the county itself, shall hold the assizes in the county court, on the day and in the place where the court meets.

This paragraph provides the basis for the petit jury provisions in the Sixth and Seventh Amendments and for restrictions in the Eighth Amendment against cruel and unusual punishments.

(20) For a trivial offence, a free man shall be fined only in proportion to the degree of his offence, and for a serious offence correspondingly, but not so heavily as to deprive him of his livelihood. In the same way, a merchant shall be spared his merchandise, and a husbandman the implements of his husbandry, if they fall upon the mercy of a royal court. None of these fines shall be imposed except by the assessment on oath of reputable men of the neighbourhood.

(38) In future no official shall place a man on trial upon his own unsupported statement, without producing credible witnesses to the truth of it.

Few principles are more important to the administration of modern criminal justice than the provisions within the Fifth and Fourteenth Amendments to the U.S. Constitution (the first applying to the national government and the second to the states) that prohibit governmental takings of "life, liberty, or property" except by "due process of law." This concept comes very close to, and was probably derived from, the Magna Carta's promise that the king would only act according to "the law of the land."

(39) No free man shall be seized or imprisoned, or stripped of his rights or possessions, or outlawed or exiled, or deprived of his standing in any other way, nor will we proceed with force against him, or send others to do so, except by the lawful judgement of his equals or by the law of the land.

(40) To no one will we sell, to no one deny or delay right or justice.

(52) To any man whom we have deprived or dispossessed of lands, castles, liberties, or rights, without the lawful judgement of his equals, we will at once restore these. In cases of dispute the matter shall be resolved by the judgement of the twenty-five barons referred to below in the clause for securing the peace (§ 61). In cases, however, where a man was deprived or dispossessed of something without the lawful judgement of his equals by our father King Henry or our brother King Richard, and it remains in our hands or is held by others under our warranty, we shall have respite for the period commonly allowed to Crusaders, unless a lawsuit had been begun, or an enquiry had been made at our order, before we took the Cross as a Crusader. On our return from the Crusade, or if we abandon it, we will at once render justice in full.

The formation of a body of 25 barons has parallels both to the formation of juries and to the creation of the English Parliament, the legislative branch that was that nation's precursor both to colonial legislatures and to the U.S. Congress. The history of English liberty was initially largely the history of the struggle between monarchs and the Parliament.

(61) SINCE WE HAVE GRANTED ALL THESE THINGS for God, for the better ordering of our kingdom, and to allay the discord that has arisen between us and our barons, and since we desire that they shall be enjoyed in their entirety, with lasting strength, for ever, we give and grant to the barons the following security:

The barons shall elect twenty-five of their number to keep, and cause to be observed with all their might, the peace and liberties granted and confirmed to them by this charter.

If we, our chief justice, our officials, or any of our servants offend in any respect against any man, or transgress any of the articles of the peace or of this security, and the offence is made known to four of the said twenty-five barons, they shall come to us—or in our absence from the kingdom to the chief justice—to declare it and claim immediate redress. If we, or in our absence abroad the chief justice, make no redress

"The barons shall elect twenty-five of their number to keep, and cause to be observed with all their might, the peace and liberties granted and confirmed to them by this charter."

within forty days, reckoning from the day on which the offence was declared to us or to him, the four barons shall refer the matter to the rest of the twenty-five barons, who may distrain upon and assail us in every way possible, with the support of the whole community of the land, by seizing our castles, lands, possessions, or anything else saving only our own person and those of the queen and our children, until they have secured such redress as they have determined upon. Having secured the redress, they may then resume their normal obedience to us.

Any man who so desires may take an oath to obey the commands of the twenty-five barons for the achievement of these ends, and to join with them in assailing us to the utmost of his power. We give public and free permission to take this oath to any man who so desires, and at no time will we prohibit any man from taking it. Indeed, we will compel any of our subjects who are unwilling to take it to swear it at our command.

If one of the twenty-five barons dies or leaves the country, or is prevented in any other way from discharging his duties, the rest of them shall choose another baron in his place, at their discretion, who shall be duly sworn in as they were.

In the event of disagreement among the twenty-five barons on any matter referred to them for decision, the verdict of the majority present shall have the same validity as a unanimous verdict of the whole twenty-five, whether these were all present or some of those summoned were unwilling or unable to appear.

The twenty-five barons shall swear to obey all the above articles faithfully, and shall cause them to be obeyed by others to the best of their power.

> *"Any man who so desires may take an oath to obey the commands of the twenty-five barons for the achievement of these ends, and to join with them in assailing us to the utmost of his power. We give public and free permission to take this oath to any man who so desires, and at no time will we prohibit any man from taking it. Indeed, we will compel any of our subjects who are unwilling to take it to swear it at our command."*

We will not seek to procure from anyone, either by our own efforts or those of a third party, anything by which any part of these concessions or liberties might be revoked or diminished. Should such a thing be procured, it shall be null and void and we will at no time make use of it, either ourselves or through a third party.

Source: English Translation of the Magna Carta. British Library. http://www.bl.uk/magna-carta/articles/magna-carta-english-translation. Used under the Creative Commons BY 4.0 license. No changes were made.

"We will not seek to procure from anyone, either by our own efforts or those of a third party, anything by which any part of these concessions or liberties might be revoked or diminished."

Against Common Right and Reason
Sir Edward Coke's Dr. Bonham's Case
1610

> **INTRODUCTION**
>
> One of England's proudest achievements was its system of common law, which judges formulated over centuries, publishing their rulings in thousands of cases that were consolidated into law reports that become legal precedents. These cases were thought to embody right reason and protect individual liberties.
>
> Sir Edward Coke (1552–1634) was one of the greatest jurists ever to sit on a British court, a position that he held before becoming a leader in Parliament. One of his most famous cases was known as "Dr. Bonham's Case." It involved a medical doctor who failed to secure a license from the College of Physicians of London, which had been given a monopoly over such licensing by the Parliament. The College had fined the doctor after he continued to practice. In invalidating this fine, Coke appeared to assert the superiority of the law even to acts of Parliament, although an alternate reading suggests that a court would never assume that Parliament intended to adopt a law against right reason.
>
> By the time of the American Revolution, the supremacy of the British Parliament had been well established; and the leading commentator on the law, Sir William Blackstone (1723–1780), argued that Parliament had the power to do anything that was not naturally impossible. American revolutionaries resorted to the earlier understanding that they had gained from a reading of Coke. The U.S. Constitution, and the subsequent Bill of Rights, incorporated a number of key concepts and institutions (for example, the petit and grand juries) that had developed from the common law system, which American colonies had adopted with special considerations to differences between the environment in Britain and that within the New World.

This paragraph is a justification both for separation of powers and for the principle that individuals should not be judges in their own cases.

The Censors cannot be Judges, Ministers, and parties; Judges, to give sentence or judgment; Ministers to make summons; and Parties, to have the [half] of the forfeiture, . . .

And it appears in our Books, that in many Cases, the Common Law does control Acts of Parliament, and sometimes shall adjudge them to be void: for when an Act of Parliament is against Common right and reason, or repugnant, or impossible to be performed, the Common Law will control it, and adjudge such Act to be void....

Source: Coke, Sir Edward. "Dr. Bonham's Case." *The Selected Writings and Speeches of Sir Edward Coke*. Vol 1. Edited by Steve Sheppard. Indianapolis, IN: Liberty Fund, 2003. http://oll.libertyfund.org/?option=com_staticxt&staticfile=show.php%3Ftitle=911&chapter=106343&layout=html&Itemid=27. Used with Permission of the Online Library of Liberty.

This paragraph served as an argument against parliamentary sovereignty during the Revolutionary War. It also served as a later justification for the doctrine of judicial review whereby courts would have the power to declare that laws duly enacted by legislative bodies were unconstitutional because they conflicted with the higher law of the Constitution.

A Civill Body Politick
The Mayflower Compact
1620

INTRODUCTION

One of the factors that distinguishes the U.S. Constitution from its English counterpart is that the former is a written document, unchangeable by ordinary legislative means. One of the earliest New World precedents for such a document is the Mayflower Compact, which was signed by the men on the *Mayflower* even before they disembarked from their ship at today's Plymouth, Massachusetts, in 1620; it was designed to pledge both Pilgrims and other non-Pilgrim settlers abroad to abide by whatever government they established. Like the U.S. Constitution that would follow, the document was followed by the names of its signatories, who were male heads of household. The Puritans, dissenters from the Anglican Church, who desired to "purify" it of what they considered to be the remaining Roman Catholic excesses, were familiar with the idea of covenants, or sacred contracts, from the Old Testament. The Mayflower Compact demonstrated a desire to establish a government of laws amid what they perceived as a wilderness.

The Pilgrims' ship had been blown off course from their intended destination in Virginia, so it seemed appropriate to indicate that they were in its northern parts. Sovereignty is the exercise of ultimate political power (in the Bible, God is referred to as sovereign). In context, the term "most meete" means most appropriate. The reference to "a civill body politick" is a reference to the need for good government. References to the king in this and other early manuscripts would later allow American colonists to say that they were bound together not by the power of the English Parliament, whose sovereignty they disputed, but by loyalty to the king in whose name they had come to America.

In the name of God, Amen. We, whose names are underwritten, the loyal subjects of our dread Sovereigne Lord, King James, by the grace of God, of Great Britaine, France and Ireland king, defender of the faith, etc. having undertaken, for the glory of God, and advancement of the Christian faith, and honour of our king and country, a voyage to plant the first colony in the Northerne parts of Virginia, doe by these presents solemnly and mutually in the presence of God and one of another, covenant and combine ourselves together into a civill body politick, for our better ordering and preservation, and furtherance of the ends aforesaid; and by virtue hereof to enacte, constitute, and frame such just and equall laws, ordinances, acts, constitutions and offices, from time to time, as shall be thought most meete and convenient for the generall good of the Colonie unto which we promise all due submission and obedience. In witness whereof we have hereunder subscribed our names at Cape-Codd the 11. of November, in the year of the raigne of our sovereigne lord, King James, of England, France and Ireland, the eighteenth, and of Scotland the fiftie-fourth. Anno Dom. 1620.

Source: Bradford, William. *Bradford's History of Plymouth Plantation, 1606–1646.* Edited by William T. Davis. New York: Charles Scribner's Sons, 1908.

No Man Be Compelled
The Petition of Right
1628

INTRODUCTION

Whereas the birth of liberty in the United States is often traced to the rejection of parliamentary sovereignty, or authority to tax, the rise of liberty in Great Britain typically pitted what was considered to be a representative Parliament against a more arbitrary monarch. Over time, Parliament became increasingly associated not simply with the nobles, but with the whole realm, against the arbitrary actions of the king. Kings needed to raise taxes to pursue foreign wars in which they could increase their own glory, but Parliament relied on the Magna Carta and other documents to insist that kings get their approval for taxes.

This petition from Parliament in 1628, which the king heeded only for a time, demonstrated the increasing role that earlier landmarks of liberty began to play in the politics of the day. Ultimately, the divisions led to civil war and to the execution of King Charles I in 1649, followed by the rule of Oliver Cromwell, before the restoration of William and Mary in 1689.

The Petition exhibited to his Majesty by the Lords Spiritual and Temporal, and Commons, in this present Parliament assembled, concerning divers Rights and Liberties of the Subjects, with the King's Majesty's royal answer thereunto in full Parliament.

To the King's Most Excellent Majesty,

Law often rests on precedent. The reference to a law passed in the reign of King Edward I (1272–1307), denying the right to tallage (a poll tax imposed on towns), and another law from the reign of King Edward III (1327–1377) demonstrates how precedents from one era can be used in another.

Humbly show unto our Sovereign Lord the King, the Lords Spiritual and Temporal, and Commons in Parliament assembles, that whereas it is declared and enacted by a statute made in the time of the reign of King Edward I, commonly called Stratutum de Tellagio non Concedendo, that no tallage or aid shall be laid or levied by the

king or his heirs in this realm, without the good will and assent of the archbishops, bishops, earls, barons, knights, burgesses, and other the freemen of the commonalty of this realm; and by authority of parliament holden in the five-and-twentieth year of the reign of King Edward III, it is declared and enacted, that from thenceforth no person should be compelled to make any loans to the king against his will, because such loans were against reason and the franchise of the land; and by other laws of this realm it is provided, that none should be charged by any charge or imposition called a benevolence, nor by such like charge; by which statutes before mentioned, and other the good laws and statutes of this realm, your subjects have inherited this freedom, that they should not be compelled to contribute to any tax, tallage, aid, or other like charge not set by common consent, in parliament.

> *"[N]o person should be compelled to make any loans to the king against his will, because such loans were against reason and the franchise of the land . . ."*

II. Yet nevertheless of late divers commissions directed to sundry commissioners in several counties, with instructions, have issued; by means whereof your people have been in divers places assembled, and required to lend certain sums of money unto your Majesty, and many of them, upon their refusal so to do, have had an oath administered unto them not warrantable by the laws or statutes of this realm, and have been constrained to become bound and make appearance and give utterance before your Privy Council and in other places, and others of them have been therefore imprisoned, confined, and sundry other ways molested and disquieted; and divers other charges have been laid and levied upon your people in several counties by lord lieutenants, deputy lieutenants, commissioners for musters, justices of peace and others, by command or direction from your Majesty, or your Privy Council, against the laws and free custom of the realm.

The terms "divers" and "sundry" are largely antiquated. Both refer to more than one. The Privy Council was a group of counselors to the king, often drawn from Parliament.

The Petition of Right

> The reference to "The Great Charter of the Liberties of England" is a reference to the Magna Carta.

III. And whereas also by the statute called "The Great Charter of the Liberties of England," it is declared and enacted, that no freeman may be taken or imprisoned or be disseized of his freehold or liberties, or his free customs, or be outlawed or exiled, or in any manner destroyed, but by the lawful judgment of his peers, or by the law of the land.

IV. And in the eight-and-twentieth year of the reign of King Edward III, it was declared and enacted by authority of parliament, that no man, of what estate or condition that he be, should be put out of his land or tenements, nor taken, nor imprisoned, nor disinherited nor put to death without being brought to answer by due process of law.

V. Nevertheless, against the tenor of the said statutes, and other the good laws and statutes of your realm to that end provided, divers of your subjects have of late been imprisoned without any cause showed; and when for their deliverance they were brought before your justices by your Majesty's writs of habeas corpus, there to undergo and receive as the court should order, and their keepers commanded to certify the causes of their detainer, no cause was certified, but that they were detained by your Majesty's special command, signified by the lords of your Privy Council, and yet were returned back to several prisons, without being charged with anything to which they might make answer according to the law.

> This concern over quartering troops in houses or castles, which was heightened by British practices in America, prefigures the Third Amendment to the U.S. Constitution.

VI. And whereas of late great companies of soldiers and mariners have been dispersed into divers counties of the realm, and the inhabitants against their wills have been compelled to receive them into their houses, and there to suffer them to sojourn against the laws and customs of

this realm, and to the great grievance and vexation of the people.

VII. And whereas also by authority of parliament, in the five-and-twentieth year of the reign of King Edward III, it is declared and enacted, that no man shall be forejudged of life or limb against the form of the Great Charter and the law of the land; and by the said Great Charter and other the laws and statutes of this your realm, no man ought to be adjudged to death but by the laws established in this your realm, either by the customs of the same realm, or by acts of parliament: and whereas no offender of what kind soever is exempted from the proceedings to be used, and punishments to be inflicted by the laws and statutes of this your realm; nevertheless of late time divers commissions under your Majesty's great seal have issued forth, by which certain persons have been assigned and appointed commissioners with power and authority to proceed within the land, according to the justice of martial law, against such soldiers or mariners, or other dissolute persons joining with them, as should commit any murder, robbery, felony, mutiny, or other outrage or misdemeanor whatsoever, and by such summary course and order as is agreeable to martial law, and is used in armies in time of war, to proceed to the trial and condemnation of such offenders, and them to cause to be executed and put to death according to the law martial.

VIII. By pretext whereof some of your Majesty's subjects have been by some of the said commissioners put to death, when and where, if by the laws and statutes of the land they had deserved death, by the same laws and statutes also they might, and by no other ought to have been judged and executed.

"[N]o man ought to be adjudged to death but by the laws established in this your realm, either by the customs of the same realm, or by acts of parliament . . ."

The Petition of Right

IX. And also sundry grievous offenders, by color thereof claiming an exemption, have escaped the punishments due to them by the laws and statutes of this your realm, by reason that divers of your officers and ministers of justice have unjustly refused or forborne to proceed against such offenders according to the same laws and statutes, upon pretense that the said offenders were punishable only by martial law, and by authority of such commissions as aforesaid; which commissions, and all other of like nature, are wholly and directly contrary to the said laws and statutes of this your realm.

> The first sentence of this section reiterates the doctrine of "no taxation without representation." The rest of this section points to rights that are generally associated with due process of laws.

> *"[T]hat no man hereafter be compelled to make or yield any gift, loan, benevolence, tax, or such like charge, without common consent by act of parliament; and that none be called to make answer, or take such oath, or to give attendance, or be confined, or otherwise molested or disquieted concerning the same or for refusal thereof..."*

X. They do therefore humbly pray your most excellent Majesty, that no man hereafter be compelled to make or yield any gift, loan, benevolence, tax, or such like charge, without common consent by act of parliament; and that none be called to make answer, or take such oath, or to give attendance, or be confined, or otherwise molested or disquieted concerning the same or for refusal thereof; and that no freeman, in any such manner as is before mentioned, be imprisoned or detained; and that your Majesty would be pleased to remove the said soldiers and mariners, and that your people may not be so burdened in time to come; and that the aforesaid commissions, for proceeding by martial law, may be revoked and annulled; and that hereafter no commissions of like nature may issue forth to any person or persons whatsoever to be executed as aforesaid, lest by color of them any of your Majesty's subjects be destroyed or put to death contrary to the laws and franchise of the land.

XI. All which they most humbly pray of your most excellent Majesty as their rights and liberties, according to the laws and statutes of this realm; and that your Majesty would also vouchsafe to declare, that the awards, doings, and proceedings, to the prejudice of your people in any of the premises, shall not be drawn hereafter into consequence or example; and that your Majesty would be also graciously pleased, for the further comfort and safety of your people, to declare your royal will and pleasure, that in the things aforesaid all your officers and ministers shall serve you according to the laws and statutes of this realm, as they tender the honor of your Majesty, and the prosperity of this kingdom.

Source: George Barnett Smith, *History of the English Parliament: Together with an Account of the Parliaments of Scotland and Ireland.* Vol 2. London: Warwick House, 1892, pp. 557–559.

"A Model of Christian Charity"
John Winthrop's Sermon
1630

INTRODUCTION

The history of early America, and especially of New England, is rife with sermons. But few have been quoted as often as this one, which was delivered on ship to another incoming group of pilgrims by John Winthrop, who later became a longtime governor of the Massachusetts colony. Although many scholars of U.S. history have commented on how American concepts of individualism were often explored in these early sermons, Winthrop's meditation focused on the need for cooperation, which was, in turn, tied to Puritan conceptions of mutual Christian charity.

Although Americans often stress opportunity, they generally focus on equality of opportunity rather than on equality of results. Even more than modern Americans, Winthrop stressed the division of individuals into classes, albeit with emphasis, similar to noblesse oblige, on the duty of those in upper classes to care for the less fortunate.

God almighty in His most holy and wise providence hath so disposed of the condition of mankind, as in all times some must be rich, some poor, some high and eminent in power and dignity, others mean and in subjection.

Reason: First, to hold conformity with the rest of His works, being delighted to show forth the glory of His wisdom in the variety and difference of the creatures and the glory of His power, in ordering all these differences for the preservation and good of the whole.

Reason: Secondly, that He might have the more occasion to manifest the work of His spirit. First, upon the wicked in moderating and restraining them, so that the rich and mighty should not eat up the poor, nor the poor and despised rise up against their superiors and shake off their yoke. Secondly, in the regenerate in exercising His graces in them, as in the great ones, their love, mercy, gentleness, temperance, etc., in the poor and inferior sort, their faith, patience, obedience, etc.

Reason: Thirdly, that every man might have need of other, and from hence they might all be knit more nearly together in the bond of brotherly affection. From hence it appears plainly that no man is made more honorable than another, or more wealthy, etc., out of any particular and singular respect to himself, but for the glory of his creator and the common good of the creature, man.

"[T]hat every man might have need of other, and from hence they might all be knit more nearly together in the bond of brotherly affection."

Thus stands the cause between God and us. We are entered into covenant with Him for this work, we have taken out a commission, the Lord hath given us leave to draw our own articles we have professed to enterprise these actions upon these and these ends, we have hereupon besought Him of favor and blessing. Now if the Lord shall please to hear us, and bring us in peace to the place we desire, then hath He ratified this covenant and sealed our commission, [and] will expect a strict performance of the articles contained in it, but if we shall neglect the observations of these articles which are the ends we have propounded, and dissembling with our God, shall fall to embrace this present world and prosecute our carnal intentions seeking great things for ourselves and our posterity, the Lord will surely break out in wrath against us, be revenged of such a perjured people, and make us know the price of the breach of such a covenant.

The idea of covenants or sacred agreements, also evident in the Mayflower Compact of 1620, was central to the thought of the Puritans. It was derived from Old Testament scriptures, which emphasized not only covenantal relationships among individuals but also with the people and with God, as in the giving and receiving of the Ten Commandments. Puritans viewed a breach of this covenant as a possible catalyst to God's wrath, or judgment.

Now the only way to avoid this shipwreck and to provide for our posterity is to follow the counsel of Micah, to do justly, to love mercy, to walk humbly with our God. For this end we must be knit together in this work as one man, we must entertain each other in brotherly affection, we must be willing to abridge ourselves of our superfluities for the supply of

"Now the only way to avoid this shipwreck and to provide for our posterity is to follow the counsel of Micah, to do justly, to love mercy, to walk humbly with our God. For this end we must be knit together in this work as one man, we must entertain each other in brotherly affection . . ."

others' necessities, we must uphold a familiar commerce together in all meekness, gentleness, patience, and liberality, we must delight in each other, make others' conditions our own, rejoice together, mourn together, labor and suffer together, always having before our eyes our commission and community in the work, our community as members of the same body. So shall we keep the unity of the spirit in the bond of peace. The Lord will be our God and delight in all our ways, so that we shall see much more of His wisdom, power, goodness, and truth than formerly we have been acquainted with. **We shall find that the God of Israel is among us, when ten of us shall be able to resist a thousand of our enemies, when He shall make us a praise and glory, that men shall say of succeeding plantations, the Lord make it like that of New England.**

For we must consider that we shall be as a city upon a hill, the eyes of all people are upon us. So that if we shall deal falsely with our God in this work we have undertaken and so cause Him to withdraw His present help from us, we shall be made a story and byword throughout the world, we shall open the mouths of enemies to speak evil of the ways of God and all professors for God's sake, we shall shame the faces of many of God's worthy servants, and cause their prayers to be turned into curses upon us till we be consumed out of the good land whither we are going. And to shut up this discourse with that exhortation of Moses, that faithful servant of the Lord in His last farewell to Israel, Deut. 30., Beloved there is now set before us life and good, death and evil, in that we are commanded this day to love the Lord our God, and to love one another, to walk in His ways and to keep His commandments and His ordinance, and His laws, and the articles of our covenant with Him that we may live and be multiplied, and that the Lord our God may bless us in the land whither we go to possess it. But if our hearts shall turn away so that

---

The Puritans saw themselves as the spiritual heirs to the nation of Israel. This sense of destiny has both propelled Americans to great causes in defense of human rights and freedoms and sometimes served to justify its mistreatment of Native Americans and slaves.

The most powerful image to emerge from this speech was borrowed from Jesus's Sermon on the Mount, in which he said that a city on a hill cannot be hidden. President Ronald Reagan often cited this speech, typically adding the word "shining" before "city," to emphasize America's distinctive role in furthering liberty. Winthrop's own take was less assertive; his tone conveyed more of a warning that if the American experiment failed, it would be seen by the entire world and would bring shame to the cause of Christianity as well as to the colony. Puritans were often conflicted in their understandings that good behavior would bring financial success and in their fears that financial prosperity could diminish focus on spiritual matters.

we will not obey, but shall be seduced and worship other Gods, our pleasures, our profits, and serve them, it is propounded unto us this day we shall surely perish out of the good land whither we pass over this vast sea to possess it. Therefore let us choose life, that we, and our seed, may live, and by obeying His voice, and cleaving to Him, for He is our life and our prosperity.

Source: Winthrop, John. "A Modell of Christian Charity." In *Collections of the Massachusetts Historical Society.* 3rd ser., vol. 7. Boston: Massachusetts Historical Society, 1838.

> *"Therefore let us choose life, that we, and our seed, may live, and by obeying His voice, and cleaving to Him, for He is our life and our prosperity."*

An Orderly and Decent Government
Fundamental Orders of Connecticut
1639

> **INTRODUCTION**
>
> Like the Mayflower Compact, the Fundamental Orders of Connecticut represent an attempt to order the affairs of a colony according to law. The Puritan origins of the colony remain evident in its blend of the secular and sacred. Although institutions were not as clearly divided as those of today, one can see a division between legislative and executive powers.

Much like Winthrop's "Model of Christian Charity," the Fundamental Orders were designed to create a Christian commonwealth. The term "commonwealth," which a number of states retain even today, describes a government on behalf of the common good.

For as much as it hath pleased Almighty God by the wise disposition of his divine providence so to order and dispose of things that we the Inhabitants and Residents of Windsor, Hartford and Wethersfield are now cohabiting and dwelling in and upon the River of Connectecotte and the lands thereunto adjoining; and well knowing where a people are gathered together the word of God requires that to maintain the peace and union of such a people there should be an orderly and decent Government established according to God, to order and dispose of the affairs of the people at all seasons as occasion shall require; do therefore associate and conjoin ourselves to be as one Public State or Commonwealth; and do for ourselves and our successors and such as shall be adjoined to us at any time hereafter, enter into Combination and Confederation together, to maintain and preserve the liberty and purity of the Gospel of our Lord Jesus which we now profess, as also, the discipline of the Churches, which according to the truth of the said Gospel is now practiced amongst us; as also in our civil affairs to be guided and governed according to such Laws, Rules, Orders and

Decrees as shall be made, ordered, and decreed as followeth:

1. It is Ordered, sentenced, and decreed, that there shall be yearly two General Assemblies or Courts, the one the second Thursday in April, the other the second Thursday in September following; the first shall be called the Court of Election, wherein shall be yearly chosen from time to time, so many Magistrates and other public Officers as shall be found requisite: Whereof one to be chosen Governor for the year ensuing and until another be chosen, and no other Magistrate to be chosen for more than one year: provided always there be six chosen besides the Governor, which being chosen and sworn according to an Oath recorded for that purpose, shall have the power to administer justice according to the Laws here established, and for want thereof, according to the Rule of the Word of God; which choice shall be made by all that are admitted freemen and have taken the Oath of Fidelity, and do cohabit within this Jurisdiction having been admitted Inhabitants by the major part of the Town wherein they live or the major part of such as shall be then present.

> Representative government is a hallmark of democracy. Although this document distinguishes between the governor and legislators, it does not distinguish between what would today be identified as separate legislative and judicial functions. Indeed, the chief legislative body is referred to as a court.

2. It is Ordered, sentenced, and decreed, that the election of the aforesaid Magistrates shall be in this manner: every person present and qualified for choice shall bring in (to the person deputed to receive them) one single paper with the name of him written in it whom he desires to have Governor, and that he that hath the greatest number of papers shall be Governor for that year. And the rest of the Magistrates or public officers to be chosen in this manner: the Secretary for the time being shall first read the names of all that are to be put to choice and then shall severally nominate them distinctly, and every one that would have the person nominated to be chosen shall bring in one single paper written upon, and he that would not have him chosen shall bring in a blank; and every one that hath more written papers than blanks shall be a Magistrate for that year; which papers shall be received and told by one or more that shall be then chosen by the court and sworn to be faithful therein; but in case there should not be six chosen as aforesaid, besides the Governor, out of those which are nominated, than he or they which have the most written papers shall be a Magistrate or Magistrates for the ensuing year, to make up the aforesaid number.

3. It is Ordered, sentenced, and decreed, that the Secretary shall not nominate any person, nor shall any person be chosen newly into the Magistracy which was not propounded in some General Court before, to be nominated the next election; and to that end it shall be lawful for each of the Towns aforesaid by their deputies to nominate any two whom they conceive fit to be put to election; and the Court may add so many more as they judge requisite.

> In colonial America, it was common to require that key leaders be members of the established church.

4. It is Ordered, sentenced, and decreed, that no person be chosen Governor above once in two years, and that the Governor be always a member of some approved Congregation, and formerly of the Magistracy within this Jurisdiction; and that all the Magistrates, Freemen of this Commonwealth; and that no Magistrate or other public officer shall execute any part of his or their office before they are severally sworn, which shall be done in the face of the court if they be present, and in case of absence by some deputed for that purpose.

5. It is Ordered, sentenced, and decreed, that to the aforesaid Court of Election the several Towns shall send their deputies, and when the Elections are ended they may proceed in any public service as at other Courts. Also the other General

Court in September shall be for making of laws, and any other public occasion, which concerns the good of the Commonwealth.

6. It is Ordered, sentenced, and decreed, that the Governor shall, either by himself or by the Secretary, send out summons to the Constables of every Town for the calling of these two standing Courts one month at least before their several times: And also if the Governor and the greatest part of the Magistrates see cause upon any special occasion to call a General Court, they may give order to the Secretary so to do within fourteen days' warning: And if urgent necessity so required, upon a shorter notice, giving sufficient grounds for it to the deputies when they meet, or else be questioned for the same; And if the Governor and major part of Magistrates shall either neglect or refuse to call the two General standing Courts or either of them, as also at other times when the occasions of the Commonwealth require, the Freemen thereof, or the major part of them, shall petition to them so to do; if then it be either denied or neglected, the said Freemen, or the major part of them, shall have the power to give order to the Constables of the several Towns to do the same, and so may meet together, and choose to themselves a Moderator, and may proceed to do any act of power which any other General Courts may.

7. It is Ordered, sentenced, and decreed, that after there are warrants given out for any of the said General Courts, the Constable or Constables of each Town, shall forthwith give notice distinctly to the inhabitants of the same, in some public assembly or by going or sending from house to house, that at a place and time by him or them limited and set, they meet and assemble themselves together to elect and choose certain deputies to be at the General Court then following to agitate the affairs of the Commonwealth; which said deputies shall

"And if the Governor and major part of Magistrates shall either neglect or refuse to call the two General standing Courts or either of them, as also at other times when the occasions of the Commonwealth require, the Freemen thereof, or the major part of them, shall petition to them so to do..."

be chosen by all that are admitted Inhabitants in the several Towns and have taken the oath of fidelity; provided that none be chosen a Deputy for any General Court which is not a Freeman of this Commonwealth. . . .

> A key to representative government is a proper allocation of representatives. This proposal provides considerable flexibility consistent with projected future growth.

8. It is Ordered, sentenced, and decreed, that Windsor, Hartford, and Wethersfield shall have power, each Town, to send four of their Freemen as their deputies to every General Court; and Whatsoever other Town shall be hereafter added to this Jurisdiction, they shall send so many deputies as the Court shall judge meet, a reasonable proportion to the number of Freemen that are in the said Towns being to be attended therein; which deputies shall have the power of the whole Town to give their votes and allowance to all such laws and orders as may be for the public good, and unto which the said Towns are to be bound.

9. It is Ordered, sentenced, and decreed, that the deputies thus chosen shall have power and liberty to appoint a time and a place of meeting together before any General Court, to advise and consult of all such things as may concern the good of the public, as also to examine their own Elections, whether according to the order, and if they or the greatest part of them find any election to be illegal they may seclude such for present from their meeting, and return the same and their reasons to the Court; and if it be proved true, the Court may fine the party or parties so intruding, and the Town, if they see cause, and give out a warrant to go to a new election in a legal way, either in part or in whole. Also the said deputies shall have power to fine any that shall be disorderly at their meetings, or for not coming in due time or place according to appointment; and they may return the said fines into the Court if it be refused to be paid, and the Treasurer to take notice of it, and to escheat or levy the same as he does other fines.

10. It is Ordered, sentenced, and decreed, that every General Court, except such as through neglect of the Governor and the greatest part of the Magistrates the Freemen themselves do call, shall consist of the Governor, or some one chosen to moderate the Court, and four other Magistrates at least, with the major part of the deputies of the several Towns legally chosen; and in case the Freemen, or major part of them, through neglect or refusal of the Governor and major part of the Magistrates, shall call a Court, it shall consist of the major part of Freemen that are present or their deputiues, with a Moderator chosen by them: In which said General Courts shall consist the supreme power of the Commonwealth, and they only shall have power to make laws or repeal them, to grant levies, to admit of Freemen, dispose of lands undisposed of, to several Towns or persons, and also shall have power to call either Court or Magistrate or any other person whatsoever into question for any misdemeanor, and may for just causes displace or deal otherwise according to the nature of the offense; and also may deal in any other matter that concerns the good of this Commonwealth, except election of Magistrates, which shall be done by the whole body of Freemen.

In which Court the Governor or Moderator shall have power to order the Court, to give liberty of speech, and silence unseasonable and disorderly speakings, to put all things to vote, and in case the vote be equal to have the casting voice. But none of these Courts shall be adjourned or dissolved without the consent of the major part of the Court.

> Even before representative governments recognized a generalized right of freedom of speech, they generally acknowledged the special need for candor from legislators and the need to allow them to express their views without fear of prosecution. Article I, Section 6 of the U.S. Constitution contains a similar provision prohibiting punishing members of Congress for the content of private conversations in chambers.

11. It is Ordered, sentenced, and decreed, that when any General Court upon the occasions of the Commonwealth have agreed upon any sum, or sums of money to be levied upon the several Towns within this Jurisdiction, that a committee be chosen to set out and appoint what shall be the proportion of every Town to pay of the said levy, provided the committee be made up of an equal number out of each Town.

14th January 1639 the 11 Orders above said are voted.

Source: Fundamental Orders of Connecticut, 1639. *The Federal and State Constitutions, Colonial Charters, and Other Organic Laws of the States, Territories, and Colonies Now or Heretofore Forming the United States of America.* Edited by Francis Newton Thorpe. Washington, DC: Government Printing Office, 1909.

The Free Fruition of Such Liberties
Massachusetts Body of Liberties
1641

INTRODUCTION

The Massachusetts Body of Liberties indicates the degree to which the colonists valued protections like those found in the Magna Carta and other English charters of liberty. Although the Puritans from England and Holland largely came to the New World in search of religious liberty, they brought with them the idea that church and state should be joined, albeit in purer versions (hence their name) than what they had seen in their home countries. This early document contains an introduction and 98 sections, which cover the gamut of human relationships. Thus, sections 79 and 80 refer to the Liberties of Women; sections 81–84, to the Liberties of Children; sections 85–88, to the Liberties of Servants; sections 89–91, to the Liberties of Foreigners and Strangers; and sections 92–93, to the liberties of "Bruite Creatures" (animals).

Notably, the liberties covered powers of both church and state, which clearly have overlapping responsibilities. In most jurisdictions, church membership was regarded as a prerequisite to citizenship.

The Body of Liberties is chiefly attributed to Nathaniel Ward, who was born in England in 1578, studied law, and came to New England in 1634. He also authored a second book called *The Simple Cobbler of Agawam* before returning to England in 1647, where he died in 1652. The Body of Liberties shows deep knowledge both of English common law (a body of precedents formulated by English judges) and of scripture.

The free fruition of such liberties Immunities and priveledges as humanitie, Civilitie, and Christianitie call for as due to every man in his place and proportion without impeachment and Infringement hath ever bene and ever will be the tranquillitie and Stabilitie of Churches and Commonwealths. And the deniall or deprivall thereof, the disturbance if not the ruine of both.

> It is probably significant that this law refers chiefly to liberties, which were generally regarded as more limited than freedoms. Puritans frequently distinguished between "liberty" and "license," the latter of which they understood to be regulated by laws.

We hould it therefore our dutie and safetie whilst we are about the further establishing of this Government to collect and expresse all such freedomes as for present we foresee may concerne us, and our posteritie after us, And to ratify them with our sollemne consent.

Wee doe therefore this day religiously and unanimously decree and confirme these following Rites, liberties and priveledges concerneing our Churches, and Civill State to be respectively impartiallie and inviolably enjoyed and observed throughout our Jurisdiction for ever.

> There are obvious parallels between these provisions and the provisions—most notably paragraph 39—of the Magna Carta. A capital case is one involving the death penalty.

1. No mans life shall be taken away, no mans honour or good name shall be stayned, no mans person shall be arested, restrayned, banished, dismembred, nor any wayes punished, no man shall be deprived of his wife or children, no mans goods or estaite shall be taken away from him, nor any way indammaged under colour of law or Countenance of Authoritie, unlesse it be by vertue or equitie of some expresse law of the Country waranting the same, established by a generall Court and sufficiently published, or in case of the defect of a law in any parteculer case by the word of God. And in Capitall cases, or in cases concerning dismembring or banishment according to that word to be judged by the Generall Court.

"Every person within this Jurisdiction, whether Inhabitant or forreiner shall enjoy the same justice and law, that is generall for the plantation, which we constitute and execute one towards another without partialitie or delay."

2. Every person within this Jurisdiction, whether Inhabitant or forreiner shall enjoy the same justice and law, that is generall for the plantation, which we constitute and execute one towards another without partialitie or delay.

3. No man shall be urged to take any oath or subscribe any articles, covenants or remonstrance, of a publique and Civill nature, but such as the Generall Court hath considered, allowed and required.

8. No mans Cattel or goods of what kinde soever shall be pressed or taken for any publique use or service, unlesse it be by warrant grounded upon some act of the generall Court, nor without such reasonable prices and hire as the ordinarie rates of the Countrie do afford. And if his Cattle or goods shall perish or suffer damage in such service, the owner shall be suffitiently recompenced.

Rites Rules and Liberties concerning Juditiall proceedings

18. No mans person shall be restrained or imprisoned by any authority whatsoever, before the law hath sentenced him thereto, if he can put in sufficient securitie, bayle or mainprise, for his appearance, and good behaviour in the meane time, unlesse it be in Crimes Capitall, and Contempts in open Court, and in such cases where some expresse act of Court doth allow

Like provisions in the U.S. Bill of Rights that would follow, this section contains provisions for individuals awaiting trial.

26. Every man that findeth himselfe unfit to plead his owne cause in any Court shall have Libertie to imploy any man against whom the Court doth not except, to helpe him, Provided he give him noe fee or reward for his paines. This shall not exempt the partie him selfe from Answering such Questions in person as the Court shall thinke meete to demand of him.

Although this law provides for the right to counsel, the provision prohibiting payment for services suggests that lawyers may not have been held in the highest regard.

27. If any plantife shall give into any Court a declaration of his cause in writing, The defendant shall also have libertie and time to give in his answer in writeing, And so in all further proceedings betwene partie and partie, So it doth not further hinder the dispach of Justice then the Court shall be willing unto.

28. The plantife in all Actions brought in any Court shall have libertie to withdraw his Action, or to be nonsuited before

Massachusetts Body of Liberties

the Jurie hath given in their verdict, in which case he shall alwaies pay full cost and chardges to the defendant, and may afterwards renew his suite at an other Court if he please.

29. In all actions at law it shall be the libertie of the plantife and defendant by mutual consent to choose whether they will be tryed by the Bensh or by a Jurie, unlesse it be where the law upon just reason hath otherwise determined. The like libertie shall be granted to all persons in Criminall cases.

> Puritans lived in a hierarchical society where certain punishments were considered too degrading to administer to those of higher classes (gentlemen). Whippings were not per se considered to be unconstitutional. Perhaps in part this resulted from the absence of prisons wherein individuals could be incarcerated for long periods of time.

43. No man shall be beaten with above 40 stripes, nor shall any true gentleman, nor any man equall to a gentleman be punished with whipping, unles his crime be very shamefull, and his course of life vitious and profligate.

45. No man shall be forced by Torture to confesse any Crime against himselfe nor any other unlesse it be in some Capitall case, where he is first fullie convicted by cleare and suffitient evidence to be guilty, After which if the cause be of that nature, That it is very apparent there be other conspiratours, or confederates with him, Then he may be tortured, yet not with such Tortures as be Barbarous and inhumane.

> *"For bodilie punishments we allow amongst us none that are inhumane Barbarous or cruel."*

46. For bodilie punishments we allow amongst us none that are inhumane Barbarous or cruel.

Liberties more peculiarlie concerning the free men

58. Civill Authoritie hath power and libertie to see the peace, ordinances and Rules of Christ observed in every church according to his word. so it be done in a Civill and not in an Ecclesiastical way.

59. Civill Authoritie hath power and libertie to deale with any Church member in a way of Civill Justice, notwithstanding any Church relation, office or interest.

60. No church censure shall degrade or depose any man from any Civill dignitie, office, or Authoritie he shall have in the Commonwealth.

Liberties of Women

80. Everie marryed woeman shall be free from bodilie correction or stripes by her husband, unlesse it be in his owne defence upon her assalt. If there be any just cause of correction complaint shall be made to Authoritie assembled in some Court, from which onely she shall receive it.

Although married women were considered to be under the authority of their husbands, the law provides limits to lessen the severity of their punishments.

Liberties of Servants

85. If any servants shall flee from the Tiranny and crueltie of their masters to the howse of any freeman of the same Towne, they shall be there protected and susteyned till due order be taken for their relife. Provided due notice thereof be speedily given to their maisters from whom they fled. And the next Assistant or Constable where the partie flying is harboured.

86. No servant shall be put of for above a yeare to any other neither in the life time of their maister nor after their death by their Executors or Administrators unlesse it be by consent of Authoritie assembled in some Court or two Assistants.

87. If any man smite out the eye or tooth of his man-servant, or maid servant, or otherwise mayme or much disfigure him, unlesse it be by meere casualtie, he shall let them goe free from his service. And shall have such further recompense as the Court shall allow him.

"If any man smite out the eye or tooth of his man-servant, or maid servant, or otherwise mayme or much disfigure him, unlesse it be by meere casualtie, he shall let them goe free from his service. And shall have such further recompense as the Court shall allow him."

Massachusetts Body of Liberties

Liberties of Forreiners and Strangers

> Puritans would have been familiar with passages in the Old Testament that reminded Israelites that they had once been held in captivity in Egypt and admonished them to give due regard to the rights of foreigners living among them.

89. If any people of other Nations professing the true Christian Religion shall flee to us from the Tiranny or oppression of their persecutors, or from famyne, warres, or the like necessary and compulsarie cause, They shall be entertayned and succoured amongst us, according to that power and prudence, god shall give us.

94. Capitall Laws.

(Deut. 13. 6, 10. Deut. 17. 2, 6. Ex. 22.20)
If any man after legall conviction shall have or worship any other god, but the lord god, he shall be put to death.

(Ex. 22. 18. Lev. 20. 27. Dut. 18. 10.)
If any man or woeman be a witch, (that is hath or consulteth with a familiar spirit,) They shall be put to death.

> This passage includes the first 3 of 12 crimes for which individuals could receive the death penalty. Notably, most are taken directly from the law of the Old Testament. Clearly, the line between church and state was a fine one. Prohibitions against witchcraft would result in the notorious Salem Witch Trials of 1692–1693, in which 20 members of a colonial Massachusetts community were hanged for this alleged offense.

(Lev. 24. 15,16.)
If any person shall Blaspheme the name of god, the father, Sonne or Holie Ghost, with direct, expresse, presumptuous or high handed blasphemie, or shall curse god in the like manner, he shall be put to death.

95. A Declaration of the Liberties the Lord Jesus hath given to the Churches.

> This passage clearly indicates that the Puritans retained control not only of purely secular matters but also of the church.

All the people of god within this Jurisdiction who are not in a church way, and be orthodox in Judgement, and not scandalous in life, shall have full libertie to gather themselves into a Church Estaite. Provided they doe it in a

Christian way, with due observation of the rules of Christ revealed in his word.

Source: Gray, F. C. "Remarks on the early laws of Massachusetts Bay; with the code adopted in 1641, and called the Body of Liberties, now first printed." In *Collections of the Massachusetts Historical Society*. 3rd ser., vol. 8. 1843, pp. 191–237.

The Peace, Safety, and Public Good of the People

John Locke's Second Treatise of Government

1689

INTRODUCTION

The English philosopher John Locke (1632–1704) had a strong influence on American political thought. In his *Two Treatises of Government,* Locke expounded on what is generally described as social contract philosophy, a point of view traced back to another English philosopher named Thomas Hobbes (1588–1679).

In his *Leviathan* (1651), Hobbes had hypothesized that men were born into a state of nature without government, which made the life of man "solitary, poor, nasty, brutish and short." This stemmed from personal insecurity that resulted from the equality of men and the ability of even the weakest to kill the strongest, and it necessitated the formation of a strong government (Hobbes preferred a monarchy) that could protect them.

Locke proceeded from similar premises of human equality (a premise that enabled him to reject the divine right of kings, which was based on the notion that authority had somehow been passed down from Adam to rulers of the present) and of the need for government. However, Locke moderated both his description of the state of nature and the degree to which he thought that individuals gave up their rights when entering into a social contract. Like subsequent American founders, Locke stressed that the role of government is preserving life, liberty, and property. He put particular emphasis on the latter.

Locke actually engaged in writing a constitution for settlers in North Carolina, but it was never implemented.

CHAP. II.

Of the State of Nature.

Sect. 4. TO understand political power right, and derive it from its original, we must consider, what state all men are naturally in, and that is, a *state of perfect freedom* to order their actions, and dispose of their possessions and persons, as they think fit, within the bounds of the law of nature, without asking leave, or depending upon the will of any other man.

A *state* also of equality wherein all the power and jurisdiction is reciprocal, no one having more than another; there being nothing more evident, than that the creatures of the same species and rank, promiscuously born to all the same advantages of nature, and the use of the same faculties, should also be equal one amongst another without subordination or subjection, unless the lord and master of them all should, by any manifest declaration of his will, set one above another, and confer on him, by an evident and clear appointment, an undoubted right to dominion and sovereignty.

Sect. 5. This *equality* of men by nature, the judicious Hooker looks upon as so evident in itself, and beyond all question, that he makes it the foundation of that obligation to mutual love amongst men, on which he builds the duties they owe one another, and from whence he derives the great maxims of justice and charity. . . .

Sect. 6. But though this be a *state of liberty*, yet it is *not a state of licence:* though man in that state have an uncontroulable liberty to dispose of his person or possessions, yet he has not liberty to destroy himself, or so much as any creature in his possession, but where some nobler use than its bare preservation calls for it. The *state of nature* has a law of nature to govern it, which obliges every one: and reason, which is that law, teaches all mankind, who will but consult it, that being all *equal and independent,* no one ought to harm another in his life, health, liberty, or possessions: for men being all the workmanship of one omnipotent, and infinitely wise maker; all the servants of one sovereign master, sent into the world by his order, and about his business; they are his property, whose

Thomas Hobbes had essentially equated the law of nature to that of self-preservation. By contrast, Locke sought to moderate the potential viciousness of the state of nature by arguing that men would still be morally obligated by natural law not only to protect themselves but also one another. He further argued that individuals in the state of nature would seek to punish lawbreakers on their own.

workmanship they are, made to last during his, not one another's pleasure: and being furnished with like faculties, sharing all in one community of nature, there cannot be supposed any such *subordination* among us, that may authorize us to destroy one another, as if we were made for one another's uses, as the inferior ranks of creatures are for our's. Every one, as he is *bound to preserve himself,* and not to quit his station wilfully, so by the like reason, when his own preservation comes not in competition, ought he, as much as he can, *to preserve the rest of mankind,* and may not, unless it be to do justice on an offender, take away, or impair the life, or what tends to the preservation of the life, the liberty, health, limb, or goods of another.

CHAP. IX.

Of the Ends of Political Society and Government.

Sec. 123. IF man in the state of nature be so free, as has been said; if he be absolute lord of his own person and possessions, equal to the greatest, and subject to no body, why will he part with his freedom? why will he give up this empire, and subject himself to the dominion and controul of any other power? To which it is obvious to answer, that though in the state of nature he hath such a right, yet the enjoyment of it is very uncertain, and constantly exposed to the invasion of others: for all being kings as much as he, every man his equal, and the greater part no strict observers of equity and justice, the enjoyment of the property he has in this state is very unsafe, very unsecure. This makes him willing to quit a condition, which, however free, is full of fears and continual dangers: and it is not without reason, that he seeks out, and is willing to join in society with others, who are already united, or have a mind to unite, for the mutual preservation of their

"[T]hough in the state of nature he hath such a right, yet the enjoyment of it is very uncertain, and constantly exposed to the invasion of others . . ."

lives, liberties and estates, which I call by the general name, property.

Sec. 124. The great and chief end, therefore, of men's uniting into commonwealths, and putting themselves under government, is the preservation of their property. To which in the state of nature there are many things wanting.

First, There wants an established, settled, known law, received and allowed by common consent to be the standard of right and wrong, and the common measure to decide all controversies between them: for though the law of nature be plain and intelligible to all rational creatures; yet men being biassed by their interest, as well as ignorant for want of study of it, are not apt to allow of it as a law binding to them in the application of it to their particular cases.

Sec. 125. Secondly, In the state of nature there wants a known and indifferent judge, with authority to determine all differences according to the established law: for every one in that state being both judge and executioner of the law of nature, men being partial to themselves, passion and revenge is very apt to carry them too far, and with too much heat, in their own cases; as well as negligence, and unconcernedness, to make them too remiss in other men's.

Sec. 126. Thirdly, In the state of nature there often wants power to back and support the sentence when right, and to give it due execution, They who by any injustice offended, will seldom fail, where they are able, by force to make good their injustice; such resistance many times

"The great and chief end, therefore, of men's uniting into commonwealths, and putting themselves under government, is the preservation of their property."

Although Locke painted the state of nature in milder hues than had Hobbes, he offered three reasons for individuals to leave such a stateless existence for one with a protecting government. First, conceptions of natural law would vary from one individual to another, with many being biased by self-interests and ignorance. Second, there would be no impartial judge to settle conflicting interpretations of law among individuals. Third, there would be no executive authority by which unbiased judgments could be enforced. Notably, these three functions are embodied in the three branches of government, with legislators agreeing to a common law, judges adjudicating conflicts that arise from this law, and the executive branch enforcing the laws.

makes the punishment dangerous, and frequently destructive, to those who attempt it.

Sec. 127. Thus mankind, notwithstanding all the privileges of the state of nature, being but in an ill condition, while they remain in it, are quickly driven into society. Hence it comes to pass, that we seldom find any number of men live any time together in this state. The inconveniencies that they are therein exposed to, by the irregular and uncertain exercise of the power every man has of punishing the transgressions of others, make them take sanctuary under the established laws of government, and therein seek the preservation of their property. It is this makes them so willingly give up every one his single power of punishing, to be exercised by such alone, as shall be appointed to it amongst them; and by such rules as the community, or those authorized by them to that purpose, shall agree on. And in this we have the original right and rise of both the legislative and executive power, as well as of the governments and societies themselves.

Sec. 128. For in the state of nature, to omit the liberty he has of innocent delights, a man has two powers.

The first is to do whatsoever he thinks fit for the preservation of himself, and others within the permission of the law of nature: by which law, common to them all, he and all the rest of mankind are one community, make up one society, distinct from all other creatures. And were it not for the corruption and vitiousness of degenerate men, there would be no need of any other; no necessity that men should separate from this great and natural community, and by positive agreements combine into smaller and divided associations.

The other power a man has in the state of nature, is the power to punish the crimes committed against that law. Both these

> *"Thus mankind, notwithstanding all the privileges of the state of nature, being but in an ill condition, while they remain in it, are quickly driven into society."*

he gives up, when he joins in a private, if I may so call it, or particular politic society, and incorporates into any commonwealth, separate from the rest of mankind.

Sec. 129. The first power, viz. of doing whatsoever he thought for the preservation of himself, and the rest of mankind, he gives up to be regulated by laws made by the society, so far forth as the preservation of himself, and the rest of that society shall require; which laws of the society in many things confine the liberty he had by the law of nature.

Sec. 130. Secondly, The power of punishing he wholly gives up, and engages his natural force, (which he might before employ in the execution of the law of nature, by his own single authority, as he thought fit) to assist the executive power of the society, as the law thereof shall require: for being now in a new state, wherein he is to enjoy many conveniencies, from the labour, assistance, and society of others in the same community, as well as protection from its whole strength; he is to part also with as much of his natural liberty, in providing for himself, as the good, prosperity, and safety of the society shall require; which is not only necessary, but just, since the other members of the society do the like.

Sec. 131. But though men, when they enter into society, give up the equality, liberty, and executive power they had in the state of nature, into the hands of the society, to be so far disposed of by the legislative, as the good of the society shall require; yet it being only with an intention in every one the better to preserve himself, his liberty and property; (for no rational creature can be supposed to change his condition with an intention to be worse) the power of the society, or legislative constituted by them, can never be supposed to extend farther, than the common good; but is obliged to secure every one's property,

"The first power, viz. of doing whatsoever he thought for the preservation of himself, and the rest of mankind, he gives up to be regulated by laws made by the society, so far forth as the preservation of himself, and the rest of that society shall require . . ."

Whereas Hobbes envisioned a strong central authority as the only means of remedying the chaos of a state of nature, Locke limited the extent of governmental powers to those that he considered to be necessary to secure life, liberty, and property. Like later American revolutionaries, Locke believed that the people had the right to overthrow governments that did not secure their rights.

by providing against those three defects above mentioned, that made the state of nature so unsafe and uneasy. And so whoever has the legislative or supreme power of any common-wealth, is bound to govern by established standing laws, promulgated and known to the people, and not by extemporary decrees; by indifferent and upright judges, who are to decide controversies by those laws; and to employ the force of the community at home, only in the execution of such laws, or abroad to prevent or redress foreign injuries, and secure the community from inroads and invasion. And all this to be directed to no other end, but the peace, safety, and public good of the people.

Source: John Locke. Second Treatise of Government. Project Gutenberg. https://www.gutenberg.org/files/7370/7370-h/7370-h.htm.

The Rights and Liberties of the Subject
English Bill of Rights
1689

> **INTRODUCTION**
>
> The early history of liberty in Great Britain was often forged from conflicts between the Parliament and the monarch. After the end of the rule of Oliver and Richard Cromwell, the Parliament had restored Charles II to the throne in 1660. His successor, James II, shared earlier notions of monarchical prerogative that conflicted with parliamentary sovereignty. He also adhered to Roman Catholicism rather than to the Anglican Church that Henry VIII had established. James II and his wife produced a Catholic heir; and William III, who was married to Charles II's daughter Mary, threatened to invade England. Leading members of the Parliament associated allegiance to the Roman church with allegiance to a foreign leader (the pope). James II fled to France, and Parliament proclaimed his Protestant daughter and her husband to be the new monarchs, but made sure that they acknowledged parliamentary authority and that the royal line would continue to be in Protestant hands.

An Act Declaring the Rights and Liberties of the Subject and Settling the Succession of the Crown

Whereas the Lords Spiritual and Temporal and Commons assembled at Westminster, lawfully, fully and freely representing all the estates of the people of this realm, did upon the thirteenth day of February in the year of our Lord one thousand six hundred eighty-eight present unto their Majesties, then called and known by the names and style of William and Mary, prince and princess of Orange, being present in their proper persons, a certain declaration in writing made by the said Lords and Commons in the words following, viz.:

> The English Parliament consisted of a lower House of Commons elected by the people and an upper House of Lords composed mostly of aristocrats. These included both English bishops, appointed by the king [Lords Spiritual] and other Lords [Temporal], who inherited their positions based on their ownership of manors.

English Bill of Rights

Whereas the late King James the Second, by the assistance of divers evil counsellors, judges and ministers employed by him, did endeavour to subvert and extirpate the Protestant religion and the laws and liberties of this kingdom;

By assuming and exercising a power of dispensing with and suspending of laws and the execution of laws without consent of Parliament;

By committing and prosecuting divers worthy prelates for humbly petitioning to be excused from concurring to the said assumed power;

By issuing and causing to be executed a commission under the great seal for erecting a court called the Court of Commissioners for Ecclesiastical Causes;

By levying money for and to the use of the Crown by pretence of prerogative for other time and in other manner than the same was granted by Parliament;

> Although the prohibition did not make it into the U.S. Constitution, many Anti-Federalists later advocated a ban on "standing" armies—permanent professional armies—which they feared monarchs would use to oppress them.

By raising and keeping a standing army within this kingdom in time of peace without consent of Parliament, and quartering soldiers contrary to law;

By causing several good subjects being Protestants to be disarmed at the same time when papists were both armed and employed contrary to law;

By violating the freedom of election of members to serve in Parliament;

By prosecutions in the Court of King's Bench for matters and causes cognizable only in Parliament, and by divers other arbitrary and illegal courses;

And whereas of late years partial corrupt and unqualified persons have been returned and served on juries in trials, and particularly divers jurors in trials for high treason which were not freeholders;

And excessive bail hath been required of persons committed in criminal cases to elude the benefit of the laws made for the liberty of the subjects;

And excessive fines have been imposed;

And illegal and cruel punishments inflicted;

And several grants and promises made of fines and forfeitures before any conviction or judgment against the persons upon whom the same were to be levied;

All which are utterly and directly contrary to the known laws and statutes and freedom of this realm;

And whereas the said late King James the Second having abdicated the government and the throne being thereby vacant, his Highness the prince of Orange (whom it hath pleased Almighty God to make the glorious instrument of delivering this kingdom from popery and arbitrary power) did (by the advice of the Lords Spiritual and Temporal and divers principal persons of the Commons) cause letters to be written to the Lords Spiritual and Temporal being Protestants, and other letters to the several counties, cities, universities, boroughs and cinque ports, for the choosing of such persons to represent them as were of right to be sent to Parliament, to meet and sit at Westminster upon the two and twentieth day of January in this year one thousand six hundred eighty and eight [old style date], in order to such an establishment as that their religion, laws and liberties might not again

"And whereas of late years partial corrupt and unqualified persons have been returned and served on juries in trials, and particularly divers jurors in trials for high treason which were not freeholders . . ."

The English Bill of Rights was structured, much like the later U.S. Declaration of Independence, as a set of indictments against the outgoing king that call for a regime change. Parliament turned power over to new monarchs based on their pledge not to repeat these abuses.

English Bill of Rights

be in danger of being subverted, upon which letters elections having been accordingly made;

And thereupon the said Lords Spiritual and Temporal and Commons, pursuant to their respective letters and elections, being now assembled in a full and free representative of this nation, taking into their most serious consideration the best means for attaining the ends aforesaid, do in the first place (as their ancestors in like case have usually done) for the vindicating and asserting their ancient rights and liberties declare

That the pretended power of suspending the laws or the execution of laws by regal authority without consent of Parliament is illegal;

That the pretended power of dispensing with laws or the execution of laws by regal authority, as it hath been assumed and exercised of late, is illegal;

That the commission for erecting the late Court of Commissioners for Ecclesiastical Causes, and all other commissions and courts of like nature, are illegal and pernicious;

"That levying money for or to the use of the Crown by pretence of prerogative, without grant of Parliament, for longer time, or in other manner than the same is or shall be granted, is illegal..."

That levying money for or to the use of the Crown by pretence of prerogative, without grant of Parliament, for longer time, or in other manner than the same is or shall be granted, is illegal;

That it is the right of the subjects to petition the king, and all commitments and prosecutions for such petitioning are illegal;

That the raising or keeping a standing army within the kingdom in time of peace, unless it be with consent of Parliament, is against law;

That the subjects which are Protestants may have arms for their defence suitable to their conditions and as allowed by law;

> These provisions are echoed in the First Amendment right to petition and the Second Amendment right to bear arms, in the U.S. Constitution.

That election of members of Parliament ought to be free;

That the freedom of speech and debates or proceedings in Parliament ought not to be impeached or questioned in any court or place out of Parliament;

That excessive bail ought not to be required, nor excessive fines imposed, nor cruel and unusual punishments inflicted;

> These provisions are echoed in the Eighth Amendment of the U.S. Constitution.

That jurors ought to be duly impanelled and returned, and jurors which pass upon men in trials for high treason ought to be freeholders;

That all grants and promises of fines and forfeitures of particular persons before conviction are illegal and void;

And that for redress of all grievances, and for the amending, strengthening and preserving of the laws, Parliaments ought to be held frequently.

And they do claim, demand and insist upon all and singular the premises as their undoubted rights and liberties, and that no declarations, judgments, doings or proceedings to the prejudice of the people in any of the said premises ought in any wise to be drawn hereafter into consequence or example; to which demand of their rights they are particularly encouraged by the declaration of his Highness the prince of Orange as being the only means for obtaining a full redress and remedy therein. Having therefore an entire confidence that his said Highness the prince of Orange will perfect the

English Bill of Rights

"I, A.B., do swear that I do from my heart abhor, detest and abjure as impious and heretical this damnable doctrine and position, that princes excommunicated or deprived by the Pope or any authority of the see of Rome may be deposed or murdered by their subjects or any other whatsoever. And I do declare that no foreign prince, person, prelate, state or potentate hath or ought to have any jurisdiction, power, superiority, pre-eminence or authority, ecclesiastical or spiritual, within this realm. So help me God."

deliverance so far advanced by him, and will still preserve them from the violation of their rights which they have here asserted, and from all other attempts upon their religion, rights and liberties, the said Lords Spiritual and Temporal and Commons assembled at Westminster do resolve that William and Mary, prince and princess of Orange, be and be declared king and queen of England, France and Ireland and the dominions thereunto belonging, to hold the crown and royal dignity of the said kingdoms and dominions to them, the said prince and princess, during their lives and the life of the survivor to them, and that the sole and full exercise of the regal power be only in and executed by the said prince of Orange in the names of the said prince and princess during their joint lives, and after their deceases the said crown and royal dignity of the same kingdoms and dominions to be to the heirs of the body of the said princess, and for default of such issue to the Princess Anne of Denmark and the heirs of her body, and for default of such issue to the heirs of the body of the said prince of Orange. And the Lords Spiritual and Temporal and Commons do pray the said prince and princess to accept the same accordingly.

And that the oaths hereafter mentioned be taken by all persons of whom the oaths have allegiance and supremacy might be required by law, instead of them; and that the said oaths of allegiance and supremacy be abrogated.

I, A.B., do sincerely promise and swear that I will be faithful and bear true allegiance to their Majesties King William and Queen Mary. So help me God.

I, A.B., do swear that I do from my heart abhor, detest and abjure as impious and heretical this damnable doctrine and position, that princes excommunicated or deprived by the Pope or any authority of the see of Rome may be deposed or murdered by their subjects or any other whatsoever. And I do declare that no foreign prince, person, prelate, state or potentate hath or ought to have any jurisdiction, power, superiority, pre-eminence or authority, ecclesiastical or spiritual, within this realm. So help me God.

Upon which their said Majesties did accept the crown and royal dignity of the kingdoms of England, France and Ireland, and the dominions thereunto belonging, according to the resolution and desire of the said Lords and Commons contained in the said declaration.... Now in pursuance of the premises the said Lords Spiritual and Temporal and Commons in Parliament assembled, for the ratifying, confirming and establishing the said declaration and the articles, clauses, matters and things therein contained by the force of law made in due form by authority of Parliament, do pray that it may be declared and enacted that all and singular the rights and liberties asserted and claimed in the said declaration are the true, ancient and indubitable rights and liberties of the people of this kingdom, and so shall be esteemed, allowed, adjudged, deemed and taken to be; and that all and every the particulars aforesaid shall be firmly and strictly holden and observed as they are expressed in the said declaration, and all officers and ministers whatsoever shall serve their Majesties and their successors according to the same in all time to come.... **And whereas it hath been found by experience that it is inconsistent with the safety and welfare of this Protestant kingdom to be governed by a popish prince, or by any king or queen marrying a papist, the said Lords Spiritual and Temporal and Commons do further pray that it may be enacted, that all and every person and persons that is, are or shall be reconciled to or shall hold communion with the see or Church of Rome, or shall profess the popish religion, or shall marry a papist, shall be excluded and be for ever incapable to inherit, possess or enjoy the crown**

"[A]ll and singular the rights and liberties asserted and claimed in the said declaration are the true, ancient and indubitable rights and liberties of the people of this kingdom, and so shall be esteemed, allowed, adjudged, deemed and taken to be . . ."

Again, in the eyes of the Parliament, association with the Roman Catholic Church was considered to be an alliance with a foreign potentate. As late as the early 1830s, some American states would continue to have an established church, and many early colonial and state constitutions required leaders to be Protestant. Notably, the U.S. Constitution prohibits "test oaths" as a condition of federal office.

and government of this realm and Ireland and the dominions thereunto belonging or any part of the same, or to have, use or exercise any regal power, authority or jurisdiction within the same; and in all and every such case or cases the people of these realms shall be and are hereby absolved of their allegiance; and the said crown and government shall from time to time descend to and be enjoyed by such person or persons being Protestants as should have inherited and enjoyed the same in case the said person or persons so reconciled, holding communion or professing or marrying as aforesaid were naturally dead; and that every king and queen of this realm who at any time hereafter shall come to and succeed in the imperial crown of this kingdom shall on the first day of the meeting of the first Parliament next after his or her coming to the crown, sitting in his or her throne in the House of Peers in the presence of the Lords and Commons therein assembled, or at his or her coronation before such person or persons who shall administer the coronation oath to him or her at the time of his or her taking the said oath (which shall first happen), make, subscribe and audibly repeat the declaration mentioned in the statute made in the thirtieth year of the reign of King Charles the Second entitled, An Act for the more effectual preserving the king's person and government by disabling papists from sitting in either House of Parliament. . . .

Source: United Kingdom. Parliament. *An Act Declaring the Rights and Liberties of the Subject and Settling the Succession of the Crown*. 1 William & Mary, Session 2, cap. 2, 1689.

There Is No Such Thing as Slavery

Samuel Sewall's *The Selling of Joseph: A Memorial*

1701

> **INTRODUCTION**
>
> One of the greatest inconsistencies in early America was that a freedom-loving people were associated with the institution of slavery. England's Samuel Johnson would ask "How is it we hear the loudest yelps for liberty among the drivers of negroes?" Although later abolitionist sentiment would have deep roots in religious principles, slavery was not unknown in the Bible, and supporters of slavery often used its text to justify the institution. The first known antislavery publication in the colonies was by Samuel Sewall, who is more notoriously known for his participation in the Salem Witch Trials, for which he later issued a public apology. Sewall's essay is a reminder that New England seamen had participated in the slave trade and that the institution originally extended outside the South. Sewall's essay focuses on the account in the book of Genesis of how Joseph was sold into slavery in Egypt by his brothers. African Americans would later take solace in the story of the exodus of Jews from Egypt as they plotted their own escapes or anticipated their own freedom.

FOR AS MUCH as Liberty is in real value next unto Life: None ought to part with it themselves, or deprive others of it, but upon most mature Consideration.

The Numerousness of Slaves at this day in the Province, and the Uneasiness of them under their Slavery, hath put many upon thinking whether the Foundation of it be firmly and well laid; so as to sustain the Vast Weight that is built upon it. It is most certain that all Men, as they are the Sons of *Adam*, are Coheirs; and have equal Right unto Liberty, and all other outward Comforts of Life.

GOD *hath given the Earth* [with all its Commodities] *unto the Sons of* Adam, *Psal* 115. 16. *And hath made of One Blood, all*

> "It is most certain that all Men, as they are the Sons of Adam, *are Coheirs; and have equal Right unto Liberty, and all other outward Comforts of Life.*"

Nations of Men, for to dwell on all the face of the Earth; and hath determined the Times before appointed, and the bounds of their habitation: That they should seek the Lord. Forasmuch then as we are the Offspring of GOD &c. Act 17.26, 27, 29. Now although the Title given by the last ADAM, doth infinitely better Mens Estates, respecting GOD and themselves; and grants them a most beneficial and inviolable Lease under the Broad Seal of Heaven, who were before only Tenants at Will: Yet through the Indulgence of GOD to our First Parents after the Fall, the outward Estate of all and every of the Children, remains the same, as to one another. So that Originally, and Naturally, there is no such thing as Slavery. *Joseph* was rightfully no more a Slave to his Brethren, then they were to him: and they had no more Authority to *Sell* him, than they had to *Slay* him. And if *they* had nothing to do to Sell him; the *Ishmaelites* bargaining with them, and paying down Twenty pieces of Silver, could not make a Title. Neither could *Potiphar* have any better Interest in him than the *Ishmaelites* had. *Gen.* 37. 20, 27, 28. For he that shall in this case plead *Alteration of Property*, seems to have forfeited a great part of his own claim to Humanity. There is no proportion between Twenty Pieces of Silver, and LIBERTY. The Commodity it self is the Claimer. If *Arabian* Gold be imported in any quantities, most are afraid to meddle with it, though they might have it at easy rates; lest if it should have been wrongfully taken from the Owners, it should kindle a fire to the Consumption of their whole Estate. 'Tis pity there should be more Caution used in buying a Horse, or a little lifeless dust; than there is in purchasing Men and Women: Whenas they are the Offspring of GOD, and their Liberty is,

—*Auro pretiosior Omni.*

And seeing GOD hath said, *He that Stealeth a Man and Selleth him, or if he be found in his hand, he shall surely be put*

The term "*Auro pretiosior Omni,*" which is found at the end of the paragraph, translates to "to each more precious than gold." Sewall is using classic natural rights arguments: God created human beings free and equal, and laws that seek to subject such individuals to slavery are based on convention rather than on nature.

to Death. Exod. 12.16. This Law being of Everlasting Equity, wherein Man Stealing is ranked amongst the most atrocious of Capital Crimes: What louder Cry can there be made of the Celebrated Warning, *Caveat Emptor!*

And all thing considered, it would conduce more to the Welfare of the Province, to have White Servants for a Term of Years, than to have Slaves for Life. Few can endure to hear of a Negro's being made free; and indeed they can seldom use their freedom well; yet their continual aspiring after their forbidden Liberty, renders them Unwilling Servants. And there is such a disparity in their Conditions, Color & Hair, that they can never embody with us, and grow up into orderly Families, to the Peopling of the Land: but still remain in our Body Politick as a kind of extra-vasat Blood. As many Negro men as there are among us, so many empty places there are in our Train Bands, and the places taken up of Men that might make Husbands for our Daughters. And the Sons and Daughters of *New England* would become more like *Jacob*, and *Rachel*, if this Slavery were thrust quite out of doors. Moreover it is too well known what Temptations Masters are under, to connive at the Fornification of their Slaves; lest they should be obliged to find them Wives, or pay their Fines. It seems to be practically pleaded that they might be Lawless; 'tis thought much of, that the Law should have Satisfaction for their Thefts, and other Immoralities; by which means, *Holiness to the Lord*, is more rarely engraven upon this sort of Servitude. It is likewise most lamentable to think, how in taking Negros out of *Africa*, and Selling of them here, That which GOD ha's joyned together men do boldly rend asunder; Men from their Country, Husbands from their Wives, Parents from their Children. How horrible is the Uncleanness, Mortality, if not Murder, that the Ships are guilty of that bring great Crouds of these miserable Men, and Women. Methinks, when we are bemoaning the barbarous Usage of our Friends and Kinsfolk

> *"And all thing considered, it would conduce more to the Welfare of the Province, to have White Servants for a Term of Years, than to have Slaves for Life. Few can endure to hear of a Negro's being made free; and indeed they can seldom use their freedom well; yet their continual aspiring after their forbidden Liberty, renders them Unwilling Servants. And there is such a disparity in their Conditions, Color & Hair, that they can never embody with us, and grow up into orderly Families, to the Peopling of the Land: but still remain in our Body Politick as a kind of extra-vasat Blood."*

in *Africa*: it might not be unseasonable to enquire whether we are not culpable in forcing the *Africans* to become Slaves amongst our selves. And it may be a question whether all the Benefit received by *Negro* Slaves, will balance the Accompt of Cash laid out upon them; and for the Redemption of our own enslaved Friends out of *Africa*. Besides all the Persons and Estates that have perished there.

Obj. 1. *These Blackamores are of the Posterity of* Cham, *and therefore are under the Curse of Slavery.* Gen. 9.25, 26, 27.

Answ. **Of all Offices, one would not begg this;** *viz.* **Uncall'd for, to be an Executioner of the Vindictive Wrath of God; the extent and duration of which is to us uncertain. If this ever was a Commission; How do we know but that it is long since out of date? Many have found it to their Cost, that a Prophetical Denunciation of Judgment against a Person or People, would not warrant them to inflict that evil. If it would,** *Hazael* **might justify himself in all he did against his Master, and the** *Israelites***, from 2** *Kings* **8. 10, 12.**

> The Biblical book of Genesis records that God punished Ham, one of the sons of Adam, after Noah became drunk and Ham failed to cover his nakedness. Many incorrectly associated the sons of Ham with members of African races and thought that slavery was a continuation of God's judgment. Without questioning the tie to race, Sewall nonetheless questioned whether the curse continued or whether it was up to humans to enforce it.

But it is possible that by cursory reading, this Text may have been mistaken. For *Canaan* is the Person Cursed three times over, without the mentioning of *Cham*. Good Expositors suppose the Curse entailed on him, and that this Prophesie was accomplished in the Extirpation of the *Canaanites*, and in the Servitude of the *Gibeonites, Vide Pareum.* Whereas the Blackmores are not descended of *Canaan*, but of *Cush. Psal.* 68. 31. *Princes shall come out of Egypt* [Mizraim] *Ethopia* [Cush] *shall soon stretch out her hands unto God.* Under which Names, all *Africa* may be comprehended; and the Promised Conversion ought to be prayed for. *Jer.* 13, 23. *Can the Ethiopian change his skin?* This shews that Black Men are the Posterity of *Cush:* Who time out of mind have been distinguished by their Colour. And for want of the true, *Ovid* assigns a fabulous cause of it.

Sanguine tum credunt in corpora summa vocato
Aethiopum populos nigrum traxisse colorem.
Metamorph. lib.2.

Obj. 2. *The* Nigers *are brought out of a Pagan Country, into places where the Gospel is Preached.*

Answ. **Evil must not be done, that good may come of it. The extraordinary and comprehensive Benefit accruing to the Church of God, and to *Joseph* personally, did not rectify his brethrens Sale of him.**

> This is a classic case of questioning whether the ends justify the means.

Obj. 3. *The* Africans *have Wars with one another: our Ships bring lawful Captives taken in those Wars.*

Answ. **For ought is known, their Wars are much such as were between *Jaob's* Sons and their Brother *Joseph*. If they be between Town and Town; Provincial, or National: Every War is upon one side Unjust. An Unlawful War can't make lawful Captives. And by Receiving, we are in danger to promote, and partake in their Barbarous Cruelties. I am sure, if some Gentlemen should go down to the *Brewsters* to take the Air, and Fish: And a stronger party from *Hull* should Surprise them, and Sell them for Slaves to a Ship outward bound: they would think themselves unjustly dealt with; both by Sellers and Buyers. And yet 'tis to be feared, we have no other kind of Title to our *Nigers*. Therefore all things whatsoever ye would that men should do to you, do ye even so to them: for this is the Law and the Prophets. Matt. 7. 12.**

> A classic justification for slavery, which dated back to classical times and which Sewall sought to refute, was that they were the appropriate fruits of war.

> *"And for men obstinately to persist in holding their Neighbours and Brethren under the Rigor of perpetual Bondage, seems to be no proper way of gaining Assurance that God ha's given them Spiritual Freedom."*

Obj. 4. Abraham *had servants bought with his Money, and born in his House.*

Answ. Until the Circumstances of *Abraham's* purchase be recorded, no Argument can be drawn from it. In the mean time, Charity obliges us to conclude, that He knew it was lawful and good.

It is Observable that the *Israelites* were strictly forbidden the buying, or selling one another for Slaves. *Levit.* 25. 39, 46. *Jer.* 34. 8–22. And GOD gaged His Blessing in lieu of any loss they might conceipt they suffered thereby. *Deut.* 15. 18. And since the partition Wall is broken down, inordinate Self love should likewise be demolished. GOD expects that Christians should be of a more Ingenuous and benign frame of spirit. Christians should carry it to all the World, as the *Israelites* were to carry it one towards another. And for men obstinately to persist in holding their Neighbours and Brethren under the Rigor of perpetual Bondage, seems to be no proper way of gaining Assurance that God ha's given them Spiritual Freedom. Our Blessed Saviour ha's altered the Measures of the Ancient Love-Song, and set it to a most Excellent New Tune, which all ought to be ambitious of Learning. *Matt.* 5. 43, 44. *John* 13. 34. These *Ethiopians*, as black as they are; seeing they are the Sons and Daughters of the First *Adam*, the Brethren and Sister of the Last ADAM, and the Offspring of GOD; They ought to be treated with a Respect agreeable.

Source: Samuel Sewall. *The Selling of Joseph: A Memorial.* Boston: Bartholomew Green and John Allen, June 24, 1700.

Liberty of Conscience
Charter of Privileges Granted to the Inhabitants of Pennsylvania and Territories
October 28, 1701

> **INTRODUCTION**
>
> English colonies in America are often divided into three types: royal colonies, owned by the king; proprietary colonies, which rested on land grants that the king had given to individuals; and self-governing colonies like Rhode Island and Connecticut that were often the offspring of a charter issued by a joint-stock company. Englishman William Penn was a prominent member of the Quaker faith. Quakers were known for their pacifism, their refusal to take off their hats in the presence of royalty, and for services with long periods of silence in which they would sometimes "quake" in the presence of God. Despite being a victim of religious persecution in Britain, William Penn received a royal grant of a large expanse of land in America in 1681 in recognition of the loyalty that his father, an admiral, showed to the crown. Penn in turn issued charters, a form of primitive constitution, to his colonies, of which this charter of 1701 to Pennsylvania is an example. Penn's guarantee of civil liberties, which was bestowed as a favor from the ruler rather than as a composition of the representatives of the people, was a historical milestone. But it arguably lacks the popular legitimacy that we associate with subsequent constitutions.

WILLIAM PENN, Proprietary and Governor of the Province of *Pensilvania* and Territories thereunto belonging, To all to whom these Presents shall come, sendeth Greeting. WHEREAS King CHARLES *the Second*, by His Letters Patents, under the Great Seal of *England*, bearing Date the *Fourth* Day of *March* in the Year *One Thousand Six Hundred and Eighty-one*, was graciously pleased to give and grant unto me, and my Heirs and Assigns for ever, this Province of Pennsilvania, with divers great Powers and Jurisdictions for the well Government thereof. . . .

Charter of Privileges Granted to the Inhabitants of Pennsylvania and Territories

AND WHEREAS I was then pleased to promise, That I would restore the said Charter to them again, with necessary Alterations, or in lieu thereof, give them another, better adapted to answer the present Circumstances and Conditions of the said Inhabitants; which they have now, by their Representatives in General Assembly met at *Philadelphia*, requested me to grant.

KNOW YE THEREFORE, That for the further Well-being and good Government of the said Province, and Territories; and in Pursuance of the Rights and Powers before-mentioned, I the said William Penn do declare, grant and confirm, unto all the Freemen, Planters and Adventurers, and other Inhabitants of this Province and Territories, these following Liberties, Franchises and Privileges, so far as in me lieth, to be held, enjoyed and kept, by the Freemen, Planters and Adventurers, and other Inhabitants of and in the said Province and Territories "hereunto annexed, for ever.

FIRST

BECAUSE no People can be truly happy, though under the greatest Enjoyment of Civil Liberties, if abridged of the Freedom of their Consciences, as to their Religious Profession and Worship: And Almighty God being the only Lord of Conscience, Father of Lights and Spirits; and the Author as well as Object of all divine Knowledge, Faith and Worship, who only doth enlighten the Minds, and persuade and convince the Understandings of People, I do hereby grant and declare, That no Person or Persons, inhabiting in this Province or Territories, who shall confess and acknowledge One almighty God, the Creator, Upholder and Ruler of the World; and profess him or themselves obliged to live quietly under the Civil Government, shall be in any Case molested or prejudiced, in his or their Person or Estate, because of his or their conscientious Persuasion or Practice, nor be compelled

"I do hereby grant and declare, That no Person or Persons, inhabiting in this Province or Territories, who shall confess and acknowledge One almighty God, the Creator, Upholder and Ruler of the World; and profess him or themselves obliged to live quietly under the Civil Government, shall be in any Case molested or prejudiced, in his or their Person or Estate, because of his or their conscientious Persuasion or Practice . . ."

to frequent or maintain any religious Worship, Place or Ministry, contrary to his or their Mind, or to do or super any other Act or Thing, contrary to their religious Persuasion.

AND that all Persons who also profess to believe in *Jesus Christ*, the Saviour of the World, shall be capable (notwithstanding their other Persuasions and Practices in Point of Conscience and Religion) to serve this Government in any Capacity, both legislatively and executively, he or they solemnly promising, when lawfully required, Allegiance to the King as Sovereign, and Fidelity to the Proprietary and Governor, and taking the Attests as now established by the Law made at *New-Castle*, in the Year *One Thousand and Seven Hundred*, entitled, *An Act directing the Attests of several Officers and Ministers*, as now amended and confirmed this present Assembly.

II

FOR the well governing of this Province and Territories, there shall be an Assembly yearly chosen, by the Freemen thereof, to consist of *Four* Persons out of each County, of most Note for Virtue, Wisdom and Ability, (or of a greater number at any Time, as the Governor and Assembly shall agree) upon the *First* Day of *October* for ever; and shall sit on the *Fourteenth* Day of the same Month, at *Philadelphia*, unless the Governor and Council for the Time being, shall see Clause to appoint another Place within the said Province or Territories: Which Assembly shall have Power to chuse a Speaker and other their Officers; and shall be Judges of the Qualifications and Elections of their own Members; sit upon their own Adjournments; appoint (committees; prepare Bills in order to pass into Laws; impeach Criminals, and redress Grievances; and shall have all other Powers and Privileges of an Assembly,

> In Great Britain, self-government was inextricably tied to representative institutions, most notably the Parliament. Penn established a similar assembly in Pennsylvania to govern local matters. The colony of Virginia had already instituted a House of Burgesses in 1619. Given the distance between the colonies and Great Britain, as well as the primitive state of communications, it was almost impossible for the colonies to be governed in their day-to-day affairs by Great Britain. This legacy of self-government would become increasingly important as the colonies began to question the authority of the distant Parliament to tax them.

according to the Rights of the free-born Subjects of *England*, and as is usual in any of the King's Plantations in *America*....

III

THAT the Freemen in each respective County at the Time and Place of Meeting for Electing their Representatives to serve in Assembly, may as often as there shall be Occasion, chuse a double Number of Persons to present to the Governor for Sheriffs and Coroners to serve for *Three* Years, if so long they behave themselves well; out of which respective Elections and Presentments, the Governor shall nominate and commissionate one for each of the said Offices, the *Third* Day after such Presentment, or else the First named in such Presentment, for each Office as aforesaid, shall stand and serve in that Office for the Time before respectively limited; and in Case of Death or Default, such Vacancies shall be supplied by the Governor, to serve to the End of the said Term.

IV

THAT the Laws of this Government shall be in this Stile, viz. *By the Governor, with the Consent and Approbations of the Freemen in General Assembly Met*; and shall be, after Confirmation by the Governor, forthwith recorded in the Rolls Office, and kept at *Philadelphia*, unless the Governor and Assembly shall agree to appoint another Place.

V

THAT all Criminals shall have the same Privileges of Witnesses and Council as their Prosecutors.

VI

THAT no Person or Persons shall or may, at any Time hereafter, be obliged to answer any Complaint, Matter or Thing whatsoever, relating to Property, before the Governor and Council, or in any other Place, but in ordinary Course of Justice, unless Appeals thereunto shall be hereafter by Law appointed.

> These guarantees are quite similar to some of those found within the Magna Carta and the English Bill of Rights as well as the future Bill of Rights to the U.S. Constitution.

VII

[omitted]

VIII

IF any person, through Temptation or Melancholy, shall destroy himself; his Estate, real and personal, shall notwithstanding descend to his Wife and Children, or Relations, as if he had died a natural Death; and if any Person shall be destroyed or killed by Casualty or Accident, there shall be no Forfeiture to the Governor by reason thereof. . . .

AND no Act, Law or Ordinance whatsoever, shall at any Time hereafter, be made or done, to alter, change or diminish the Form or Effect of this Charter, or of any Part or Clause therein, contrary to the true Intent and Meaning thereof, without the Consent of the Governor for the Time being, and *Six* Parts of *Seven* of the Assembly met.

> These two clauses mark significant landmarks in political thought. They recognize that written charters sometimes require changes (what we call constitutional amendments), but they also recognize that certain rights are so fundamental that to deny them would be contrary to the purposes of government. Penn tried to bridge this gap by providing for changing the constitution by a supermajority of six-sevenths of the assembly while shielding liberties of conscience from any changes.

BUT because the Happiness of Mankind depends so much upon the Enjoying of Liberty of their Consciences as aforesaid, I do hereby solemnly declare, promise and grant, for me, my Heirs and Assigns, That the *First* Article of this Charter relating to Liberty of Conscience, and every Part and Clause therein, according to the true

> **Intent and Meaning thereof, shall be kept and remain, without any Alteration, inviolably for ever.**

NOTWITHSTANDING which Separation of the Province and Territories, in Respect of Legislation, I do hereby promise, grant and declare, That the Inhabitants of both Province and Territories, shall separately enjoy all other Liberties, Privileges and Benefits, granted jointly to them in this Charter, any Law, Usage or Custom of this Government heretofore made and practiced, or any Law made and passed by this General Assembly, to the Contrary hereof, notwithstanding.

WILLIAM PENN.

THIS CHARTER of PRIVILEGES *being distinctly read in Assembly; and the whole and every Part thereof, being approved of and agreed to, by Us, we do thankfully receive the same from, our Proprietary and Governor, at* Philadelphia, *this* Twenty-Eighth *Day of* October, One Thousand Seven Hundred and One. *Signed on Behalf, and by Order of the Assembly*,

per JOSEPH GROWDON, *Speaker.*
EDWARD SHIPPEN,
PHINEAS PEMBERTON,
SAMUEL CARPENTER,
GRIFFITH OWEN,
CALEB PUSEY,
THOMAS STORY,
Proprietary and Governor's Council.

Source: William Penn. Charter of Privileges Granted to the Inhabitants of Pennsylvania and Territories, October 28, 1701. *The Federal and State Constitutions, Colonial Charters, and Other Organic Laws of the States, Territories, and Colonies Now or Heretofore Forming the United States of America.* Edited by Francis Newton Thorpe. Washington, DC: Government Printing Office, 1909.

Proclaim Liberty
Liberty Bell Inscription
1751

INTRODUCTION

One can tell much about a people and their values by examining their most cherished symbols. The Liberty Bell is one of America's most iconic landmarks. Originally commissioned in 1751 (perhaps in commemoration of the 50th anniversary of Penn's 1701 Charter of Privileges), the first bell was cast by the Whitechapel Foundry in London later that year. It cracked on its first ringing, however, and was melted down by John Pass and John Stow and recast in Philadelphia in 1753. It was taken down and hidden throughout much of the Revolutionary War period (for a time in the basement of the Zion Reformed Church in Allentown, Pennsylvania) so that it could not be melted down by the enemy for weapons. It was among the bells that pealed for the ratification of the U.S. Constitution.

In the 1840s, after nearly 100 years of use in the State House (today's Independence Hall), the Liberty Bell cracked again. Attempts to fix it proved unsuccessful, but while it would never ring again, the bell was increasingly viewed as a symbol, first of the abolitionist movement, then of unity after the Civil War (when it traveled from city to city), and later of women's suffrage and other causes. The bell is now on permanent exhibit in a building outside Independence Hall, near the Constitution Center in Philadelphia. The bell weighs approximately 2,080 pounds, is made of bronze, and is yoked to wood from an American elm.

Proclaim LIBERTY throughout all the Land unto all the Inhabitants thereof Lev. XXV X By Order of the ASSEMBLY of the Province of PENSYLVANIA for the State House in Philada

The inscription on the bell is from the biblical book of Leviticus and refers to the Year of Jubilee, an event that was to occur every 50 years and would result in the freeing of all slaves.

Source: National Park Service. "The Liberty Bell." Accessed January 14, 2015. http://www.nps.gov/inde/historyculture/stories-libertybell.htm.

Join, or Die

Benjamin Franklin's Sketch

May 9, 1754

INTRODUCTION

Benjamin Franklin was one of the greatest geniuses of the American Founding Era. He earned his early reputation in the area of journalism. Shortly before he proposed the Albany Plan of Union, Franklin drew this famous sketch, which is widely regarded as the first political cartoon. Beginning with the New England states and including most others (omitting Georgia), the figure suggests that the colonists' only hope for survival is unity. This was a perpetual theme throughout the American Revolution and the struggle for a constitution. It seems a bit odd to portray the colonies as a snake, but it has been argued that the undulations of its body somewhat paralleled those of America's eastern coastline. Early revolutionary flags would follow with the picture of a snake and the words "Don't Tread On Me!"

Source: Benjamin Franklin. Woodcut from *Pennsylvania Gazette* (Philadelphia), May 9, 1754. Library of Congress. Accessed January 14, 2015. http://www.loc.gov/exhibits/creating-the-united-states/revolution-of-the-mind.html#obj19.

Mutual Defence and Security
The Albany Plan of Union
July 10, 1754

INTRODUCTION

Founded and governed independently, the original 13 colonies dealt individually with Great Britain. But they also shared common threats, most notably from Native Americans and the French, which would eventually result in the French and Indian War (1754–1763). Long before they considered uniting against Great Britain, then, the colonists weighed whether they should unite, under Britain's protection, to achieve common goals. (The New England states had in fact joined together in a New England Confederation that lasted from 1643 to 1685).

The Albany Plan of Union, which was chiefly the work of Benjamin Franklin, was presented at an Albany Congress in 1754 and later become something of a model for the Articles of Confederation. It consisted of a preamble and 23 sections. The English, who had their own concerns about colonial unity, rejected the Albany Plan in favor of sending troops to the New World to defend the colonies from the French and indigenous tribes. The expense of housing these soldiers in the colonies, however, eventually led to parliamentary attempts to tax the colonies, which in turn sparked the Revolutionary War.

PLAN of a Proposed Union of the Several Colonies of Masachusets-bay, New Hampshire, Coneticut, Rhode Island, New York, New Jerseys, Pensilvania, Maryland, Virginia, North Carolina, and South Carolina, For their Mutual Defence and Security, and for Extending the British Settlements in North America.

THAT humble Application be made for an Act of the Parliament of Great Britain, by Virtue of which, one General Government may be formed in America, including all the said Colonies, within and under which Government, each Colony may retain its present Constitution, except in the Particulars

> The Articles of Confederation would later follow a similar pattern in individually listing the colonies that were participating rather than including them, as would the Constitution, under a broader rubric like "We the People."

The Albany Plan of Union

wherein a Change may be directed by the said Act, as hereafter follows.

> This presents the outline of both executive and legislative authorities.

President General
Grand Council
That the said General Government be administred by a President General, To be appointed and Supported by the Crown, and a Grand Council to be Chosen by the Representatives of the People of the Several Colonies, met in their respective Assemblies.

Election of Members

> Representation was to be apportioned according to rough population estimates rather than, as under the later Articles of Confederation, equally. In this respect, the document was arguably more democratic than the Articles of Confederation that would follow.

That within Months after the passing of such Act, The House of Representatives in the Several Assemblies, that Happen to be Sitting within that time or that shall be Specially for that purpose Convened, may and Shall Choose Members for the Grand Council in the following Proportions, that is to say.

Masachusets-Bay	7.
New Hampshire	2.
Conecticut	5.
Rhode-Island	2.
New-York	4.
New-Jerseys	3.
Pensilvania	6.
Maryland	4.
Virginia	7.
North-Carolina	4.
South-Carolina	4.
	48.

Place of first meeting

Who shall meet for the first time at the City of Philadelphia, in Pensilvania, being called by the President General as soon as conveniently may be, after his Appointment.

> Philadelphia was at the time the largest city in North America, and it was fairly centrally located. It would be the site of the two continental congresses and of the Constitutional Convention of 1787.

New Election

That there shall be a New Election of Members for the Grand Council every three years; And on the Death or Resignation of any Member his Place shall be Supplyed by a New Choice at the next Sitting of the Assembly of the Colony he represented.

Proportion of Members after first 3 years

That after the first three years, when the Proportion of Money arising out of each Colony to the General Treasury can be known, The Number of Members to be Chosen, for each Colony shall from time to time in all ensuing Elections be regulated by that proportion (yet so as that the Number to be Chosen by any one Province be not more than Seven nor less than Two).

> Delegates to the Constitutional Convention of 1787 would later consider using state contributions to allocate representation within Congress, but chose instead a compromise based on population in one house and on equality in the other.

Meetings of Grand Council.
Call.
That the Grand Council shall meet once in every Year, and oftner if Occasion require, at such Time and place as they shall adjourn to at the last preceeding meeting, or as they shall be called to meet at by the President General, on any Emergency, he having first obtained in Writing the Consent of seven of the Members to such call, and sent due and timely Notice to the whole.

Speaker.
Continuance.

That the Grand Council have Power to Chuse their Speaker, and shall neither be Dissolved, prorogued nor Continue Sitting longer than Six Weeks at one Time without their own Consent, or the Special Command of the Crown.

Member's Allowance

That the Members of the Grand Council shall be Allowed for their Service ten shillings Sterling per Diem, during their Sessions or Journey to and from the Place of Meeting; Twenty miles to be reckoned a days Journey.

Assent of President General. His Duty.

That the Assent of the President General be requisite, to all Acts of the Grand Council, and that it be His Office, and Duty to cause them to be carried into Execution.

Power of President and Grand Council. Peace and War.
Indian Purchases.
New Settlements
Laws to Govern them.
That the President General with the Advice of the Grand Council, hold or Direct all Indian Treaties in which the General Interest or Welfare of the Colony's may be Concerned; And make Peace or Declare War with the Indian Nations. That they make such Laws as they Judge Necessary for regulating all Indian Trade. That they make all Purchases from Indians for the Crown, of Lands not within the Bounds of Particular Colonies, or that shall not be within their Bounds when some of them are reduced to more Convenient Dimensions. That they make New Settlements on such Purchases, by Granting Lands in the Kings Name, reserving a Quit Rent to the Crown, for the use of the General Treasury. That they make Laws for regulating and Governing such new Settlements, till the Crown shall think fit to form them into Particular Governments.

Raise Soldiers &c. Lakes.
Not to Impress
Power to make Laws Duties &c.
Treasurer.
Money how to Issue.
That they raise and pay Soldiers, and build Forts for the Defence of any of the Colonies, and equip Vessels of Force to Guard the Coasts and Protect the Trade on the Ocean, Lakes, or Great Rivers; But they shall not Impress Men in any Colonies, without the Consent of its Legislature. That for these purposes they have Power to make Laws And lay and Levy such General Duties, Imposts, or Taxes, as to them shall appear most equal and Just, Considering the Ability and other Circumstances of the Inhabitants in the Several Colonies, and such as may be Collected with the least Inconvenience to the People, rather discouraging Luxury, than Loading Industry with unnecessary Burthens. That they may a General Treasurer and a Particular Treasurer in each Government, when Necessary, And from Time to Time may Order the Sums in the Treasuries of each Government, into the General Treasury, or draw on them for Special payments as they find most Convenient; Yet no money to Issue, but by joint Orders of the President General and Grand Council Except where Sums have been Appropriated to particular Purposes, And the President General is previously impowered By an Act to draw for such Sums.

Accounts.
That the General Accounts shall be yearly Settled and Reported to the Several Assembly's.

Quorum.
Laws to be Transmitted.

> Although this section deals almost exclusively with matters involving security and defense, it otherwise resembles the list of governmental powers later articulated in Article I, Section 8 of the U.S. Constitution. Had the colonists and Britain agreed to a plan whereby a general government in the colonies could raise taxes, it might have eased future controversies over the colonists' assertion that "taxation without representation" was improper.

The Albany Plan of Union

That a Quorum of the Grand Council impower'd to Act with the President General, do consist of Twenty-five Members, among whom there shall be one, or more from a Majority of the Colonies. That the Laws made by them for the Purposes aforesaid, shall not be repugnant but as near as may be agreeable to the Laws of England, and Shall be transmitted to the King in Council for Approbation, as Soon as may be after their Passing and if not disapproved within Three years after Presentation to remain in Force.

Death of President General.
That in case of the Death of the President General The Speaker of the Grand Council for the Time Being shall Succeed, and be Vested with the Same Powers, and Authority, to Continue until the King's Pleasure be known.

Officers how Appointed.
Vacancies how Supplied.
Each Colony may defend itself on Emergency.

> These provisions make for interesting comparisons with those in the U.S. Constitution for the appointment and confirmation of key officials as well as with provisions in Article IV relating to the rights of states to defend themselves against invasions.

That all Military Commission Officers Whether for Land or Sea Service, to Act under this General Constitution, shall be Nominated by the President General But the Approbation of the Grand Council, is to be Obtained before they receive their Commissions, And all Civil Officers are to be Nominated, by the Grand Council, and to receive the President General's Approbation, before they Officiate; But in Case of Vacancy by Death or removal of any Officer Civil or Military under this Constitution, The Governor of the Province, in which such Vacancy happens, may Appoint till the Pleasure of the President General and Grand Council can be known. That the Particular Military as well as Civil Establishments in each Colony remain in their present State, this General Constitution Notwithstanding. And that on Sudden Emergencies any Colony may Defend itself, and lay the Accounts of

Expence thence Arisen, before the President General and Grand Council, who may allow and order payment of the same As far as they Judge such Accounts Just and reasonable.

Source: Albany Plan of Union, July 10, 1754. "Documents Illustrative of the Formation of the Union of the American States." Washington, DC: Government Printing Office, 1927. House Document No. 398.

Section II: The Revolutionary and Confederal Periods

Life, Liberty, and Property
Declaration and Resolves of the First Continental Congress
October 14, 1774

INTRODUCTION

After the English Parliament sought to impose taxes on the colonies to pay for the protection that they had provided during the French and Indian War (referred to in this document as "the last war"), the colonists objected. Relying upon the principle of "no taxation without representation" contained in the Magna Carta, they charged that Parliament had no power to tax them because they were unrepresented in the body. As the Parliament continued asserting its authority, delegates from 12 of the colonies (all but Georgia) met in Philadelphia to draft a list of their grievances and to agree to a nonimportation agreement to pressure the British. Students should find it useful to compare the grievances that the colonists articulated in this document with those outlined later in the Declaration of Independence. Whereas the Declaration of Independence would assert the natural rights that Americans thought all human beings shared, this document put far greater focus on the rights that the colonists, who still considered themselves Englishmen, had brought with them to the New World. Interestingly, a number of 19th-century texts refer to this document, rather than the first 10 amendments to the U.S. Constitution, as the Bill, or declaration, of Rights.

Whereas, since the close of the last war, the British parliament, claiming a power, of right, to bind the people of America by statutes in all cases whatsoever, hath, in some acts, expressly imposed taxes on them, and in others, under various presences, but in fact for the purpose of raising a revenue, hath imposed rates and duties payable in these colonies, established a board of commissioners, with unconstitutional powers, and extended the jurisdiction of courts of admiralty, not only for collecting the said duties, but for the trial of causes merely arising within the body of a county:

And whereas, in consequence of other statutes, judges, who before held only estates at will in their offices, have been made dependant on the crown alone for their salaries, and standing armies kept in times of peace: And whereas it has lately been resolved in parliament, that by force of a statute, made in the thirty-fifth year of the reign of King Henry the Eighth, colonists may be transported to England, and tried there upon accusations for treasons and misprisions, or concealments of treasons committed in the colonies, and by a late statute, such trials have been directed in cases therein mentioned:

And whereas, in the last session of parliament, three statutes were made; one entitled, "An act to discontinue, in such manner and for such time as are therein mentioned, the landing and discharging, lading, or shipping of goods, wares and merchandise, at the town, and within the harbour of Boston, in the province of Massachusetts-Bay in New England;" another entitled, "An act for the better regulating the government of the province of Massachusetts-Bay in New England;" and another entitled, "An act for the impartial administration of justice, in the cases of persons questioned for any act done by them in the execution of the law, or for the suppression of riots and tumults, in the province of the Massachusetts-Bay in New England;" and another statute was then made, "for making more effectual provision for the government of the province of Quebec, etc." All which statutes are impolitic, unjust, and cruel, as well as unconstitutional, and most dangerous and destructive of American rights:

And whereas, assemblies have been frequently dissolved, contrary to the rights of the people, when they attempted to deliberate on grievances; and their dutiful, humble, loyal, and reasonable petitions to the crown for redress, have been

"And whereas, in the last session of parliament, three statutes were made; one entitled, "An act to discontinue, in such manner and for such time as are therein mentioned, the landing and discharging, lading, or shipping of goods, wares and merchandise, at the town, and within the harbour of Boston, in the province of Massachusetts-Bay in New England;" another entitled, "An act for the better regulating the government of the province of Massachusetts-Bay in New England;" and another entitled, "An act for the impartial administration of justice, in the cases of persons questioned for any act done by them in the execution of the law, or for the suppression of riots and tumults, in the province of the Massachusetts-Bay in New England . . ."

repeatedly treated with contempt, by his Majesty's ministers of state:

> As in the later Articles of Confederation, the colonists listed their names separately, almost as though each were a separate nation, rather than collectively, as in "We the People," the opening words to the U.S. Constitution.

The good people of the several colonies of New-Hampshire, Massachusetts-Bay, Rhode Island and Providence Plantations, Connecticut, New-York, New-Jersey, Pennsylvania, Newcastle, Kent, and Sussex on Delaware, Maryland, Virginia, North-Carolina and South-Carolina, justly alarmed at these arbitrary proceedings of parliament and administration, have severally elected, constituted, and appointed deputies to meet, and sit in general Congress, in the city of Philadelphia, in order to obtain such establishment, as that their religion, laws, and liberties, may not be subverted: Whereupon the deputies so appointed being now assembled, in a full and free representation of these colonies, taking into their most serious consideration, the best means of attaining the ends aforesaid, do, in the first place, as Englishmen, their ancestors in like cases have usually done, for asserting and vindicating their rights and liberties, DECLARE,

> Whereas the Declaration of Independence would later appeal to the belief in common natural rights, that idea is one of only three grounds invoked in this document, which understands the colonists in America to be British subjects.

That the inhabitants of the English colonies in North-America, by the immutable laws of nature, the principles of the English constitution, and the several charters or compacts, have the following RIGHTS:

> The rights identified here are similar to the three identified in the opening paragraph of the Declaration of Independence. "N. C. D." stands for the Latin *nemine contra dicente,* meaning "no one contradicting."

Resolved, N.C.D. 1. **That they are entitled to life, liberty and property: and they have never ceded to any foreign power whatever, a right to dispose of either without their consent.**

Resolved, N.C.D. 2. That our ancestors, who first settled these colonies, were at the time of their emigration from the mother country, entitled to all the rights, liberties, and immunities of free and natural-born subjects, within the realm of England.

Resolved, N.C.D. 3. That by such emigration they by no means forfeited, surrendered, or lost any of those rights, but that they were, and their descendants now are, entitled to the exercise and enjoyment of all such of them, as their local and other circumstances enable them to exercise and enjoy.

Resolved, N.C.D. 4. That the foundation of English liberty, and of all free government, is a right in the people to participate in their legislative council: and as the English colonists are not represented, and from their local and other circumstances, cannot properly be represented in the British parliament, they are entitled to a free and exclusive power of legislation in their several provincial legislatures, where their right of representation can alone be preserved, in all cases of taxation and internal polity, subject only to the negative of their sovereign, in such manner as has been heretofore used and accustomed: But, from the necessity of the case, and a regard to the mutual interest of both countries, we cheerfully consent to the operation of such acts of the British parliament, as are bonfide, restrained to the regulation of our external commerce, for the purpose of securing the commercial advantages of the whole empire to the mother country, and the commercial benefits of its respective members; excluding every idea of taxation internal or external, for raising a revenue on the subjects, in America, without their consent.

Resolved, N.C.D. 5. **That the respective colonies are entitled to the common law of England, and more especially to the great and inestimable privilege of being tried by their peers of the vicinage, according to the course of that law.**

Resolved, N.C.D. 6. That they are entitled to the benefit of such of the English statutes, as existed at the time of their colonization; and which they have, by experience,

"That by such emigration they by no means forfeited, surrendered, or lost any of those rights . . ."

"That the foundation of English liberty, and of all free government, is a right in the people to participate in their legislative council: and as the English colonists are not represented, and from their local and other circumstances, cannot properly be represented in the British parliament, they are entitled to a free and exclusive power of legislation in their several provincial legislatures . . ."

The British common law was a set of judge-made rules that emerged from cases and were collected within casebooks as precedents. Trial by jury was a key right that would later be reaffirmed both in the U.S. Constitution and in the Bill of Rights.

> *"That these, his Majesty's colonies, are likewise entitled to all the immunities and privileges granted and confirmed to them by royal charters, or secured by their several codes of provincial laws."*

respectively found to be applicable to their several local and other circumstances.

Resolved, N.C.D. 7. That these, his Majesty's colonies, are likewise entitled to all the immunities and privileges granted and confirmed to them by royal charters, or secured by their several codes of provincial laws.

Resolved, N.C.D. 8. That they have a right peaceably to assemble, consider of their grievances, and petition the king; and that all prosecutions, prohibitory proclamations, and commitments for the same, are illegal.

Resolved, N.C.D. 9. That the keeping a standing army in these colonies, in times of peace, without the consent of the legislature of that colony, in which such army is kept, is against law.

Resolved, N.C.D. 10. It is indispensably necessary to good government, and rendered essential by the English constitution, that the constituent branches of the legislature be independent of each other; that, therefore, the exercise of legislative power in several colonies, by a council appointed, during pleasure, by the crown, is unconstitutional, dangerous and destructive to the freedom of American legislation.

All and each of which the aforesaid deputies, in behalf of themselves, and their constituents, do claim, demand, and insist on, as their indubitable rights and liberties, which cannot be legally taken from them, altered or abridged by any power whatever, without their own consent, by their representatives in their several provincial legislature.

In the course of our inquiry, we find many infringements and violations of the foregoing rights, which, from an ardent desire, that harmony and mutual intercourse of affection and interest may be restored, we pass over for the present, and proceed to state such acts and measures as have been adopted since the last war, which demonstrate a system formed to enslave America.

Resolved, N.C.D. That the following acts of parliament are infringements and violations of the rights of the colonists; and that the repeal of them is essentially necessary, in order to restore harmony between Great Britain and the American colonies, viz. . . . [*Here the document goes on to list various statutes that the colonists believe violate colonial rights.*]

To these grievous acts and measures, Americans cannot submit, but in hopes their fellow subjects in Great Britain will, on a revision of them, restore us to that state, in which both countries found happiness and prosperity, we have for the present, only resolved to pursue the following peaceable measures: 1. To enter into a non-importation, non-consumption, and non-exportation agreement or association. 2. To prepare an address to the people of Great-Britain, and a memorial to the inhabitants of British America: and 3. To prepare a loyal address to his majesty, agreeable to resolutions already entered into.

Source: *Documents Illustrative of the Formation of the American States.* Selected by Charles C. Tansill. Washington, DC: Government Printing Office, 1927.

"To these grievous acts and measures, Americans cannot submit, but in hopes their fellow subjects in Great Britain will, on a revision of them, restore us to that state, in which both countries found happiness and prosperity, we have for the present, only resolved to pursue the following peaceable measures . . ."

So Void of Common Sense

Washington Forbids Soldiers from Celebrating Guy Fawkes Day

November 5, 1775

> **INTRODUCTION**
>
> As the 13 colonies sought allies in the fighting against Great Britain, George Washington, whom the Second Continental Congress had appointed commander of colonial forces on May 9, 1775, got word that some of his soldiers were planning to celebrate Guy Fawkes Day. Widely commemorated in England as the day that Guy Fawkes had been arrested for attempting to blow up the Parliament and kill King James I, the celebrations included burning the pope in effigy. Washington recognized that this would undercut plans by the 13 colonies to secure the help of Canada, but he also expressed genuine dismay at the thought of his soldiers participating in an event that would stir religious animosities.

This pronouncement, which came long before the adoption of the First Amendment guaranteeing free exercise of religion, makes for a fascinating comparison to Washington's letter to a Jewish congregation in Rhode Island, which is included in Section IV of this book. Washington would welcome individuals of all faiths in the fight against Great Britain, making it clear that the war was not to be pursued for sectarian purposes.

As the Commander in Chief has been apprized of a design form'd for the observance of that ridiculous and childish custom of burning the Effigy of the pope—He cannot help expressing his surprise that there should be Officers and Soldiers in this army so void of common sense, as not to see the impropriety of such a step at this Juncture; at a Time when we are soliciting, and have really obtain'd the friendship and alliance of the people of Canada, whom we ought to consider as Brethren embarked in the same Cause. The defense of the general Liberty of America: At such a juncture, and in such Circumstances, to be insulting their Religion, is so monstrous, as not to be suffered or excused; indeed instead of offering the most remote insult, it is our duty to address public thanks to these our Brethren, as to them we are so much indebted for every late happy Success over the common Enemy in Canada.

Source: Order in Quarters issued by General George Washington, November 5, 1775. *The Writings of George Washington from the Original Manuscript Sources, 1745–1799, Volume 4.* Edited by John C. Fitzpatrick. Washington, DC: Government Printing Office, 1931, pp. 64–65.

'Tis Time to Part
Thomas Paine's *Common Sense*
1776

INTRODUCTION

Long after they had renounced parliamentary sovereignty, and even after fighting broke out between Americans and the British at Lexington and Concord, Massachusetts, in April 1775, many Americans continued to identify with the British king and to hope for eventual reconciliation. As the king continued to side with Parliament against the colonies, however, Thomas Paine, an immigrant from Britain, published *Common Sense* in January 1776 to encourage the colonists to renounce their loyalty to the king. Although his later publication of *The Rights of Man* demonstrated that his own views of Christianity were fairly unconventional, in *Common Sense* Paine based his call for independence on fairly traditional arguments from scripture, most of which were designed to show that the Bible had not intended for the Israelites to have a king.

"Society is produced by our wants, and government by our wickedness; the former promotes our happiness positively by uniting our affections, the latter negatively by restraining our vices."

Paine began with a very minimalistic view of the role of government, not unlike that shared by many modern-day libertarians. Although Paine viewed government as necessitated by human imperfections, he saw it as chiefly designed to secure human life and liberty. When it failed to do so, he thought the people had the right to replace it.

Chapter 1
Of the Origin and Design of Government in General. With Concise Remarks on the English Constitution.

Some writers have so confounded society with government, as to leave little or no distinction between them; whereas they are not only different, but have different origins. Society is produced by our wants, and government by our wickedness; the former promotes our happiness positively by uniting our affections, the latter negatively by restraining our vices. The one encourages intercourse, the other creates distinctions. The first is a patron, the last a punisher.

Society in every state is a blessing, but government even in its best state is but a necessary evil; in its worst state an

intolerable one; for when we suffer, or are exposed to the same miseries by a government, which we might expect in a country without government, our calamities is heightened by reflecting that we furnish the means by which we suffer. Government, like dress, is the badge of lost innocence; the palaces of kings are built on the ruins of the bowers of paradise. For were the impulses of conscience clear, uniform, and irresistibly obeyed, man would need no other lawgiver; but that not being the case, he finds it necessary to surrender up a part of his property to furnish means for the protection of the rest; and this he is induced to do by the same prudence which in every other case advises him out of two evils to choose the least. Wherefore, security being the true design and end of government, it unanswerably follows that whatever form thereof appears most likely to ensure it to us, with the least expence and greatest benefit, is preferable to all others.

"Government, like dress, is the badge of lost innocence; the palaces of kings are built on the ruins of the bowers of paradise."

Chapter 2
Of Monarchy and Hereditary Succession

Mankind being originally equals in the order of creation, the equality could only be destroyed by some subsequent circumstance; the distinctions of rich, and poor, may in a great measure be accounted for, and that without having recourse to the harsh, ill-sounding names of oppression and avarice. Oppression is often the consequence, but seldom or never the means of riches; and though avarice will preserve a man from being necessitously poor, it generally makes him too timorous to be wealthy.

But there is another and greater distinction for which no truly natural or religious reason can be assigned, and that is, the distinction of men into KINGS and

Whereas many contemporaries took the division of mankind into kings and subjects for granted, Paine did not. In this chapter, he criticizes the practice of hereditary succession whereby rulers passed down their thrones to their offspring. He further associates monarchs with war and oppression, argues that scriptures warn against monarchy, and asserts that continued association with Britain will mean that Americans will continue to be needlessly involved in wars.

> *"[H]ow a race of men came into the world so exalted above the rest, and distinguished like some new species, is worth enquiring into, and whether they are the means of happiness or of misery to mankind."*
>
> As its title suggests, Paine devoted this chapter to arguing that it was time for Americans to declare their independence.

SUBJECTS. Male and female are the distinctions of nature, good and bad the distinctions of heaven; but how a race of men came into the world so exalted above the rest, and distinguished like some new species, is worth enquiring into, and whether they are the means of happiness or of misery to mankind. . . .

Thoughts on the Present State of American Affairs

Europe is too thickly planted with kingdoms to be long at peace, and whenever a war breaks out between England and any foreign power, the trade of America goes to ruin, because of her connection with Britain. The next war may not turn out like the last, and should it not, the advocates for reconciliation now will be wishing for separation then, because, neutrality in that case, would be a safer convoy than a man of war. Every thing that is right or natural pleads for separation. The blood of the slain, the weeping voice of nature cries, 'TIS TIME TO PART. Even the distance at which the Almighty hath placed England and America, is a strong and natural proof, that the authority of the one, over the other, was never the design of Heaven. The time likewise at which the continent was discovered, adds weight to the argument, and the manner in which it was peopled encreases the force of it. The reformation was preceded by the discovery of America, as if the Almighty graciously meant to open a sanctuary to the persecuted in future years, when home should afford neither friendship nor safety. . . .

> Although the Second Continental Congress was in session, it had not yet proposed the Articles of Confederation. Paine proceeds to provide a sketchy outline of what he thinks will work.

If there is any true cause of fear respecting independance, it is because no plan is yet laid down. Men do not see their way out–Wherefore, as an opening into that business, I offer the following hints; at the same time modestly affirming, that I have no other opinion of them myself,

than that they may be the means of giving rise to something better. Could the straggling thoughts of individuals be collected, they would frequently form materials for wise and able men to improve to useful matter.

LET the assemblies be annual, with a President only. The representation more equal. Their business wholly domestic, and subject to the authority of a Continental Congress.

Let each colony be divided into six, eight, or ten, convenient districts, each district to send a proper number of delegates to Congress, so that each colony send at least thirty. The whole number in Congress will be at least 390. Each Congress to sit and to choose a president by the following method. When the delegates are met, let a colony be taken from the whole thirteen colonies by lot, after which let the whole Congress choose (by ballot) a president from out of the delegates of that province. In the next Congress, let a colony be taken by lot from twelve only, omitting that colony from which the president was taken in the former Congress, and so proceeding on till the whole thirteen shall have had their proper rotation. And in order that nothing may pass into a law but what is satisfactorily just, not less than three fifths of the Congress to be called a majority.-He that will promote discord, under a government so equally formed as this, would join Lucifer in his revolt.

But as there is a peculiar delicacy, from whom, or in what manner, this business must first arise, and as it seems most agreeable and consistent, that it should come from some intermediate body between the governed and the governors, that is between the Congress and the people, let a CONTINENTAL CONFERENCE be held, in the following manner, and for the following purpose.

A committee of twenty-six members of Congress, viz. two for each colony. Two members for each house of assembly, or Provincial convention; and five representatives of the people at large, to be chosen in the capital city or town of each province, for, and in behalf of the whole province, by as many qualified voters as shall think proper to attend from all parts of the province for that purpose; or, if more convenient, the representatives may be chosen in two or three of the most populous parts thereof. In this conference, thus assembled, will be united, the two grand principles of business, knowledge and power. The members of Congress, Assemblies, or Conventions, by having had experience in national concerns, will be able and useful counsellors, and the whole, being impowered by the people will have a truly legal authority.

> Constitutions are known not only for creating institutions of government, but for establishing the parameters of those powers, especially with respect to the exercise of individual rights. Paine suggests that this should be accomplished through what he calls "a Continental Charter."

The conferring members being met, let their business be to frame a CONTINENTAL CHARTER, or Charter of the United Colonies; (answering to what is called the Magna Charta of England) fixing the number and manner of choosing members of Congress, members of Assembly, with their date of sitting, and drawing the line of business and jurisdiction between them: (Always remembering, that our strength is continental, not provincial:) Securing freedom and property to all men, and above all things the free exercise of religion, according to the dictates of conscience; with such other matter as is necessary for a charter to contain. Immediately after which, the said conference to dissolve, and the bodies which shall he chosen conformable to the said charter, to be the legislators and governors of this continent for the time being: Whose peace and happiness, may God preserve, Amen.

Should any body of men be hereafter delegated for this or some similar purpose, I offer them the following extracts from that wise observer on governments Dragonetti. "The science" says he, "of the politician consists in fixing the true point of happiness and freedom. Those men would deserve the gratitude of ages, who should discover a mode of government that contained the greatest sum of individual happiness, with the least national expence. Dragonetti on Virtue and Rewards."

But where says some is the King of America? I'll tell you Friend, he reigns above, and doth not make havock of mankind like the Royal—of Britain. Yet that we may not appear to be defective even in earthly honors, let a day be solemnly set apart for proclaiming the charter; let it be brought forth placed on the divine law, the word of God; let a crown be placed thereon, by which the world may know, that so far as we approve of monarchy, that in America THE LAW IS KING. For as in absolute governments the King is law, so in free countries the law ought to be King; and there ought to be no other. But lest any ill use should afterwards arise, let the crown at the conclusion of the ceremony be demolished, and scattered among the people whose right it is.

In what may be the most important pronouncement in this work, Paine suggests that Americans should replace the rule of a monarch with the rule of law. After "crowning" such a document, he further recommends destroying the crown, lest it be used for oppressive purposes.

A government of our own is our natural right: And when a man seriously reflects on the precariousness of human affairs, he will become convinced, that it is infinitely wiser and safer, to form a constitution of our own in a cool deliberate manner, while we have it in our power, than to trust such an interesting event to time and chance.

Having urged Americans to declare their independence, Paine could no longer appeal based on the rights of English citizenship; he appealed on the basis of human, or natural, rights. Much of the rest of this essay emphasizes that Americans can prevail in a struggle against Britain.

Source: Thomas Paine. *Common Sense*. Philadelphia, PA: R. Bell, 1776. American Imprint Collection, Rare Book and Special Collections Division, Library of Congress.

Remember the Ladies
Abigail and John Adams, Correspondence on Women's Issues
March–August 1776

> **INTRODUCTION**
>
> The Adams family was one of the most distinguished in early American history. John Adams would serve as the nation's second president, and his son John Quincy Adams would serve as the nation's sixth. John's involvement in the American Revolution and his extended service abroad as a U.S. diplomat meant that he was often separated from his beloved wife Abigail—the well-read, home-educated educated daughter of a pastor—with whom he carried on a lively correspondence. One of their most prescient exchanges occurred while John was attending the Second Continental Congress. John further elaborated on his views in correspondence with James Sullivan, a Massachusetts state judge who was sympathetic to women's rights.
>
> Although the initial letters were written before the Declaration of Independence's assertion that all men were created equal (a phrase that was likely intended to include humankind in general), Abigail's letter to her husband indicates that the spirit of liberty was in the air. She, at least, was applying the lessons to the relationship between the sexes as well as that of the colonists toward the king.

"And, by the way, in the new code of laws which I suppose it will be necessary for you to make, I desire you would remember the ladies and be more generous and favorable to them than your ancestors. Do not put such unlimited power into the hands of the husbands. Remember, all men would be tyrants if they could."

Letter from Abigail Adams to John Adams, March 31, 1776

I long to hear that you have declared an independency. And, by the way, in the new code of laws which I suppose it will be necessary for you to make, I desire you would remember the ladies and be more generous and favorable to them than your ancestors. Do not put such unlimited power into the hands of the husbands. Remember, all men would be tyrants if they could.

If particular care and attention is not paid to the ladies, we are determined to foment a rebellion, and will not hold ourselves bound by any laws in which we have no voice or representation.

That your sex are naturally tyrannical is a truth so thoroughly established as to admit of no dispute; but such of you as wish to be happy willingly give up the harsh title of master for the more tender and endearing one of friend.

Why, then, not put it out of the power of the vicious and the lawless to use us with cruelty and indignity with impunity? Men of sense in all ages abhor those customs which treat us only as the vassals of your sex; regard us then as beings placed by Providence under your protection, and in imitation of the Supreme Being make use of that power only for our happiness.

> Few phrases are better known from the Founding Period than Abigail's plea that John and his corevolutionaries "remember the ladies" in their deliberations. It is difficult to tease out the degree to which Abigail was being completely serious (did she have particular legal abuses, like the control of property, which was almost always in the husband's name, in mind?) and the degree to which her correspondence was intended to be somewhat playful. The last paragraph suggests that Abigail was comfortable with at least some aspects of conventional gender roles (the man as woman's protector rather than tyrant).

John Adams Responds on April 14, 1776

As to your extraordinary code of laws, I cannot but laugh. We have been told that our struggle has loosened the bonds of government everywhere; that children and apprentices were disobedient; that schools and colleges were grown turbulent; that Indians slighted their guardians, and negroes grew insolent to their masters. But your letter was the first intimation that another tribe, more numerous and powerful than all the rest, were grown discontented.—This is rather too coarse a Compliment but you are so saucy, I won't blot it out.

"As to your extraordinary code of laws, I cannot but laugh."

Depend upon it, we know better than to repeal our masculine systems. Although they are in full force, you know they are little more than theory. We dare not exert our power in its full latitude. We are obliged to go fair and softly, and, in practice, you know we are the subjects. We have only the name of masters, and rather than give up

> John Adams appears to treat Abigail's pleas almost as though they are a joke, and yet her words seem to confirm the fears of those who worried that political revolution would also lead to social revolution. Like Abigail's initial letter, Adams's response indicates an understanding that political power could not fully be gauged by power at the ballot box. His reference to women as members of a "tribe" seems unusual, and (given contemporary white attitudes toward Native Americans) not particularly helpful for the cause of women's rights.

this, which would completely subject us to the despotism of the petticoat, I hope General Washington and all our brave heroes would fight; I am sure every good politician would plot, as long as he would against despotism, empire, monarchy, aristocracy, oligarchy, or ochlocracy.

Letter from Abigail Adams to John Adams, August 14, 1776

If you complain of neglect of education in sons, what shall I say with regard to daughters, who every day experience the want of it? With regard to the education of my own children, I find myself soon out of my depth, and destitute and deficient in every part of education....

> This letter, written at a time when most education above the grade school level was reserved for men, seems more closely tied to hopes for equality of educational opportunity than political power. With a husband so frequently absent from the home, Abigail had special reason to feel the difficulty of educating her children when her own formal education was so deficient by comparison to that of her husband, a Harvard graduate.

I most sincerely wish that some more liberal plan might be laid and executed for the benefit of the rising generation, and that our new constitution may be distinguished for learning and virtue. If we mean to have heroes, statesmen and philosophers, we should have learned women. The world perhaps would laugh at me, and accuse me of vanity, but you I know have a mind too enlarged and liberal to disregard the sentiment. If much depends as is allowed upon the early education of youth and the first principles which are instilled take the deepest root, great benefit must arise from literary accomplishments in women.

Letter from John Adams to James Sullivan, May 26, 1776

"It is certain in Theory, that the only moral Foundation of Government is the Consent of the People, But to what an Extent Shall We carry this Principle?"

It is certain in Theory, that the only moral Foundation of Government is the Consent of the People, But to what an Extent Shall We carry this Principle? Shall We Say that every Individual of the Community, old and young, male and female, as well as rich and poor, must consent, expressly to every Act of Legislation? No, you will Say. This is impossible. How then does the Right arise in the Majority to govern the Minority, against their Will? Whence arises the Right of the Men to govern Women, without their Consent? Whence the Right of the old to bind the Young, without theirs.

But let us first Suppose, that the whole Community of every Age, Rank, Sex, and Condition, has a Right to vote. This Community, is assembled—a Motion is made and carried by a Majority of one Voice. The Minority will not agree to this. Whence arises the Right of the Majority to govern, and the Obligation of the Minority to obey? from Necessity, you will Say, because there can be no other Rule. But why exclude Women? You will Say, because their Delicacy renders them unfit for Practice and Experience, in the great Business of Life, and the hardy Enterprises of War, as well as the arduous Cares of State. Besides, their attention is So much engaged with the necessary Nurture of their Children, that Nature has made them fittest for domestic Cares. And Children have not Judgment or Will of their own.

True. But will not these Reasons apply to others? Is it not equally true, that Men in general in every Society, who are wholly destitute of Property, are also too little acquainted with public Affairs to form a Right Judgment, and too dependent upon other Men to have a Will of their own? If this is a Fact, if you give to every Man, who has no Property, a Vote, will you not make a fine encouraging Provision for Corruption by your fundamental Law? Such is the Frailty of the human Heart, that very few Men, who have no Property, have any Judgment of their own. They talk and vote as they are directed by Some Man of Property, who has attached their Minds to his Interest.

Some revolutionaries, like Adams, who wanted freedom from Britain did not associate such freedom with equal suffrage and had serious doubts about extending the vote to women or men with limited property. The U.S. Constitution would leave voting qualifications to the states. In 1848, delegates to the Seneca Falls Convention adopted a declaration, patterned after the Declaration of Independence, that declared that all men and women were created equal. But it was not until the ratification of the Nineteenth Amendment in 1920 that women throughout the United States gained the right to vote.

Abigail and John Adams, Correspondence on Women's Issues

"Depend upon it, sir, it is dangerous to open So fruitfull a Source of Controversy and Altercation, as would be opened by attempting to alter the Qualifications of Voters."

Depend upon it, sir, it is dangerous to open So fruitfull a Source of Controversy and Altercation, as would be opened by attempting to alter the Qualifications of Voters. There will be no End of it. New Claims will arise. Women will demand a Vote. Lads from 12 to 21 will think their Rights not enough attended to, and every Man, who has not a Farthing, will demand an equal Voice with any other in all Acts of State. It tends to confound and destroy all Distinctions, and prostrate all Ranks, to one common Level.

Sources: Charles Francis Adams, ed. *Familiar Letters of John Adams and His Wife Abigail Adams, During the Revolution.* Cambridge, MA: Houghton, 1875, pp. 149–50, 213, 144.

Letter from John Adams to James Sullivan, *The Works of John Adams*. Vol. 9. Edited by Charles Francis Adams. Boston: Little, Brown and Company, 1854, pp. 375–78. Online Library of Liberty, http://oll.libertyfund.org/titles/2107.

Adopt Such Government

Resolution of Second Continental Congress

May 10, 1776

INTRODUCTION

This resolution, introduced by John Adams and adopted by the Second Continental Congress on May 10, 1776, set in motion a period of state constitution writing that would provide models for the national government. Initial state constitutions were not as uniform as they would become after the adoption of the U.S. Constitution, but most of them elevated the legislative branch above relatively weak executives and judiciaries.

Resolved, That it be recommended to the respective assemblies and conventions of the United Colonies, where no government sufficient to the exigencies of their affairs have been hitherto established, to adopt such government as shall, in the opinion of the representatives of the people, best conduce to the happiness and safety of their constituents in particular, and America in general.

> The colonists recognized that the governments hitherto administered by Britain would need to be replaced by new documents, better adapted to new circumstances. In this resolution, it is clear that they regarded constitutions as a means of securing the public good.

Source: *Journals of Continental Congress, Volume 4.* Edited by Worthington Chauncey Ford. Washington, DC: Government Printing Office, 1906, p. 342.

Absolved from All Allegiance
Richard Henry Lee's Resolutions
June 7, 1776

> **INTRODUCTION**
>
> Virginia's Richard Henry Lee introduced three historically important resolutions in Congress on June 7, 1776. Each led to an important political development. The resolutions carried particular weight because they came from a delegate from the most populous colony, whose support would be absolutely essential to the successful prosecution of a war with Great Britain.

This resolution led to the writing and adoption of the Declaration of Independence, which incorporates the motion within its final paragraph. The decision came after months of deliberating and petitioning the English king in hopes that he would seek to overturn parliamentary assertions of authority (especially taxation) over the colonies.

Resolved, That these United Colonies are, and of right ought to be, free and independent States, that they are absolved from all allegiance to the British Crown, and that all political connection between them and the State of Great Britain is, and ought to be, totally dissolved.

The colonists realized that Great Britain was the most formidable power in the world of their day and that they needed allies if they hoped to gain their independence. French naval help would prove to be especially critical at Yorktown, Virginia, in the final days of the Revolutionary War.

That it is expedient forthwith to take the most effectual measures for forming foreign Alliances.

This final resolution demonstrates the colonists' understanding that they would need to act in a more unified manner if they hoped to defeat the British. The resolution led Congress to draw up the Articles of Confederation, which served as the nation's official government from 1781 through 1789, when the new Constitution fully went into effect.

That a plan of confederation be prepared and transmitted to the respective Colonies for their consideration and approbation.

Source: *Journals of the Continental Congress 1774–1779.* Edited by Worthington Chauncey Ford. Washington, DC: Government Printing Office, 1905.

The Basis and Foundation of Government
The Virginia Declaration of Rights
Ratified on June 12, 1776

INTRODUCTION

George Mason, a planter and longtime neighbor of George Washington, was the key figure in drafting both the Virginia constitution (Jefferson drafted a plan but it arrived in the Virginia legislature too late for consideration) and the Virginia Declaration of Rights, which was somewhat modified by the convention and ratified on June 12, 1776. Phrased more like a set of aspirations than a set of judicially enforceable norms (as in the U.S. Constitution), the Declaration of Rights, like Jefferson's Declaration of Independence that followed one month later, highlighted the colonists' belief in natural rights and their continuing concern for due process.

George Mason later served as a delegate to the Constitutional Convention of 1787. Although he engaged actively in its proceedings, he was one of three remaining delegates who refused to sign the document, largely because it did not include a bill of rights.

A declaration of rights made by the representatives of the good people of Virginia, assembled in full and free convention; which rights do pertain to them and their posterity, as the basis and foundation of government.

> Although state legislatures adopted some early constitutions and accompanying declarations, this was adopted, like the later U.S. Constitution, by a special convention called for that purpose.

SEC. 1. That all men are by nature equally free and independent and have certain inherent rights, of which, when they enter into a state of society, they cannot, by any compact, deprive or divest their posterity; namely, the enjoyment of life and liberty, with the means of acquiring and possessing property, and pursuing and obtaining happiness and safety.

> There are obvious parallels between these sentiments and those of the Declaration of Independence, although the latter elevates the trio of liberties connected to "life, liberty, and the pursuit of happiness." George Mason owned many slaves. The phrase "when they enter into a state of society" was proposed by Edmund Pendleton, in hopes that it would thus not be considered to apply to slaves.

SEC. 2. That all power is vested in, and consequently derived from, the people; that magistrates are their trustees and servants and at all times amenable to them.

> Echoed by the reference to "We the People" in the U.S. Constitution, Mason emphasizes that government rests upon popular consent.

The Virginia Declaration of Rights

> Here, as in the writings of John Locke and the Declaration of Independence, the Virginia declaration views the right of revolution as a logical complement to the notion that governments that do not fulfill basic human purposes are subject to dissolution and replacement by governments that can and will so do.

SEC. 3. That government is, or ought to be, instituted for the common benefit, protection, and security of the people, nation, or community; of all the various modes and forms of government, that is best which is capable of producing the greatest degree of happiness and safety and is most effectually secured against the danger of maladministration; and that, when any government shall be found inadequate or contrary to these purposes, a majority of the community hath an indubitable, inalienable, and indefeasible right to reform, alter, or abolish it, in such manner as shall be judged most conducive to the public weal.

SEC. 4. That no man, or set of men, are entitled to exclusive or separate emoluments or privileges from the community, but in consideration of public services; which, not being descendible, neither ought the offices of magistrate, legislator, or judge to be hereditary.

> Defenders of the U.S. Constitution would claim that the entire document was a bill of rights in that it provided for checks against arbitrary government. Clearly, Mason and his compatriots viewed the principles of separation of powers and of periodic elections as means to securing personal liberty.

SEC. 5. That the legislative and executive powers of the state should be separate and distinct from the judiciary; and that the members of the two first may be restrained from oppression, by feeling and participating the burdens of the people, they should, at fixed periods, be reduced to a private station, return into that body from which they were originally taken, and the vacancies be supplied by frequent, certain, and regular elections, in which all, or any part, of the former members, to be again eligible, or ineligible, as the laws shall direct.

SEC. 6. That elections of members to serve as representatives of the people, in assembly, ought to be free; and that all men, having sufficient evidence of permanent common interest with, and attachment to, the community, have the right of suffrage and cannot be taxed or deprived of their property for public uses without their own consent, or that of their representatives so elected, nor bound by any law to which they have not, in like manner, assented for the public good.

SEC. 7. That all power of suspending laws, or the execution of laws, by any authority, without consent of the representatives of the people, is injurious to their rights and ought not to be exercised.

SEC. 8. That in all capital or criminal prosecutions a man hath a right to demand the cause and nature of his accusation, to be confronted with the accusers and witnesses, to call for evidence in his favor, and to a speedy trial by an impartial jury of twelve men of his vicinage, without whose unanimous consent he cannot be found guilty; nor can he be compelled to give evidence against himself; that no man be deprived of his liberty, except by the law of the land or the judgment of his peers.

SEC. 9. That excessive bail ought not to be required, nor excessive fines imposed, nor cruel and unusual punishments inflicted.

SEC. 10. That general warrants, whereby an officer or messenger may be commanded to search suspected places without evidence of a fact committed, or to seize any person or persons not named, or whose offense is not particularly described and supported by evidence, are grievous and oppressive and ought not to be granted.

SEC. 11. That in controversies respecting property, and in suits between man and man, the ancient trial by jury is preferable to any other and ought to be held sacred.

"That general warrants, whereby an officer or messenger may be commanded to search suspected places without evidence of a fact committed, or to seize any person or persons not named, or whose offense is not particularly described and supported by evidence, are grievous and oppressive and ought not to be granted."

The Virginia Declaration of Rights

Many of these provisions, which put strong emphasis on the rights of criminal defendants, would later be incorporated into the first 10 amendments to the U.S. Constitution.

SEC. 12. That the freedom of the press is one of the great bulwarks of liberty and can never be restrained but by despotic governments.

Mason joined other "republican" thinkers who feared that leaders would use "standing armies" to threaten the liberties of the people. Although the Constitution would provide for civilian control of the military, it did not specifically prohibit professional standing military forces.

SEC. 13. That a well-regulated militia, or composed of the body of the people, trained to arms, is the proper, natural, and safe defense of a free state; that standing armies, in time of peace, should be avoided as dangerous to liberty; and that in all cases the military should be under strict subordination to, and governed by, the civil power.

SEC. 14. That the people have a right to uniform government; and, therefore, that no government separate from or independent of the government of Virginia ought to be erected or established within the limits thereof.

SEC. 15. That no free government, or the blessings of liberty, can be preserved to any people, but by a firm adherence to justice, moderation, temperance, frugality, and virtue, and by frequent recurrence to fundamental principles.

Originally phrased to provide "toleration" of all religions, this may be the single most important provision to emerge from this declaration. James Madison, who served on the drafting committee along with Mason and thought that the term "toleration" suggested a matter of grace rather than of rights, insisted on inserting the "free exercise" language, which the First Amendment of the U.S. Constitution (in which Madison also had an influential part) later repeated.

SEC. 16. That religion, or the duty which we owe to our Creator, and the manner of discharging it, can be directed only by reason and conviction, not by force or violence; and therefore all men are equally entitled to the free exercise of religion, according to the dictates of conscience; and that it is the mutual duty of all to practice Christian forbearance, love, and charity toward each other.

Source: *The Federal and State Constitutions, Colonial Charters, and Other Organic Laws of the States, Territories, and Colonies Now or Heretofore Forming the United States of America.* Vol 7. Edited by Francis Newton Thorpe. Washington, DC: GPO, 1909.

We Hold These Truths
The Declaration of Independence
July 4, 1776

> **INTRODUCTION**
>
> Few documents, if any, are more important than this explanation of the causes for the colonists' decision to revolt against the mother country and their attempt to gain support for their cause. Although conflict had broken out between the colonists and the British at Lexington and Concord in April of 1775, the colonists had continued to petition the king for redress of grievances against Parliament in hope of reconciliation. In June of 1776, Richard Henry Lee of Virginia proposed three resolutions, including one for independence and the others for securing foreign allies and creating a new system of government to replace that which the British had administered. Congress appointed a committee consisting of Thomas Jefferson, John Adams, Benjamin Franklin, Roger Sherman, and Robert Livingston to draw up an explanation of the colonists' actions, which the Second Continental Congress then debated and altered, much to the discomfort of its central author, Thomas Jefferson. On July 2, 1776, the Congress adopted a resolution for independence, and on July 4 it adopted the Declaration as a formal explanation for its actions and in hopes of mustering both domestic and international support. Note that while not all delegates had agreed to it (some wanted to send still more petitions), the Declaration was unanimously adopted by the states.

WHEN, in the Course of human Events, it becomes necessary for one People to dissolve the Political Bands which have connected them with another, and to assume, among the Powers of the Earth, the separate and equal Station to which the Laws of Nature and of Nature's GOD entitle them, a decent Respect to the Opinions of Mankind requires that they should declare the Causes which impel them to the Separation.

> The Declaration was not intended to create a new government (something that would come later) but to explain the former colonists' reasons for seeking separation from the mother country. The opening sentence plays upon the manner in which Americans, like Thomas Paine, thought that they were part of a worldwide movement for liberty. Their reference to God lends peculiar solemnity to their Declaration.

The Declaration of Independence

> This is the most quoted paragraph of the Declaration because it provides a philosophy not only for revolution but for the creation of new governments. The notion that men were equally entitled to the rights of "life, liberty, and the pursuit of happiness" was consistent with the natural rights philosophy of John Locke (although he probably would have used the word "property" rather than "pursuit of happiness"), as was the idea that government was based on popular consent rather than on divine right. Because government was formed by the people to protect their rights, they had the right to replace a government that was not securing its objects. The Declaration recognized that revolution should not proceed for trivial measures and attempted to show that the colonists had patiently petitioned the British for redress of grievances and that the colonists had only proceeded to revolution after it was clear that such measures had failed. It is important to realize that Jefferson, and many of his fellow delegates to the Second Continental Congress, had been trained as attorneys. The accusations that follow are phrased much like an indictment or legal brief. Jefferson and the Congress used heightened rhetoric that sought to magnify the extent of their own grievances. In the grievances that follow, "He" refers to King George III. By describing what they consider abuses of government, the Congress is at least indirectly pointing to what it thinks good government would require.

We hold these Truths to be self-evident, that all Men are created equal, that they are endowed, by their CREATOR, with certain unalienable Rights, that among these are Life, Liberty, and the Pursuit of Happiness.—That to secure these Rights, Governments are instituted among Men, deriving their just Powers from the Consent of the Governed, that whenever any Form of Government becomes destructive of these Ends, it is the Right of the People to alter or to abolish it, and to institute new Government, laying its Foundation on such Principles, and organizing its Powers in such Form, as to them shall seem most likely to effect their Safety and Happiness. Prudence, indeed, will dictate, that Governments long established, should not be changed for light and transient Causes; and accordingly all Experience hath shewn, that Mankind are more disposed to suffer, while Evils are sufferable, than to right themselves by abolishing the Forms to which they are accustomed. But when a long Train of Abuses and Usurpations, pursuing invariably the same Object, evinces a Design to reduce them under absolute Despotism, it is their Right, it is their Duty, to throw off such Government, and to provide new Guards for their future Security. Such has been the patient Sufferance of these Colonies; and such is now the Necessity which constrains them to alter their former Systems of Government. The History of the present King of Great-Britain is a History of repeated Injuries and Usurpations, all having in direct Object the Establishment of an absolute Tyranny over these States. To prove this, let Facts be submitted to a candid World.

HE has refused his Assent to Laws, the most wholesome and necessary for the public Good.

HE has forbidden his Governors to pass Laws of immediate and pressing Importance, unless suspended in their Operation till his Assent should be obtained; and when so suspended, he has utterly neglected to attend to them.

HE has refused to pass other Laws for the Accommodation of large Districts of People, unless those People would relinquish the Right of Representation in the Legislature, a Right inestimable to them, and formidable to Tyranny only.

HE has called together Legislative Bodies at Places unusual, uncomfortable, and distant from the Depository of their public Records, for the sole Purpose of fatiguing them into Compliance with his Measures.

HE has dissolved Representative Houses repeatedly, for opposing with manly Firmness his Invasions on the Rights of the People.

HE has refused for a long Time, after such Dissolutions, to cause others to be elected; whereby the Legislative Powers, incapable of Annihilation, have returned to the People at large for their exercise; the State remaining, in the mean Time, exposed to all the Dangers of Invasion from without, and Convulsions within.

HE has endeavoured to prevent the Population of these States; for that Purpose obstructing the Laws for Naturalization of Foreigners; refusing to pass others to encourage their Migrations hither, and raising the Conditions of new Appropriations of Lands.

HE has obstructed the Administration of Justice, by refusing his Assent to Laws for establishing Judiciary Powers.

HE has made Judges dependent on his Will alone, for the Tenure of their Offices, and the Amount and Payment of their Salaries.

"HE has dissolved Representative Houses repeatedly, for opposing with manly Firmness his Invasions on the Rights of the People."

The Declaration of Independence

HE has erected a Multitude of new Offices, and sent hither Swarms of Officers to harrass our People, and eat out their Substance.

HE has kept among us, in Times of Peace, Standing Armies, without the Consent of our Legislatures.

HE has affected to render the Military independent of and superior to the Civil Power.

HE has combined with others to subject us to a Jurisdiction foreign to our Constitution, and unacknowledged by our Laws; giving his Assent to their Acts of pretended Legislation:

> Whereas the accusations to this point have involved the British king, the remainder of the indictment includes accusations against the Parliament as well. The reference "with others" is indirect because the colonists had much earlier indicated that they had not accepted the authority or sovereignty of Parliament because they were not represented therein.

FOR quartering large Bodies of Armed Troops among us:

FOR protecting them, by a mock Trial, from Punishment for any Murders which they should commit on the Inhabitants of these States:

FOR cutting off our Trade with all Parts of the World:

FOR imposing Taxes on us without our Consent:

FOR depriving us, in many Cases, of the Benefits of Trial by Jury:

FOR transporting us beyond Seas to be tried for pretended Offences:

FOR abolishing the free System of English Laws in a neighbouring Province, establishing therein an arbitrary Government, and enlarging its Boundaries, so as to render it at once an Example and fit Instrument for introducing the same absolute Rule into these Colonies:

FOR taking away our Charters, abolishing our most valuable Laws, and altering fundamentally the Forms of our Governments:

> This accusation reinforces the extent to which the colonists regarded their charters as constitutions designed to protect their liberties.

FOR suspending our own Legislatures, and declaring themselves invested with Power to legislate for us in all Cases whatsoever.

HE has abdicated Government here, by declaring us out of his Protection, and waging War against us.

HE has plundered our Seas, ravaged our Coasts, burnt our Towns, and destroyed the Lives of our People.

HE is, at this Time, transporting large Armies of foreign Mercenaries to complete the Works of Death, Desolation, and Tyranny, already begun with Circumstances of Cruelty and Perfidy, scarcely paralleled in the most barbarous Ages, and totally unworthy the Head of a civilized Nation.

HE has constrained our Fellow-Citizens, taken Captive on the high Seas, to bear Arms against their Country, to become the Executioners of their Friends and Brethren, or to fall themselves by their Hands.

"HE has abdicated Government here, by declaring us out of his Protection, and waging War against us."

HE has excited domestic Insurrections amongst us, and has endeavoured to bring on the Inhabitants of our Frontiers, the merciless Indian Savages, whose known Rule of Warfare, is an undistinguished Destruction, of all Ages, Sexes, and Conditions.

> Jefferson switches essentially from peacetime to wartime grievances, focusing on atrocities that he accuses the king of having engaged in since the beginning of hostilities at Lexington and Concord. The first part of the last sentence indicts the king for encouraging African American slaves to take up arms against their masters. Jefferson had originally drawn up a much stronger indictment, but fellow delegates tamped down the language, undoubtedly recognizing the hypocrisy of blaming the king for urging individuals whom the colonists hoped to keep in subjection to seek their freedom.

IN every Stage of these Oppressions we have Petitioned for Redress in the most humble Terms: Our repeated Petitions have been answered only by repeated Injury. A Prince, whose Character is thus marked by every Act which may define a Tyrant, is unfit to be the Ruler of a free People.

The Declaration of Independence

The Declaration reiterates the patience of the colonists up to this point. The tone appears to be one of sorrow rather than triumph, disappointment that the British people, from whom most of the colonists had sprung, had not given greater heed to their protests. As the author of A Summary View of the Rights of British America *(1774), Jefferson believed that Americans had brought their rights with them. This is why he reminds his audience "of the Circumstances of our Emigration and Settlement" here.*

NOR have we been wanting in Attentions to our British Brethren. We have warned them, from Time to Time, of Attempts by their Legislature to extend an unwarrantable Jurisdiction over us. We have reminded them of the Circumstances of our Emigration and Settlement here. We have appealed to their native Justice and Magnanimity, and we have conjured them by the Ties of our common Kindred to disavow these Usurpations, which would inevitably interrupt our Connexions and Correspondence. They too have been deaf to the Voice of Justice and of Consanguinity. We must, therefore, acquiesce in the Necessity, which denounces our Separation, and hold them, as we hold the Rest of Mankind, Enemies in War, in Peace Friends.

This final paragraph incorporates the resolution for independence that Richard Henry Lee had introduced in the Congress in June. As in the first paragraph, the document includes a reference to Providence. In pledging mutual support, members of Congress recognized that their actions were considered treasonous by the British and that conviction for treason carried the penalty of death.

WE, therefore, the Representatives of the UNITED STATES OF AMERICA, in GENERAL CONGRESS Assembled, appealing to the Supreme Judge of the World for the Rectitude of our Intentions, do, in the Name, and by Authority of the good People of these Colonies, solemnly Publish and Declare, That these United Colonies are, and of Right ought to be, FREE AND INDEPENDENT STATES; that they are absolved from all Allegiance to the British Crown, and that all political Connexion between them and the State of Great-Britain, is, and ought to be, totally dissolved; and that as FREE AND INDEPENDENT STATES, they have full Power to levy War, conclude Peace, contract Alliances, establish Commerce, and to do all other Acts and Things which INDEPENDENT STATES may of Right do. And for the Support of this Declaration, with a firm Reliance on the Protection of DIVINE PROVIDENCE, we mutually pledge to each other our *Lives*, our *Fortunes*, and our *sacred Honour*.

John Hancock.

GEORGIA, *Button Gwinnett, Lyman Hall, Geo. Walton.*

NORTH-CAROLINA, *Wm. Hooper, Joseph Hewes, John Penn.*

SOUTH-CAROLINA, *Edward Rutledge, Thos Heyward, junr. Thomas Lynch, junr. Arthur Middleton.*

MARYLAND, *Samuel Chase, Wm. Paca, Thos. Stone, Charles Carroll, of Carrollton.*

VIRGINIA, *George Wythe, Richard Henry Lee, Ths. Jefferson, Benja. Harrison, Thos. Nelson, jr. Francis Lightfoot Lee, Carter Braxton.*

PENNSYLVANIA, *Robt. Morris, Benjamin Rush, Benja. Franklin, John Morton, Geo. Clymer, Jas. Smith, Geo. Taylor, James Wilson, Geo. Ross.*

DELAWARE, *Caesar Rodney, Geo. Read.*

NEW-YORK, *Wm. Floyd, Phil. Livingston, Frank Lewis, Lewis Morris.*

NEW-JERSEY, *Richd. Stockton, Jno. Witherspoon, Fras. Hopkinson, John Hart, Abra. Clark.*

NEW-HAMPSHIRE, *Josiah Bartlett, Wm. Whipple, Matthew Thornton.*

MASSACHUSETTS-BAY, *Saml. Adams, John Adams, Robt. Treat Paine, Elbridge Gerry.*

RHODE-ISLAND AND PROVIDENCE, &c. *Step. Hopkins, William Ellery.*

CONNECTICUT, *Roger Sherman, Saml. Huntington, Wm. Williams, Oliver Wolcott.*

IN CONGRESS, JANUARY 18, 1777.

ORDERED,

THAT an authenticated Copy of the DECLARATION OF INDEPENDENCY, with the Names of the MEMBERS of CONGRESS, subscribing the same, be sent to each of the UNITED STATES, and that they be desired to have the same put on RECORD.

By Order of CONGRESS,

JOHN HANCOCK, *President.*

In the original document, John Hancock's signature, as president of the Second Continental Congress, is so prominent that it remains common to tell someone to sign their "John Hancock" to a legal manuscript.

Source: Declaration of Independence. National Archives and Records Administration Charters of Freedom website. Accessed January 14, 2015. http://www.archives.gov/exhibits/charters/declaration.html.

The Natural Rights of Mankind
A Bill for Establishing Religious Freedom
Introduced June 18, 1779; adopted 1786

> **INTRODUCTION**
>
> Although many colonists came to America seeking religious freedom, they were not always anxious to extend it to others. Many established an official church, and some persecuted those who were not members. Thomas Jefferson was among those who favored separating church and state. Indeed, among three accomplishments that he wanted listed on his tombstone was the adoption of the Virginia Statute for Religious Freedom, the text of which follows. Although Jefferson introduced this bill, the primary work in getting it passed belongs to James Madison, who would also play a key role in the later adoption of the First Amendment to the U.S. Constitution. Madison also authored a Memorial and Remonstrance Against Religious Assessments in June 1785, in which he registered strong objections to a plan supported by Governor Patrick Henry to use state monies to fund religious instructors.

Well aware that the opinions and belief of men depend not on their own will, but follow involuntarily the evidence proposed to their minds; that **Almighty God hath created the mind free,** *and manifested his supreme will that free it shall remain by making it altogether insusceptible of restraint*; that all attempts to influence it by temporal punishments, or burthens, or by civil incapacitations, tend only to beget habits of hypocrisy and meanness, and are a departure from the plan of the holy author of our religion, who being lord both of body and mind, yet chose not to propagate it by coercions on either, as was in his Almighty power to do, *but to extend it by its influence on reason alone;* that the impious presumption of legislators and rulers, civil as well as ecclesiastical, who, being themselves but fallible and uninspired men, have assumed dominion over the faith of others,

> For generations men had thought that one of the purposes of government was the care of human souls. By contrast, this law argued that secular rulers were incapable of supervising such matters, which rested on individual consciences, which would only be corrupted if men were forced outwardly to support that which they did not inwardly believe. The law was particularly concerned about the forcing of individuals to give financial support to religions that they did not support, a principle that has continued to guide interpretations of the establishment clause of the First Amendment to the U.S. Constitution.

A Bill for Establishing Religious Freedom

> *"That to compel a man to furnish contributions of money for the propagation of opinions which he disbelieves* and abhors, *is sinful and tyrannical; that even the forcing him to support this or that teacher of his own religious persuasion, is depriving him of the comfortable liberty of giving his contributions to the particular pastor whose morals he would make his pattern, and whose powers he feels most persuasive to righteousness . . ."*

setting up their own opinions and modes of thinking as the only true and infallible, and as such endeavoring to impose them on others, hath established and maintained false religions over the greatest part of the world and through all time: That to compel a man to furnish contributions of money for the propagation of opinions which he disbelieves *and abhors,* is sinful and tyrannical; that even the forcing him to support this or that teacher of his own religious persuasion, is depriving him of the comfortable liberty of giving his contributions to the particular pastor whose morals he would make his pattern, and whose powers he feels most persuasive to righteousness; and is withdrawing from the ministry those temporary rewards, which proceeding from an approbation of their personal conduct, are an additional incitement to earnest and unremitting labours for the instruction of mankind; that our civil rights have no dependance on our religious opinions, any more than our opinions in physics or geometry; that therefore the proscribing any citizen as unworthy the public confidence by laying upon him an incapacity of being called to offices of trust and emolument, unless he profess or renounce this or that religious opinion, is depriving him injuriously of those privileges and advantages to which, in common with his fellow citizens, he has a natural right; that it tends also to corrupt the principles of that *very* religion it is meant to encourage, by bribing, with a monopoly of worldly honours and emoluments, those who will externally profess and conform to it; that though indeed these are criminal who do not withstand such temptation, yet neither are those innocent who lay the bait in their way; *that the opinions of men are not the object of civil government, nor under its jurisdiction*; that to suffer the civil magistrate to intrude his powers into the field of opinion and to restrain the profession or propagation of principles on supposition of their ill tendency is a dangerous falacy, which at once destroys all religious liberty, because he being of course judge of that tendency will make his opinions the rule of judgment, and approve or condemn the sentiments of others only as they shall square with or differ from his own; that it is time enough for the rightful purposes of civil government for its officers to interfere when principles break out into overt acts against peace and good order; and finally, that truth is great and will prevail if left to herself; that she is the proper and sufficient antagonist to error, and has nothing to fear from the conflict unless by human interposition disarmed of her natural weapons, free argument and debate; errors ceasing to be dangerous when it is permitted freely to contradict them.

We the General Assembly of Virginia do enact that no man shall be compelled to frequent or support any religious worship, place, or ministry whatsoever, nor shall be enforced, restrained, molested, or burthened in his body or goods, nor shall otherwise suffer, on account of his religious opinions or belief; but that all men shall be free to profess, and by argument to maintain, their opinions in matters of religion, and that the same shall in no wise diminish, enlarge, or affect their civil capacities.

And though we well know that this Assembly, elected by the people for the ordinary purposes of legislation only, have no power to restrain the acts of succeeding Assemblies, constituted with powers equal to our own, and that therefore to declare this act irrevocable would be of no effect in law; yet we are free to declare, and do declare, that the rights hereby asserted are of the natural rights of mankind, and that if any act shall be hereafter passed to repeal the present or to narrow its operation, such act will be an infringement of natural right.

"We the General Assembly of Virginia do enact that no man shall be compelled to frequent or support any religious worship, place, or ministry whatsoever, nor shall be enforced, restrained, molested, or burthened in his body or goods, nor shall otherwise suffer, on account of his religious opinions or belief; but that all men shall be free to profess, and by argument to maintain, their opinions in matters of religion . . ."

This may be one of the most profound thoughts from the Founding Era. Because this act was a state law and not part of a more permanent constitution, Jefferson knew that the legislature could repeal this law. But he insisted that the natural rights principle that the law embodied was eternal and that anyone who sought to repeal the central provision of the law would therefore be seeking to undermine such rights. Such a sentiment would explain the desire for Jefferson and other founders to secure such rights in both state and national constitutions.

Source: Thomas Jefferson. "A Bill for Establishing Religious Freedom." National Archives and Records Administration Founders Online website. Accessed January 15, 2015. http://founders.archives.gov/documents/Jefferson/01-02-02-0132-0004-0082.

Mutual Friendship and Intercourse

Articles of Confederation

Written in 1776; adopted in 1781

INTRODUCTION

Although the First and Second Continental Congresses served as a de facto government during the period leading up to and immediately following the American Revolution, each was understood to be a temporary body. When the Second Continental Congress considered independence, it was simultaneously working on obtaining foreign allies and drawing up a more permanent government.

John Dickinson, the reluctant revolutionary and "penman of the Revolution," took the lead in drafting the Articles of Confederation. He probably drew, in part, from Benjamin Franklin's earlier Albany Plan of Union in composing the Articles. The plan was debated in Congress in 1777 where, at the insistence of Thomas Burke of North Carolina, it was modified to increase the power of the states and sent to them for approval. The Articles of Confederation required unanimous consent, and Maryland, which was concerned about the western land claims of the larger states, held out until 1781.

The Articles laid the framework for what was arguably less a true national government than a confederation organized around principles of mutual defense. Article II stressed that sovereignty remained with the states, each of which had a single vote in the unicameral Congress. The president of the Congress was the instrument of, rather than a counterweight to, the Congress, and there was no system of independent national courts. In time the perceived weaknesses of the Articles of Confederation would lead to calls for a new Constitution.

To all to whom these Presents shall come, we the undersigned Delegates of the States affixed to our Names send greeting.

Articles of Confederation and perpetual Union between the states of New Hampshire, Massachusetts-bay Rhode Island and Providence Plantations, Connecticut, New

> This formulation is similar to that of the Albany Plan of Union and a striking contrast to the more generic reference to "We the People" in the U.S. Constitution.

York, New Jersey, Pennsylvania, Delaware, Maryland, Virginia, North Carolina, South Carolina and Georgia.

I.

The Stile of this Confederacy shall be "The United States of America."

II.

> This provision is arguably key to understanding the Articles. Primary authority, or sovereignty, rested with individual states rather than with Congress, which exercised a limited number of enumerated powers, which themselves often required supermajority agreement.

Each state retains its sovereignty, freedom, and independence, and every power, jurisdiction, and right, which is not by this Confederation expressly delegated to the United States, in Congress assembled.

III.

> *"The said States hereby severally enter into a firm league of friendship with each other, for their common defense, the security of their liberties, and their mutual and general welfare . . ."*

The said States hereby severally enter into a firm league of friendship with each other, for their common defense, the security of their liberties, and their mutual and general welfare, binding themselves to assist each other, against all force offered to, or attacks made upon them, or any of them, on account of religion, sovereignty, trade, or any other pretense whatever.

IV.

The better to secure and perpetuate mutual friendship and intercourse among the people of the different States in this Union, the free inhabitants of each of these States, paupers, vagabonds, and fugitives from justice excepted, shall be entitled to all privileges and immunities of free citizens in the several States; and the people of each State shall freely ingress and regress to and from any other

State, and shall enjoy therein all the privileges of trade and commerce, subject to the same duties, impositions, and restrictions as the inhabitants thereof respectively, provided that such restrictions shall not extend so far as to prevent the removal of property imported into any State, to any other State, of which the owner is an inhabitant; provided also that no imposition, duties or restriction shall be laid by any State, on the property of the United States, or either of them.

If any person guilty of, or charged with, treason, felony, or other high misdemeanor in any State, shall flee from justice, and be found in any of the United States, he shall, upon demand of the Governor or executive power of the State from which he fled, be delivered up and removed to the State having jurisdiction of his offense.

Full faith and credit shall be given in each of these States to the records, acts, and judicial proceedings of the courts and magistrates of every other State.

> These provisions guaranteed freedom of movement from one state to another and state recognition of the legal judgments of fellow states. It makes for an interesting comparison with Article IV of the current U.S. Constitution, which addresses the respective rights and responsibilities of the national government and the states.

V.

For the most convenient management of the general interests of the United States, delegates shall be annually appointed in such manner as the legislatures of each State shall direct, to meet in Congress on the first Monday in November, in every year, with a power reserved to each State to recall its delegates, or any of them, at any time within the year, and to send others in their stead for the remainder of the year.

No State shall be represented in Congress by less than two, nor more than seven members; and no person shall be capable of being a delegate for more than three years in any term of six years; nor shall any person, being a delegate, be capable of holding any office under the United States, for which he, or another for his benefit, receives any salary, fees or emolument of any kind.

Each State shall maintain its own delegates in a meeting of the States, and while they act as members of the committee of the States.

> The most distinctive aspect of the Articles of Confederation was that it represented each state equally. This provision was especially important to the less populous states, which would lose power if representation were awarded instead on the basis of population. These states proved very reluctant to part with this equality when they assembled at the Constitutional Convention of 1787. As a result, the 1787 Convention preserved equality of state representation in the U.S. Senate.

In determining questions in the United States in Congress assembled, each State shall have one vote.

Freedom of speech and debate in Congress shall not be impeached or questioned in any court or place out of Congress, and the members of Congress shall be protected in their persons from arrests or imprisonments, during the time of their going to and from, and attendence on Congress, except for treason, felony, or breach of the peace.

VI.

No State, without the consent of the United States in Congress assembled, shall send any embassy to, or receive any embassy from, or enter into any conference, agreement, alliance or treaty with any King, Prince or State; nor shall any person holding any office of profit or trust under the United States, or any of them, accept any present, emolument, office or title of any kind whatever from any King, Prince or foreign State; nor shall the United States in Congress assembled, or any of them, grant any title of nobility.

No two or more States shall enter into any treaty, confederation or alliance whatever between them, without the consent of the United States in Congress assembled, specifying accurately the purposes for which the same is to be entered into, and how long it shall continue.

No State shall lay any imposts or duties, which may interfere with any stipulations in treaties, entered into by the United States in Congress assembled, with any King, Prince or State, in pursuance of any treaties already proposed by Congress, to the courts of France and Spain.

No vessel of war shall be kept up in time of peace by any State, except such number only, as shall be deemed necessary by the United States in Congress assembled, for the defense of such State, or its trade; nor shall any body of forces be kept up by any State in time of peace, except such number only, as in the judgement of the United States in Congress assembled, shall be deemed requisite to garrison the forts necessary for the defense of such State; but every State shall always keep up a well-regulated and disciplined militia, sufficiently armed and accoutered, and shall provide and constantly have ready for use, in public stores, a due number of filed pieces and tents, and a proper quantity of arms, ammunition and camp equipage.

No State shall engage in any war without the consent of the United States in Congress assembled, unless such State be actually invaded by enemies, or shall have received certain advice of a resolution being formed by some nation of Indians to invade such State, and the danger is so imminent as not to admit of a delay till the United States in Congress assembled can be consulted; nor shall any State grant commissions to any ships or vessels of war, nor letters of marque or reprisal, except it be after a declaration of war by the United States in Congress assembled, and then only against the Kingdom or State and the subjects thereof, against which war has been so declared, and under such regulations as shall be established by the United States in Congress assembled, unless such State be infested by pirates, in which case vessels of war may be fitted out for that occasion, and kept so long as the danger shall continue, or until the United States in Congress assembled shall determine otherwise.

VII.

When land forces are raised by any State for the common defense, all officers of or under the rank of colonel, shall be appointed by the legislature of each State respectively, by whom such forces shall be raised, or in such manner as such State shall direct, and all vacancies shall be filled up by the State which first made the appointment.

VIII.

All charges of war, and all other expenses that shall be incurred for the common defense or general welfare, and allowed by the United States in Congress assembled, shall be defrayed out of a common treasury, which shall be supplied by the several States in proportion to the value of all land within each State, granted or surveyed for any person, as such land and the buildings and improvements thereon shall be estimated according to such mode as the United States in Congress assembled, shall from time to time direct and appoint.

> Today the government created under the Articles of Confederation is known as a confederal government. In such an arrangement, the national authorities do not act directly on individual citizens, as they do in unitary governments like England and France, but must operate through the states. Although the delegates in Congress could agree to allocate expenses among the states, there was no way to compel them to do so.

The taxes for paying that proportion shall be laid and levied by the authority and direction of the legislatures of the several States within the time agreed upon by the United States in Congress assembled.

IX.

The United States in Congress assembled, shall have the sole and exclusive right and power of determining on peace and war, except in the cases mentioned in the sixth article—of sending and receiving ambassadors—entering into treaties and alliances, provided that no treaty of commerce shall be made whereby the legislative power of the respective States shall be restrained from imposing such imposts and duties on foreigners, as their own people are subjected to, or from prohibiting the exportation or importation of any species of goods or commodities whatsoever—of establishing rules for deciding in all cases, what captures on land or water shall be legal, and in what manner prizes taken by land or naval forces in the service of the United States shall be divided or appropriated—of granting letters of marque and reprisal in times of peace—appointing courts for the trial of piracies and felonies commited on the high seas and establishing courts for receiving and determining finally appeals in all cases of captures, provided that no member of Congress shall be appointed a judge of any of the said courts.

The United States in Congress assembled shall also be the last resort on appeal in all disputes and differences now subsisting or that hereafter may arise between two or more States concerning boundary, jurisdiction or any other causes whatever; which authority shall always be exercised in the manner following. Whenever the legislative or executive authority or lawful agent of any State in controversy with another shall present a petition to Congress stating the matter in question and praying for a hearing, notice thereof shall be given by order of Congress to the legislative or executive authority of the other State in controversy, and a day assigned for the appearance of the parties by their lawful agents, who shall then be directed to appoint by joint consent, commissioners or judges to constitute a court for hearing and determining the matter in

Although the Articles of Confederation did not create a separate system of courts, it did provide a mechanism for the peaceful resolution of land disputes among the colonies, which could be considered to be something of a precursor to such courts.

question: but if they cannot agree, Congress shall name three persons out of each of the United States, and from the list of such persons each party shall alternately strike out one, the petitioners beginning, until the number shall be reduced to thirteen; and from that number not less than seven, nor more than nine names as Congress shall direct, shall in the presence of Congress be drawn out by lot, and the persons whose names shall be so drawn or any five of them, shall be commissioners or judges, to hear and finally determine the controversy, so always as a major part of the judges who shall hear the cause shall agree in the determination: and if either party shall neglect to attend at the day appointed, without showing reasons, which Congress shall judge sufficient, or being present shall refuse to strike, the Congress shall proceed to nominate three persons out of each State, and the secretary of Congress shall strike in behalf of such party absent or refusing; and the judgement and sentence of the court to be appointed, in the manner before prescribed, shall be final and conclusive; and if any of the parties shall refuse to submit to the authority of such court, or to appear or defend their claim or cause, the court shall nevertheless proceed to pronounce sentence, or judgement, which shall in like manner be final and decisive, the judgement or sentence and other proceedings being in either case transmitted to Congress, and lodged among the acts of Congress for the security of the parties concerned: provided that every commissioner, before he sits in judgement, shall take an oath to be administered by one of the judges of the supreme or superior court of the State, where the cause shall be tried, "well and truly to hear and determine the matter in question, according to the best of his judgement, without favor, affection or hope of reward": provided also, that no State shall be deprived of territory for the benefit of the United States.

All controversies concerning the private right of soil claimed under different grants of two or more States, whose jurisdictions as they may respect such lands, and the States which passed such grants are adjusted, the said grants or either of them being at the same time claimed to have originated antecedent to such settlement of jurisdiction, shall on the petition of either party to the Congress of the United States, be finally determined as near as may be in the same manner as is before prescribed for deciding disputes respecting territorial jurisdiction between different States.

The United States in Congress assembled shall also have the sole and exclusive right and power of regulating the alloy and value of coin struck by their own authority, or by that of the respective States—fixing the standards of weights and measures throughout the United States—regulating the trade and managing all affairs with the Indians, not members of any of the States, provided that the legislative right of any State within its own limits be not infringed or violated—establishing or regulating post offices from one State to another, throughout all the United States, and exacting such postage on the papers passing through the same as may be requisite to defray the expenses of the said office—appointing all officers of the land forces, in the service of the United States, excepting regimental officers—appointing all the officers of the naval forces, and commissioning all officers whatever in the service of the United States—making rules for the government and regulation of the said land and naval forces, and directing their operations.

The United States in Congress assembled shall have authority to appoint a committee, to sit in the recess of Congress, to be denominated "A Committee of the States," and to consist of one delegate from each State; and to appoint such other committees and civil officers

This provision for "A Committee of the States" was designed, much like today's presidency, to provide for contingencies between congressional sessions, but it was drawn from Congress rather than from an independent executive branch.

as may be necessary for managing the general affairs of the United States under their direction—to appoint one of their members to preside, provided that no person be allowed to serve in the office of president more than one year in any term of three years; to ascertain the necessary sums of money to be raised for the service of the United States, and to appropriate and apply the same for defraying the public expenses—to borrow money, or emit bills on the credit of the United States, transmitting every half-year to the respective States an account of the sums of money so borrowed or emitted—to build and equip a navy—to agree upon the number of land forces, and to make requisitions from each State for its quota, in proportion to the number of white inhabitants in such State; which requisition shall be binding, and thereupon the legislature of each State shall appoint the regimental officers, raise the men and cloath, arm and equip them in a solid-like manner, at the expense of the United States; and the officers and men so cloathed, armed and equipped shall march to the place appointed, and within the time agreed on by the United States in Congress assembled. But if the United States in Congress assembled shall, on consideration of circumstances judge proper that any State should not raise men, or should raise a smaller number of men than the quota thereof, such extra number shall be raised, officered, cloathed, armed and equipped in the same manner as the quota of each State, unless the legislature of such State shall judge that such extra number cannot be safely spread out in the same, in which case they shall raise, officer, cloath, arm and equip as many of such extra number as they judge can be safely spared. And the officers and men so cloathed, armed, and equipped, shall march to the place appointed, and within the time agreed on by the United States in Congress assembled.

The United States in Congress assembled shall never engage in a war, nor grant letters of marque or reprisal in time of peace, nor enter into any treaties or alliances, nor coin money, nor regulate the value thereof, nor ascertain the sums and expenses necessary for the defense and welfare of the United States, or any of them, nor emit bills, nor borrow money on the credit of the United States, nor appropriate money, nor agree upon the number of vessels of war, to be built or purchased, or the number of land or sea forces to be raised, nor appoint a commander in chief of the army or navy, unless nine States assent to the same: nor shall a question on any other point, except for adjourning from day to day be determined, unless by the votes of the majority of the United States in Congress assembled.

Perhaps in part because each state was represented equally, states required concurrence of nine or more states on most key measures. This supermajority requirement, combined with the fairly routine absence of some states, made collective action quite difficult.

The Congress of the United States shall have power to adjourn to any time within the year, and to any place within the United States, so that no period of adjournment be for a longer duration than the space of six months, and shall publish the journal of their proceedings monthly, except such parts thereof relating to treaties, alliances or military operations, as in their judgement require secrecy; and the yeas and nays of the delegates of each State on any question shall be entered on the journal, when it is desired by any delegates of a State, or any of them, at his or their request shall be furnished with a transcript of the said journal, except such parts as are above excepted, to lay before the legislatures of the several States.

X.

The Committee of the States, or any nine of them, shall be authorized to execute, in the recess of Congress, such of the powers of Congress as the United States in Congress

"The Committee of the States, or any nine of them, shall be authorized to execute, in the recess of Congress, such of the powers of Congress as the United States in Congress assembled, by the consent of the nine States, shall from time to time think expedient to vest them with . . ."

assembled, by the consent of the nine States, shall from time to time think expedient to vest them with; provided that no power be delegated to the said Committee, for the exercise of which, by the Articles of Confederation, the voice of nine States in the Congress of the United States assembled be requisite.

XI.

Canada acceding to this confederation, and adjoining in the measures of the United States, shall be admitted into, and entitled to all the advantages of this Union; but no other colony shall be admitted into the same, unless such admission be agreed to by nine States.

> The 13 colonies seemed to have something of a love/hate relationship with Canada to their north. One of their grievances against the British had been that the British had extended freedom of worship to the Catholic majority in the Quebec Act of 1774, and yet the colonies also knew that their war with Britain would have a better chance for success if they could get the Canadians to join them. The American desire to incorporate Canada was even greater during the War of 1812, when they unsuccessfully attempted to secure Canadian territory through force rather than through persuasion.

XII.

All bills of credit emitted, monies borrowed, and debts contracted by, or under the authority of Congress, before the assembling of the United States, in pursuance of the present confederation, shall be deemed and considered as a charge against the United States, for payment and satisfaction whereof the said United States, and the public faith are hereby solemnly pledged.

XIII.

Every State shall abide by the determination of the United States in Congress assembled, on all questions which by this confederation are submitted to them. And the Articles of this Confederation shall be inviolably observed by every State, and the Union shall be perpetual; nor shall any alteration at any time hereafter be made in any of them; unless such alteration be agreed to in a Congress of the United States, and be afterwards confirmed by the legislatures of every State.

And Whereas it hath pleased the Great Governor of the World to incline the hearts of the legislatures we respectively represent in Congress, to approve of, and to authorize us to ratify the said Articles of Confederation and perpetual Union. Know Ye that we the undersigned delegates, by virtue of the power and authority to us given for that purpose, do by these presents, in the name and in behalf of our respective constituents, fully and entirely ratify and confirm each and every of the said Articles of Confederation and perpetual Union, and all and singular the matters and things therein contained: And we do further solemnly plight and engage the faith of our respective constituents, that they shall abide by the determinations of the United States in Congress assembled, on all questions, which by the said Confederation are submitted to them. And that the Articles thereof shall be inviolably observed by the States we respectively represent, and that the Union shall be perpetual.

> Although the Articles of Confederation did not provide for an established church, they did, like the Declaration of Independence, include an acknowledgment of God.

In Witness whereof we have hereunto set our hands in Congress. Done at Philadelphia in the State of Pennsylvania the ninth day of July in the Year of our Lord One Thousand Seven Hundred and Seventy-Eight, and in the Third Year of the independence of America.

Agreed to by Congress 15 November 1777 In force after ratification by Maryland, 1 March 1781.

Source: Articles of Confederation and Perpetual Union, July 9, 1778. Library of Congress website. Accessed January 15, 2015. http://memory.loc.gov/cgi-bin/ampage?collId=llsl&fileName=001/llsl001.db&recNum=127.

E Pluribus Unum
Great Seal of the United States
1782

INTRODUCTION

A nation's history and values are often embodied in its most treasured symbols. Today's U.S. flag hearkens back both to the original 13 states (the red and white stripes) and the 50 existing ones (the stars). Early congresses expended considerable amounts of time attempting to formulate a great seal to be used to certify official documents that would represent the values and aspirations of the nation.

Congress actually appointed the first committee to formulate a great seal in 1776. Reflecting the colonists' view that they were waging a holy fight, a committee consisting of Benjamin Franklin, Thomas Jefferson, and John Adams formulated several suggestions. Franklin visualized a seal depicting the children of Israel crossing the Red Sea and surrounded by the motto, "Rebellion to Tyrants is Obedience to God." Jefferson played on the same theme and suggested including the biblical cloud that led by day and the pillar of fire to that led at night. Adams suggested depicting Hercules choosing between a life of indulgence and a life of duty. Pierre Eugene du Simitiere, a Philadelphia artist whom the committee had consulted, in turn proposed a shield depicting six nations from which the colonists had derived and the initials of the original 13 states along with the Latin phrase *e pluribus unum* ("from many, one") and the year 1776 (in which the colonists had declared their independence) in Roman numerals.

Congress did not act on this recommendation but created a second committee in March 1780 consisting of James Lovell, John Morin Scott, and William Churchill Houston, who were advised by Francis Hopkinson. They suggested adding red and white stripes and 13 stars to the seal, but their efforts were stymied by congressional inaction.

In May 1782, Congress appointed a third committee of John Rutledge, Arthur Middleton, and Elias Boudinot. They requested help from William Barton, who contributed an eagle (a symbol of strength) to their proposed design. Congress passed the work of all three committees to Charles Thomson, the secretary of Congress.

The resulting seal, adopted later in 1782, features an eagle with outstretched wings, with a shield of 13 stripes on its chest, an olive branch symbolizing peace in its left claw, and a sheaf of 13 arrows in its right, suggesting a willingness to use force when needed. It holds a banner in its mouth proclaiming e *pluribus unum,* and clouds with 13 stars sit above its head.

The reverse side features a pyramid with the triangular eye of Providence at the top under the words *annuit coeptis*, which indicates God's favor on the nation. A scroll below the pyramid containes the words *novus ordo seclorum*, meaning "a new order of the ages." Both sides of the seal are displayed on the back of current one-dollar bills.

Source: Gaillard Hunt. *The Seal of the United States: How It was Developed and Adopted.* Washington, DC: Department of State, 1892, p. 26.

The Interest of the Community

George Washington's Circular to the States

June 8, 1783

> **INTRODUCTION**
>
> Although the Articles of Confederation provided a transitional government from that of Great Britain to the Constitution of 1787, there were early signs that the Articles were not adequately providing for national unity, particularly on matters related to foreign affairs. No American better symbolized the struggle for independence than George Washington, who had successfully led patriot forces in the conflict with Britain during the Revolutionary War, and would soon resign his military commission and retire to private life as a plantation owner of Mount Vernon, Virginia.

Washington sought to gain the nation's attention by reminding citizens of their success in gaining their independence. One of the difficulties that the nation faced under the Articles was that it no longer focused on a common enemy.

When we consider the magnitude of the prize we contended for, the doubtful nature of the contest, and the favorable manner in which it has terminated, we shall find the greatest possible reason for gratitude and rejoicing; this is a theme that will afford infinite delight to every benevolent and liberal mind, whether the event in contemplation, be considered as the source of present enjoyment or the parent of future happiness; and we shall have equal occasion to felicitate ourselves on the lot which Providence has assigned us, whether we view it in a natural, a political or moral point of light.

Although it is far more common to identify other American founders with collegiate educations as products of Enlightenment thinking, this passage indicates that Washington, who had no such education, also had a sense that the nation profited from living in a time known as "The Age of Reason." Interestingly, by also referring to "the pure and benign light of Revelation," Washington references the important positive influence that he believes Christianity has exerted on contemporary thought. He will repeat this praise of religious influence at the end of his second term as president in his farewell address.

The Citizens of America, placed in the most enviable condition, as the sole Lords and Proprietors of a vast Tract of Continent, comprehending all the various soils and climates of the World, and abounding with all the necessaries and conveniencies of life, are now by the late satisfactory pacification, acknowledged to be possessed of absolute freedom and Independency; They are, from this period, to be considered as the Actors on a most conspicuous Theatre, which seems to be peculiarly designated by Providence for the display of human greatness and felicity; Here, they are not only surrounded with every thing which can contribute to the completion of private and domestic enjoyment, but Heaven has crowned all its other blessings, by giving a fairer oppertunity for political happiness, than any other Nation has ever been favored with. Nothing can illustrate these observations more forcibly, than a recollection of the happy conjuncture of times and circumstances, under which our Republic assumed its rank among the Nations; The foundation of our Empire was not laid in the gloomy age of Ignorance and Superstition, but at an Epocha when the rights of mankind were better understood and more clearly defined, than at any former period, the researches of the human mind, after social happiness, have been carried to a great extent, the Treasures of knowledge, acquired by the labours of Philosophers, Sages and Legislatures, through a long succession of years, are laid open for our use, and their collected wisdom may be happily applied in the Establishment of our forms of Government; the free cultivation of Letters, the unbounded extension of Commerce, the progressive refinement of Manners, the growing liberality of sentiment, and above all, the pure and benign light of Revelation, have had a meliorating influence on mankind and increased the blessings of Society. At this auspicious period, the United States came into existence as a Nation, and if their Citizens should not be completely free and happy, the fault will be intirely their own.

Such is our situation, and such are our prospects: but notwithstanding the cup of blessing is thus reached out to us, notwithstanding happiness is ours, if we have a disposition

> *"The foundation of our Empire was not laid in the gloomy age of Ignorance and Superstition, but at an Epocha when the rights of mankind were better understood and more clearly defined, than at any former period, the researches of the human mind, after social happiness, have been carried to a great extent, the Treasures of knowledge, acquired by the labours of Philosophers, Sages and Legislatures, through a long succession of years, are laid open for our use, and their collected wisdom may be happily applied in the Establishment of our forms of Government . . ."*

George Washington's Circular to the States

> *"This is the time of their political probation, this is the moment when the eyes of the whole World are turned upon them, this is the moment to establish or ruin their national Character forever, this is the favorable moment to give such a tone to our Federal Government, as will enable it to answer the ends of its institution, or this may be the ill-fated moment for relaxing the powers of the Union, annihilating the cement of the Confederation..."*

As much as any of the founders, Washington had a sense of his presence on the public stage and of the importance of deferring to civilian authorities. In this passage, he is attempting to assure the nation of his good intentions.

to seize the occasion and make it our own; yet, it appears to me there is an option still left to the United States of America, that it is in their choice, and depends upon their conduct, whether they will be respectable and prosperous, or contemptable and miserable as a Nation; This is the time of their political probation, this is the moment when the eyes of the whole World are turned upon them, this is the moment to establish or ruin their national Character forever, this is the favorable moment to give such a tone to our Federal Government, as will enable it to answer the ends of its institution, or this may be the ill-fated moment for relaxing the powers of the Union, annihilating the cement of the Confederation, and exposing us to become the sport of European politics, which may play one State against another to prevent their growing importance, and to serve their own interested purposes. For, according to the system of Policy the States shall adopt at this moment, they will stand or fall, and by their confirmation or lapse, it is yet to be decided, whether the Revolution must ultimately be considered as a blessing or a curse: a blessing or a curse, not to the present age alone, for with our fate will the destiny of unborn Millions be involved.

With this conviction of the importance of the present Crisis, silence in me would be a crime; I will therefore speak to your Excellency, the language of freedom and of sincerity, without disguise; I am aware, however, that those who differ from me in political sentiment, may perhaps remark, I am stepping out of the proper line of my duty, and they may possibly ascribe to arrogance or ostentation, what I know is alone the result of the purest intention, but the rectitude of my own heart, which disdains such unworthy motives, the part I have hitherto acted in life, the determination I have formed, of not taking any

share in public business hereafter, the ardent desire I feel, and shall continue to manifest, of quietly enjoying in private life, after all the toils of War, the benefits of a wise and liberal Government, will, I flatter myself, sooner or later convince my Countrymen, that I could have no sinister views in delivering with so little reserve, the opinions contained in this Address.

There are four things, which I humbly conceive, are essential to the well being, I may even venture to say, to the existence of the United States as an Independent Power:

1st. An indissoluble Union of the States under one Federal Head.

2dly. A Sacred regard to Public Justice.

3dly. The adoption of a proper Peace Establishment, and

4thly. The prevalence of that pacific and friendly Disposition, among the People of the United States, which will induce them to forget their local prejudices and policies, to make those mutual concessions which are requisite to the general prosperity, and in some instances, to sacrifice their individual advantages to the interest of the Community.

> Each of the keys to national well-being identified by Washington were, arguably, defects in the Articles of Confederation. Significantly, both his first and last points emphasize the need for a stronger national union.

These are the Pillars on which the glorious Fabrick of our Independency and National Character must be supported; Liberty is the Basis, and whoever would dare to sap the foundation, or overturn the Structure, under whatever specious pretexts he may attempt it, will merit the bitterest execration, and the severest punishment which can be inflicted by his injured Country.

> "That unless the States will suffer Congress to exercise those prerogatives, they are undoubtedly invested with by the Constitution, every thing must very rapidly tend to Anarchy and confusion, That it is indispensable to the happiness of the individual States, that there should be lodged somewhere, a Supreme Power to regulate and govern the general concerns of the Confederated Republic . . ."

On the three first Articles I will make a few observations, leaving the last to the good sense and serious consideration of those immediately concerned.

Under the first head, altho' it may not be necessary or proper for me in this place to enter into a particular disquisition of the principles of the Union, and to take up the great question which has been frequently agitated, whether it be expedient and requisite for the States to delegate a larger proportion of Power to Congress, or not, Yet it will be a part of my duty, and that of every true Patriot, to assert without reserve, and to insist upon the following positions, That unless the States will suffer Congress to exercise those prerogatives, they are undoubtedly invested with by the Constitution, every thing must very rapidly tend to Anarchy and confusion, That it is indispensable to the happiness of the individual States, that there should be lodged somewhere, a Supreme Power to regulate and govern the general concerns of the Confederated Republic, without which the Union cannot be of long duration. That there must be a faithfull and pointed compliance on the part of every State, with the late proposals and demands of Congress, or the most fatal consequences will ensue, That whatever measures have a tendency to dissolve the Union, or contribute to violate or lessen the Sovereign Authority, ought to be considered as hostile to the Liberty and Independency of America, and the Authors of them treated accordingly, and lastly, that unless we can be enabled by the concurrence of the States, to participate of the fruits of the Revolution, and enjoy the essential benefits of Civil Society, under a form of Government so free and uncorrupted, so happily guarded against the danger of oppression, as has been devised and adopted by the Articles of Confederation, it will be a subject of regret, that so much blood and treasure have been lavished for no purpose, that so many sufferings have been encountered without a compensation, and that so many sacrifices have been made in vain. **Many other considerations might here be adduced to prove, that without an entire conformity to the Spirit of the Union, we cannot exist as an Independent Power;** it will be sufficient for my purpose to mention but one or two which seem to me of the greatest importance. It is only in our united Character as an Empire, that our Independence is acknowledged, that our power can be regarded, or our Credit supported among Foreign Nations. The Treaties of the European Powers with the United States of America, will have no validity on a dissolution of the Union. We shall be left nearly in a state of Nature, or we may find by our own unhappy experience, that there is a natural and necessary progression, from the extreme of anarchy to the extreme of Tyranny; and that arbitrary power is most easily established on the ruins of Liberty abused to licentiousness.

> Again, Washington emphasizes the need for national unity. His reference to "a state of Nature" expresses his concern that the nation might break up into individual states, which would be inadequate to meet the threat posed by foreign nations on their boundaries.

Source: George Washington. Circular to the States, June 8, 1783. *The Writings of George Washington from the Original Manuscript Sources, 1745–1799.* Vol. 26. Edited by John C. Fitzpatrick. Washington, DC: Government Printing Office, 1931–1944, pp. 484–89.

A Firm and Perpetual Peace
Treaty of Paris
September 3, 1783

> INTRODUCTION
>
> When Lord Cornwallis surrendered to American forces at Yorktown on October 19, 1781, the bloodshed of the American Revolutionary War came to an end. But it took the two sides another two years to negotiate a formal end to the war. Hostilities finally came to an end with the signing of the Treaty of Paris on September 3, 1783, by three American negotiators and a representative of Great Britain.

God was often viewed, as in oaths, as the Guarantor of solemn agreements. This phrase was written prior to the adoption of the First Amendment and indicates that both nations were predominately peopled by Christian believers in the Trinity.

"[T]o establish such a beneficial and satisfactory Intercourse between the two countries upon the ground of reciprocal Advantages and mutual Convenience as may promote and secure to both perpetual Peace and Harmony . . ."

In the Name of the most Holy & undivided Trinity.

It having pleased the Divine Providence to dispose the Hearts of the most Serene and most Potent Prince George the Third, by the Grace of God, King of Great Britain, France, and Ireland, Defender of the Faith, Duke of Brunswick and Lunebourg, Arch-Treasurer and Prince Elector of the Holy Roman Empire etc. and of the United States of America, to forget all past Misunderstandings and Differences that have unhappily interrupted the good Correspondence and Friendship which they mutually wish to restore; and to establish such a beneficial and satisfactory Intercourse between the two countries upon the ground of reciprocal Advantages and mutual Convenience as may promote and secure to both perpetual Peace and Harmony; and having for this desirable End already laid the Foundation of Peace & Reconciliation by the Provisional Articles signed at Paris on the 30th of November 1782, by the Commissioners empowered on each Part, which Articles were agreed to be inserted in and constitute the Treaty of Peace proposed to be concluded between the Crown of Great

Britain and the said United States, but which Treaty was not to be concluded until Terms of Peace should be agreed upon between Great Britain & France, and his Britannic Majesty should be ready to conclude such Treaty accordingly: and the treaty between Great Britain & France having since been concluded, his Britannic Majesty & the United States of America, in Order to carry into full Effect the Provisional Articles above mentioned, according to the Tenor thereof, have constituted & appointed, that is to say his Britannic Majesty on his Part, David Hartley, Esqr., Member of the Parliament of Great Britain, and the said United States on their Part,—John Adams, Esqr., late a Commissioner of the United States of America at the Court of Versailles, late Delegate in Congress from the State of Massachusetts, and Chief Justice of the said State, and Minister Plenipotentiary of the said United States to their High Mightinesses the States General of the United Netherlands; which Benjamin Franklin, Esqr., late Delegate in Congress from the State of Pennsylvania, President of the Convention of the said State, and Minister Plenipotentiary from the United States of America at the Court of Versailles; John Jay, Esqr., late President of Congress and Chief Justice of the state of New York, and Minister Plenipotentiary from the said United States at the Court of Madrid; to be Plenipotentiaries for the concluding and signing the Present Definitive Treaty; who after having reciprocally communicated their respective full Powers have agreed upon and confirmed the following Articles.

Article 1st:

His Brittanic Majesty acknowledges the said United States, viz., New Hampshire, Massachusetts Bay, Rhode Island and Providence Plantations, Connecticut, New York, New Jersey, Pennsylvania, Delaware, Maryland,

> Perhaps because they were part of a confederation, each state was listed individually (from North to South), much as in the preamble to the Articles of Confederation. Prior to the adoption of the U.S. Constitution, many European diplomats were unsure whether the union of North American states would continue to endure.

Treaty of Paris

Virginia, North Carolina, South Carolina and Georgia, to be free sovereign and Independent States; that he treats with them as such, and for himself his Heirs & Successors, relinquishes all claims to the Government, Propriety, and Territorial Rights of the same and every Part thereof.

Article 2d:

> The document proceeds to describe boundaries that extended to the Mississippi River, thus recognizing American claims outside the boundaries of the existing 13 states.

And that all Disputes which might arise in future on the subject of the Boundaries of the said United States may be prevented, it is hereby agreed and declared, that the following are and shall be their Boundaries,

Article 3d:

It is agreed that the People of the United States shall continue to enjoy unmolested the Right to take Fish of every kind on the Grand Bank and on all the other Banks of Newfoundland, also in the Gulf of Saint Lawrence and at all other Places in the Sea, where the Inhabitants of both Countries used at any time heretofore to fish. And also that the Inhabitants of the United States shall have Liberty to take Fish of every Kind on such Part of the Coast of Newfoundland as British Fishermen shall use, (but not to dry or cure the same on that Island) And also on the Coasts, Bays & Creeks of all other of his Brittanic Majesty's Dominions in America; and that the American Fishermen shall have Liberty to dry and cure Fish in any of the unsettled Bays, Harbors, and Creeks of Nova Scotia, Magdalen Islands, and Labrador, so long as the same shall remain unsettled, but so soon as the same or either of them shall be settled, it shall not be lawful for the said Fishermen to dry or cure Fish at such Settlement without a previous Agreement for that purpose with the Inhabitants, Proprietors, or Possessors of the Ground.

Article 4th:

It is agreed that Creditors on either Side shall meet with no lawful Impediment to the Recovery of the full Value in Sterling Money of all bona fide Debts heretofore contracted.

> Many Americans had used the Revolutionary War as an excuse not to pay debts owed to the English. This treaty recognized that such debts remained.

Article 5th:

It is agreed that Congress shall earnestly recommend it to the Legislatures of the respective States to provide for the Restitution of all Estates, Rights, and Properties, which have been confiscated belonging to real British Subjects; and also of the Estates, Rights, and Properties of Persons resident in Districts in the Possession on his Majesty's Arms and who have not borne Arms against the said United States. And that Persons of any other Description shall have free Liberty to go to any Part or Parts of any of the thirteen United States and therein to remain twelve Months unmolested in their Endeavors to obtain the Restitution of such of their Estates—Rights & Properties as may have been confiscated. And that Congress shall also earnestly recommend to the several States a Reconsideration and Revision of all Acts or Laws regarding the Premises, so as to render the said Laws or Acts perfectly consistent not only with Justice and Equity but with that Spirit of Conciliation which on the Return of the Blessings of Peace should universally prevail. And that Congress shall also earnestly recommend to the several States that the Estates, Rights, and Properties of such last mentioned Persons shall be restored to them, they refunding to any Persons who may be now in Possession the Bona fide Price (where any has been given) which such Persons may have paid on purchasing any of the said Lands, Rights, or Properties since the Confiscation.

> One of the more unseemly aspects of the Revolution is that it often resulted in the confiscation of properties of American Tories who had supported Britain during the war. Perhaps in recognition of the limited power of the government under the Articles of Confederation, Congress committed itself to recommending that states remedy such encroachments on property without being able to guarantee that they would do so.

And it is agreed that all Persons who have any Interest in confiscated Lands, either by Debts, Marriage Settlements, or otherwise, shall meet with no lawful Impediment in the Prosecution of their just Rights.

Article 6th:

That there shall be no future Confiscations made nor any Prosecutions commenced against any Person or Persons for, or by Reason of the Part, which he or they may have taken in the present War, and that no Person shall on that Account suffer any future Loss or Damage, either in his Person, Liberty, or Property; and that those who may be in Confinement on such Charges at the Time of the Ratification of the Treaty in America shall be immediately set at Liberty, and the Prosecutions so commenced be discontinued.

Article 7th:

> At the time of the Constitutional Convention, the British had yet to remove all their troops from the American northwest, and one impetus for constructing a stronger national authority than the Articles of Confederation was the hope that it would have power to insist that this part of the treaty be obeyed.

There shall be a firm and perpetual Peace between his Britanic Majesty and the said States, and between the Subjects of the one and the Citizens of the other, wherefore all Hostilities both by Sea and Land shall from henceforth cease: All prisoners on both Sides shall be set at Liberty, and his Britanic Majesty shall with all convenient speed, and without causing any Destruction, or carrying away any Negroes or other Property of the American inhabitants, withdraw all his Armies, Garrisons & Fleets from the said United States, and from every Post, Place and Harbour within the same; leaving in all Fortifications, the American Artillery that may be therein: And shall also Order & cause all Archives, Records, Deeds & Papers belonging to any of the said States, or their Citizens, which in the Course of the War may have fallen into

the hands of his Officers, to be forthwith restored and delivered to the proper States and Persons to whom they belong.

Article 8th:

The Navigation of the river Mississippi, from its source to the Ocean, shall forever remain free and open to the Subjects of Great Britain and the Citizens of the United States.

> The Mississippi River was a lifeline for states like Virginia and North Carolina, which at the time of the signing of the Treaty of Paris extended to the river's shores. In the years leading up to the Constitutional Convention of 1787, representatives from northern states sometimes showed a willingness to exchange this right for the right to trade with Britain and/or fish in northern waters, and concern over access to the Mississippi was evident in debates at the Constitutional Convention of 1787.

Article 9th:

In case it should so happen that any Place or Territory belonging to great Britain or to the United States should have been conquered by the Arms of either from the other before the Arrival of the said Provisional Articles in America, it is agreed that the same shall be restored without Difficulty and without requiring any Compensation.

Article 10th:

The solemn Ratifications of the present Treaty expedited in good & due Form shall be exchanged between the contracting Parties in the Space of Six Months or sooner if possible to be computed from the Day of the Signature of the present Treaty. In witness whereof we the undersigned their Ministers Plenipotentiary have in their Name and in Virtue of our Full Powers, signed with our Hands the present Definitive Treaty, and caused the Seals of our Arms to be affixed thereto.

Done at Paris, this third day of September in the year of our Lord, one thousand seven hundred and eighty-three.

D HARTLEY (SEAL)
JOHN ADAMS (SEAL)
B FRANKLIN (SEAL)
JOHN JAY (SEAL)

Source: Treaty of Paris, 1783; International Treaties and Related Records, 1778–1974; General Records of the United States Government, Record Group 11; National Archives.

An Affectionate Farewell

George Washington's Address on Resigning His Commission

December 23, 1783

> **INTRODUCTION**
>
> Revolutions often end in dictatorships directed by rebel military leaders. The emergence of Napoleon from the French Revolution, Lenin from the Russian Revolution, and Castro from the Cuban Revolution are examples. George Washington took a different path. Faced with a Congress that did not always honor its financial commitment to those who had fought for independence, Washington refused as a military commander to use his soldiers to force Congress's hands. Moreover, once the Treaty of Paris was signed on September 3, 1783, Washington decided to resign from his military duties and return to his beloved plantation in Virginia. In so doing, Washington consciously followed the example of the Roman general Cincinnatus (519–430 BCE), who left his farm to assume command of the military when the Roman Empire was threatened by foreign invaders—and then returned to private life when the danger to Rome had passed.

Mr. President: The great events on which my resignation depended having at length taken place; I have now the honor of offering my sincere Congratulations to Congress and of presenting myself before them to surrender into their hands the trust committed to me, and to claim the indulgence of retiring from the Service of my Country.

Happy in the confirmation of our Independence and Sovereignty, and pleased with the oppertunity afforded the United States of becoming a respectable Nation, I resign with satisfaction the Appointment I accepted with diffidence. A diffidence in my abilities to accomplish so arduous a task, which however was superseded by a confidence in the rectitude of our Cause, the support of the supreme Power of the Union, and the patronage of Heaven.

> Washington expressed humility in his remarks, attributing the outcome of the Revolution not to his own efforts but to the rectitude of the colonial cause and the intervention of Providence.

George Washington's Address on Resigning His Commission

The Successful termination of the War has verified the most sanguine expectations, and my gratitude for the interposition of Providence, and the assistance I have received from my Countrymen, encreases with every review of the momentous Contest.

A good leader is often characterized by a willingness to share credit. Although he had refused to use military force to obtain such ends, Washington continued to remind Congress of its obligation to those who have served on the nation's behalf.

While I repeat my obligations to the Army in general, I should do injustice to my own feelings not to acknowledge in this place the peculiar Services and distinguished merits of the Gentlemen who have been attached to my person during the War. It was impossible the choice of confidential Officers to compose my family should have been more fortunate. Permit me Sir, to recommend in particular those, who have continued in Service to the present moment, as worthy of the favorable notice and patronage of Congress.

I consider it an indispensable duty to close this last solemn act of my Official life, by commending the Interests of our dearest Country to the protection of Almighty God, and those who have the superintendence of them, to his holy keeping.

Washington anticipated that his military commission would be his last public service. Citizens were later willing to trust him with the presidency because they believed that his service derived from a sense of duty rather than from the need for further public accolades.

Having now finished the work assigned to me, I retire from the great theatre of Action; and bidding an Affectionate farewell to this August body under whose orders I have so long acted, I here offer my Commission, and take my leave of all the employments of public life.

Source: George Washington. Address to Congress on Resigning His Commission, December 23, 1783. *The Writings of George Washington, Volume 27.* Edited by John C. Fitzpatrick. Washington, DC: Government Printing Office, 1938, pp. 284–285.

No Powers but What Were Given

Thomas Jefferson's Notes on the State of Virginia

1785

INTRODUCTION

When the influential French naturalist Georges Louis Leclerc, Comte de Buffon asserted that the flora, fauna, and people of America were inferior to their counterparts in Europe, Thomas Jefferson, who served as an ambassador to France, responded with *Notes on the State of Virginia* (1785). In this famous work, Jefferson argued vehemently that the natural world of the North American continent and the people and wildlife within were fully equal to—if not superior—to Europe. Although Jefferson would assert in the Declaration of Independence that all men were created equal, he shared views of African Americans and of Native Americans that were similar to those of his contemporaries. Jefferson's *Notes* were divided into a series of 23 answers to queries from François Barbé-Marbois, the secretary of the French delegation to the United States. The sections below pertain to Native Americans and to Virginia's constitutional framework.

QUERY XI. A description of the Indians established in that state?

Aborigines When the first effectual settlement of our colony was made, which was in 1607, the country from the sea-coast to the mountains, and from Patowmac to the most southern waters of James river, was occupied by upwards of forty different tribes of Indians. Of these the **Powhatans**, the **Mannahoacs**, and **Monacans**, were the most powerful. Those between the sea-coast and falls of the rivers, were in amity with one another, and attached to the **Powhatans** as their link of union. Those between the falls of the rivers and the mountains, were divided into two confederacies; the tribes inhabiting the head waters of Patowmac and Rappahanoc being attached to the **Mannahoacs**; and those on the upper parts of James river to the **Monacans**. But the **Monacans** and their friends were in amity with the **Mannahoacs** and their friends, and waged joint and perpetual war against the **Powhatans**. We are told that the **Powhatans**, **Mannahoacs**, and **Monacans**, spoke languages so radically different, that interpreters were necessary when they transacted business. Hence we may conjecture, that this was not the case between all the tribes, and probably that each spoke the language of the nation to which it was attached; which we know to have been the case in many particular instances. Very possibly there may have been antiently three different stocks, each of which multiplying in a long course of time, had separated into so many little societies. **This practice results from the circumstance of their having never submitted themselves to any laws, any coercive power, any shadow of government. Their only controuls are their manners, and that moral sense of right and wrong, which, like the sense of tasting and feeling, in every man makes a part of his nature. An offence against these is punished by contempt, by exclusion from society, or, where the case is serious, as that of murder, by the individuals whom it concerns. Imperfect as this species of coercion may seem, crimes are very rare among them: insomuch that were it made a question, whether no law, as among the savage Americans, or too much law, as among the civilized Europeans, submits man to the greatest evil, one who has seen both conditions of existence would pronounce it to be the last: and that the sheep are happier of themselves, than under care of the wolves. It will be said, that great societies cannot exist without government. The Savages therefore break them into small ones. . . .**

> The French philosopher Jean-Jacques Rousseau (1712–1778) had portrayed men in the state of nature as "noble savages," whereas many American colonists saw them as little more than heathens. Jefferson adopted something of a middle posture. He accepted their humanity, hence their "moral sense of right and wrong" (the idea of "moral sense" was common to adherents to Scottish "common sense" philosophy) but indicated that their government was primitive, and associated their division into tribes with the weakness of their institutions.

. . . What would be the melancholy sequel of their history, may however be augured from the census of 1669; by which we discover that the tribes therein enumerated were, in the space of 62 years, reduced to about one-third of their former numbers. Spirituous liquors, the small-pox, war, and an abridgment of territory, to a people who lived principally on the spontaneous productions of nature, had committed terrible havock among them, which generation, under the obstacles opposed to it among them, was not likely to make good. **That the lands of this country were taken from them by conquest, is not so general a truth as is supposed. I find in our historians and records, repeated proofs of purchase, which cover a considerable part of the lower country; and many more would doubtless be found on further search. The upper country we know has been acquired altogether by purchases made in the most unexceptionable form....**

> Although he may be considered to be among the more enlightened of the colonists with regard to the humanity of Native Americans, Jefferson attributed their decline less to colonial aggression than to unintended factors like disease. He sought to exonerate the colonists from charges that they stole the Indian lands, pointing to colonial purchases.

...A knowledge of their several languages would be the most certain evidence of their derivation which could be produced. In fact, it is the best proof of the affinity of nations which ever can be referred to. How many ages have elapsed since the English, the Dutch, the Germans, the Swiss, the Norwegians, Danes and Swedes have separated from their common stock? Yet how many more must elapse before the proofs of their common origin, which exist in their several languages, will disappear? It is to be lamented then, very much to be lamented, that we have suffered so many of the Indian tribes already to extinguish, without our having previously collected and deposited in the records of literature, the general rudiments at least of the languages they spoke. Were vocabularies formed of all the languages spoken in North and South America, preserving their appellations of the most common objects in nature, of those which must be present to every nation barbarous or civilised, with the inflections of their nouns and verbs, their principles of regimen and concord, and these deposited in all the public libraries, it would furnish opportunities to those skilled

> Jefferson recognized the humanity of Native Americans and was troubled by the disappearance of so many tribes because he thought it would make it more difficult to trace their ancestry to other human civilizations.

in the languages of the old world to compare them with these, now, or at any future time, and hence to construct the best evidence of the derivation of this part of the human race.

> Jefferson begins this section with an extended discussion of the charter under which Virginia had been settled, stressing that the colonists had come with the understanding that they were bringing their rights with them.

Query XIII The constitution of the state, and its several charters?

> Jefferson reiterated the grievances of the colonists that led to the Revolution, much as he had done in the Declaration of Independence.

The colony supposed, that, by this solemn convention, entered into with arms in their hands, they had secured the (* 1) antient limits of their country, (* 2) its free trade, its exemption from (* 3) taxation but by their own assembly, and exclusion of (* 4) military force from among them. Yet in every of these points was this convention violated by subsequent kings and parliaments, and other infractions of their constitution, equally dangerous, committed. Their General Assembly, which was composed of the council of state and burgesses, sitting together and deciding by plurality of voices, was split into two houses, by which the council obtained a separate negative on their laws. Appeals from their supreme court, which had been fixed by law in their General Assembly, were arbitrarily revoked to England, to be there heard before the king and council. Instead of four hundred miles on the sea coast, they were reduced, in the space of thirty years, to about one hundred miles. Their trade with foreigners was totally suppressed, and, when carried to Great-Britain, was there loaded with imposts. It is unnecessary, however, to glean up the several instances of injury, as scattered through American and British history, and the more especially as, by passing on to the accession of the present king, we shall find specimens of them all, aggravated, multiplied and crouded within a small compass of time, so as to evince a fixed design of considering our rights natural, conventional and chartered as mere

nullities. The following is an epitome of the first fifteen years of his reign. The colonies were taxed internally and externally; their essential interests sacrificed to individuals in Great-Britain; their legislatures suspended; charters annulled; trials by juries taken away; their persons subjected to transportation across the Atlantic, and to trial before foreign judicatories; their supplications for redress thought beneath answer; themselves published as cowards in the councils of their mother country and courts of Europe; armed troops sent among them to enforce submission to these violences; and actual hostilities commenced against them. No alternative was presented but resistance, or unconditional submission. Between these could be no hesitation. They closed in the appeal to arms. They declared themselves independent States. They confederated together into one great republic; thus securing to every state the benefit of an union of their whole force.

In each state separately a new form of government was established. Of ours particularly the following are the outlines. The executive powers are lodged in the hands of a governor, chosen annually, and incapable of acting more than three years in seven. He is assisted by a council of eight members. The judiciary powers are divided among several courts, as will be hereafter explained. Legislation is exercised by two houses of assembly, the one called the house of Delegates, composed of two members from each county, chosen annually by the citizens possessing an estate for life in 100 acres of uninhabited land, or 25 acres with a house on it, or in a house or lot in some town: the other called the Senate, consisting of 24 members, chosen quadrennially by the same electors, who for this purpose are distributed into 24 districts. The

"The colonies were taxed internally and externally; their essential interests sacrificed to individuals in Great-Britain; their legislatures suspended; charters annulled; trials by juries taken away; their persons subjected to transportation across the Atlantic, and to trial before foreign judicatories; their supplications for redress thought beneath answer; themselves published as cowards in the councils of their mother country and courts of Europe . . ."

Jefferson provides a brief summary of the Virginia Constitution. Like other constitutions of the time, it had, as Jefferson knew from his own experience in the office, a relatively weak executive who served for one-year terms.

"No alternative was presented but resistance, or unconditional submission."

concurrence of both houses is necessary to the passage of a law. They have the appointment of the governor and council, the judges of the superior courts, auditors, attorney-general, treasurer, register of the land office, and delegates to congress. As the dismemberment of the state had never had its confirmation, but, on the contrary, had always been the subject of protestation and complaint, that it might never be in our own power to raise scruples on that subject, or to disturb the harmony of our new confederacy, the grants to Maryland, Pennsylvania, and the two Carolinas, were ratified.

> Jefferson attributed the defects of the Virginia Constitution not to ill will or incompetence but to inexperience.

This constitution was formed when we were new and unexperienced in the science of government. It was the first too which was formed in the whole United States. No wonder then that time and trial have discovered very capital defects in it.

> One of the most difficult aspects of representative government is that of providing fair representation. Jefferson was writing before the general widening of the suffrage movement, which largely took place in the early nineteenth century.

1. The majority of the men in the state, who pay and fight for its support, are unrepresented in the legislature, the roll of freeholders intitled to vote, not including generally the half of those on the roll of the militia, or of the tax-gatherers.

> Jefferson proceeds to provide examples.

2. Among those who share the representation, the shares are very unequal. . . .

> Although clearly favoring bicameralism, Jefferson argued that the similarity between Virginia's two legislative branches deprived the government of the advantages it would have otherwise derived from this mechanism. At the national level, delegates to the Constitutional Convention of 1787 would seek to avoid repetition of this mistake by providing for somewhat different qualifications, term lengths, and different methods of selection for the two legislative bodies.

3. The senate is, by its constitution, too homogeneous with the house of delegates. Being chosen by the same electors, at the same time, and out of the same subjects, the choice falls of course on men of the same description. The purpose of establishing different houses of legislation is to introduce the influence of different interests or different principles. Thus in Great-Britain it is said their

constitution relies on the house of commons for honesty, and the lords for wisdom; which would be a rational reliance if honesty were to be bought with money, and if wisdom were hereditary. In some of the American states the delegates and senators are so chosen, as that the first represent the persons, and the second the property of the state. But with us, wealth and wisdom have equal chance for admission into both houses. We do not therefore derive from the separation of our legislature into two houses, those benefits which a proper complication of principles is capable of producing, and those which alone can compensate the evils which may be produced by their dissensions.

4. **All the powers of government, legislative, executive, and judiciary, result to the legislative body. The concentrating these in the same hands is precisely the definition of despotic government. It will be no alleviation that these powers will be exercised by a plurality of hands, and not by a single one. 173 despots would surely be as oppressive as one.** Let those who doubt it turn their eyes on the republic of Venice. As little will it avail us that they are chosen by ourselves. An *elective despotism* was not the government we fought for; but one which should not only be founded on free principles, but in which the powers of government should be so divided and balanced among several bodies of magistracy, as that no one could transcend their legal limits, without being effectually checked and restrained by the others. For this reason that convention, which passed the ordinance of government, laid its foundation on this basis, that the legislative, executive and judiciary departments should be separate and distinct, so that no person should exercise the powers of more than one of them at the same time. But no barrier was

> Jefferson argued that Virginia had instituted separation of powers more in name than in reality, which meant that the legislature acted with few constitutional restraints. Most state constitutions of the time provided for legislative predominance.

> *"The judiciary and executive members were left dependant on the legislative, for their subsistence in office, and some of them for their continuance in it. If therefore the legislature assumes executive and judiciary powers, no opposition is likely to be made; nor, if made, can it be effectual; because in that case they may put their proceedings into the form of an act of assembly, which will render them obligatory on the other branches."*

provided between these several powers. The judiciary and executive members were left dependant on the legislative, for their subsistence in office, and some of them for their continuance in it. If therefore the legislature assumes executive and judiciary powers, no opposition is likely to be made; nor, if made, can it be effectual; because in that case they may put their proceedings into the form of an act of assembly, which will render them obligatory on the other branches. They have accordingly, in many instances, decided rights which should have been left to judiciary controversy: and the direction of the executive, during the whole time of their session, is becoming habitual and familiar. And this is done with no ill intention. The views of the present members are perfectly upright. When they are led out of their regular province, it is by art in others, and inadvertence in themselves. And this will probably be the case for some time to come. But it will not be a very long time. Mankind soon learn to make interested uses of every right and power which they possess, or may assume. The public money and public liberty, intended to have been deposited with three branches of magistracy, but found inadvertently to be in the hands of one only, will soon be discovered to be sources of wealth and dominion to those who hold them; distinguished too by this tempting circumstance, that they are the instrument, as well as the object of acquisition. With money we will get men, said Caesar, and with men we will get money. Nor should our assembly be deluded by the integrity of their own purposes, and conclude that these unlimited powers will never be abused, because themselves are not disposed to abuse them. They should look forward to a time, and that not a distant one, when corruption in this, as in the country from which we derive our origin, will have seized the heads of government, and be spread by them through the body of the people; when they will purchase the voices of the people, and make them pay the price.

Human nature is the same on every side of the Atlantic, and will be alike influenced by the same causes. The time to guard against corruption and tyranny, is before they shall have gotten hold on us. It is better to keep the wolf out of the fold, than to trust to drawing his teeth and talons after he shall have entered. To render these considerations the more cogent, we must observe in addition,

5. That the ordinary legislature may alter the constitution itself. On the discontinuance of assemblies, it became necessary to substitute in their place some other body, competent to the ordinary business of government, and to the calling forth the powers of the state for the maintenance of our opposition to Great-Britain. Conventions were therefore introduced, consisting of two delegates from each county, meeting together and forming one house, on the plan of the former house of Burgesses, to whose places they succeeded. These were at first chosen anew for every particular session. But in March 1775, they recommended to the people to chuse a convention, which should continue in office a year. This was done accordingly in April 1775, and in the July following that convention passed an ordinance for the election of delegates in the month of April annually. It is well known, that in July 1775, a separation from Great-Britain and establishment of Republican government had never yet entered into any person's mind. A convention therefore, chosen under that ordinance, cannot be said to have been chosen for purposes which certainly did not exist in the minds of those who passed it. Under this ordinance, at the annual election in April 1776, a convention for the year was chosen. Independance, and the establishment of a new form of government, were not even yet the objects of the people at large. One extract from the pamphlet called Common Sense had appeared in the Virginia papers in February, and copies of the pamphlet itself had got into a few hands.

"That the ordinary legislature may alter the constitution itself."

Thomas Jefferson's Notes on the State of Virginia

At the beginning of the American Revolution, state legislators sometimes found themselves not only legislating but also drawing up new constitutions. Jefferson recognized that this provided inadequate popular grounding for government and effectively made the legislature sovereign. Jefferson advocated the creation of a new state constitution through a convention specifically vested with this authority. This is the procedure that the nation would follow in calling the Constitutional Convention of 1787 and in providing for its ratification not by existing state legislatures but by special conventions called for this specific task.

But the idea had not been opened to the mass of the people in April, much less can it be said that they had made up their minds in its favor. So that the electors of April 1776, no more than the legislators of July 1775, not thinking of independance and a permanent republic, could not mean to vest in these delegates powers of establishing them, or any authorities other than those of the ordinary legislature. So far as a temporary organization of government was necessary to render our opposition energetic, so far their organization was valid. But they received in their creation no powers but what were given to every legislature before and since. They could not therefore pass an act transcendant to the powers of other legislatures. If the present assembly pass any act, and declare it shall be irrevocable by subsequent assemblies, the declaration is merely void, and the act repealable, as other acts are. So far, and no farther authorized, they organized the government by the ordinance entitled a Constitution or Form of government. It pretends to no higher authority than the other ordinances of the same session; it does not say, that it shall be perpetual; that it shall be unalterable by other legislatures; that it shall be transcendant above the powers of those, who they knew would have equal power with themselves. . . .

6. That the assembly exercises a power of determining the Quorum of their own body which may legislate for us. . . .

Source: Thomas Jefferson. "Query XI" and "Query XIII," *Notes on the State of Virginia.* Richmond, VA: J. W. Randolph, 1785.

The Sole and Exclusive Right
Congressional Proposal for Revising the Articles of Confederation
August 7, 1786

> **INTRODUCTION**
>
> Given that Congress wrote the Articles of Confederation when its primary attentions were devoted to overseeing a war for independence from Great Britain, it is not surprising that experience demonstrated the need for alterations. The document seemingly provided for amendments at the request of Congress and the unanimous approval of state legislatures, but on a number of occasions, the Congress came a single state short of having proposals adopted. Although the following resolutions, proposed on August 7, 1786, did not make it out of Congress, they demonstrated what some leading members thought were the central weaknesses of the existing arrangements.

THAT the first paragraph of the ninth of the articles of confederation be altered, so as to read thus, viz.

> *Section 9 of the Articles outlined congressional powers.*

The United States in Congress assembled, shall have the sole and exclusive right and power of determining on peace and war, except in the cases mentioned in the sixth article—of sending and receiving ambassadors—entering into treaties and alliances—of regulating the trade of the states, as well with foreign nations, as with each other, and of laying such impost and duties, upon imports and exports, as may be necessary for the purpose; provided, that the citizens of the states, shall in no instance be subjected to pay higher imposts and duties, than those imposed on the subjects of foreign powers; provided also, that the legislative power of the several states, shall not be restrained from prohibiting the importation or exportation of any species of goods or commodities whatsoever;

> *Congress identified two chief weaknesses within the Articles. One was that the states did not present a united front in its dealings with other nations. A second defect was that the document did not vest Congress with the power over interstate and foreign commerce. Under such circumstances, states taxed the commerce of goods from and to neighboring states, leaving those with ports with far greater resources than those without them, and leaving the national government, which depended on requisitions on states, with no independent source of revenue. The committee introducing this resolution followed with an explanation of why greater unity was required in dealing with foreign nations.*

provided also, that all such duties as may be imposed, shall be collected under the authority and accrue to the rise of the state, in which the same shall be payable. And provided lastly, that every act of Congress for the above purpose, shall have the assent of nine states in Congress assembled—of establishing rules for deciding in all cases, what captures on land or water shall be legal, and in what manner prizes taken by land or naval forces in the service of the United States shall be divided or appropriated, of granting letters of marque and reprisal in time of peace— appointing courts for the trial of piracies and felonies committed on the high seas, and establishing courts for receiving and determining finally appeals in all cases of captures; provided that no member of Congress shall be appointed judge of any of the said courts.

Source: Library of Congress. Documents from the Continental Congress and the Constitutional Convention, 1774–1789. Accessed January 15, 2015. http://hdl.loc.gov/loc.rbc/bdsdcc.11801.

Section III: Calling and Convening the Constitutional Convention

Defects in the System
Annapolis Convention Resolution
1786

> **INTRODUCTION**
>
> After delegates from Maryland and Virginia successfully met at George Washington's house at Mount Vernon in March 1785 to discuss common issues of navigation, the Virginia legislature adopted a resolution on January 21, 1786, appointing five delegates to yet another convention in Annapolis, Maryland, to discuss issues of interstate trade and commerce. It also sent a circular letter in February encouraging other states to send delegates. Although delegations from only five states showed up for the meeting, which was held in the old senate chamber of the Maryland State House, the Convention met from September 11 through September 13. Afterward, it issued a call for what would become the Constitutional Convention of 1787 to discuss a broader range of issues of import to all the states.

To the Honorable, The Legislatures of Virginia, Delaware, Pennsylvania, New Jersey, and New York—assembled at Annapolis, humbly beg leave to report.

That, pursuant to their several appointments, they met, at Annapolis in the State of Maryland on the eleventh day of September Instant, and having proceeded to a Communication of their Powers; they found that the States of New York, Pennsylvania, and Virginia, had, in substance, and nearly in the same terms, authorized their respective Commissions "to meet such other Commissioners as were, or might be, appointed by the other States in the Union, at such time and place as should be agreed upon by the said Commissions to take into consideration the trade and commerce of the United States, to consider how far a uniform system in their commercial intercourse and regulations might be necessary to their common interest and permanent harmony, and to report to the several States such an Act, relative to this great object, as when unanimously by them would enable the United States in Congress assembled effectually to proved for the same."

That the State of New Jersey had enlarged the object of their appointment, empowering their Commissioners, "to consider how far a uniform system in their commercial regulations and other important matters, mighty be necessary to the common interest and permanent harmony of the several States," and to report such an Act on the subject, as when ratified by them, "would enable the United States in Congress assembled, effectually to provide for the exigencies of the Union."

That appointments of Commissioners have also been made by the States of New Hampshire, Massachusetts, Rhode Island, and North Carolina, none of whom, however, have attended; but that no information has been received by your Commissioners, of any appointment having been made by the States of Connecticut, Maryland, South Carolina or Georgia.

That the express terms of the powers of your Commissioners supposing a deputation from all the States, and having for object the Trade and Commerce of the United States, Your Commissioners did not conceive it advisable to proceed on the business of their mission, under the Circumstances of so partial and defective a representation.

Essentially, the delegates are claiming that their meeting failed not for lack of state interest in the problem under the Articles of Confederation but because states found the scope of the meeting to be too limited.

Deeply impressed, however, with the magnitude and importance of the object confided to them on this occasion, your Commissioners cannot forbear to indulge an expression of their earnest and unanimous wish, that speedy measures be

Annapolis Convention Resolution

taken, to effect a general meeting, of the States, in a future Convention, for the same, and such other purposes, as the situation of public affairs may be found to require.

If in expressing this wish, or in intimating any other sentiment, your Commissioners should seem to exceed the strict bounds of their appointment, they entertain a full confidence, that a conduct, dictated by an anxiety for the welfare of the United States, will not fail to receive an indulgent construction.

> Again, the delegates suggested that it was impossible to discuss the issue of interstate trade without considering other aspects of government under the existing Articles of Confederation.

In this persuasion, your Commissioners submit an opinion, that the Idea of extending the powers of their Deputies, to other objects, than those of Commerce, which has been adopted by the State of New Jersey, was an improvement on the original plan, and will deserve to be incorporated into that of a future Convention; they are the more naturally led to this conclusion, as in the course of their reflections on the subject, they have been induced to think, that the power of regulating trade is of such comprehensive extent, and will enter so far into the general System of the federal government, that to give it efficacy, and to obviate questions and doubts concerning its precise nature and limits, may require a correspondent adjustment of other parts of the Federal System.

> Although the delegates declined to list all the defects that they perceived in the Articles of Confederation, they did indicate that the defects were both internal and external.

That there are important defects in the system of the Federal Government is acknowledged by the Acts of all those States, which have concurred in the present Meeting; That the defects, upon a closer examination, may be found greater and more numerous, than even these acts imply, is at least so far probable, from the embarrassments which characterize the present State of our national affairs, foreign and domestic, as may reasonably be

supposed to merit a deliberate and candid discussion, in some mode, which will unite the Sentiments and Councils of all the States. In the choice of the mode, your Commissioners are of opinion, that a Convention of Deputies from the different States, for the special and sole purpose of entering into this investigation, and digesting a plan for supplying such defects as may be discovered to exist, will be entitled to a preference from considerations, which will occur without being particularized.

Your Commissioners decline an enumeration of those national circumstances on which their opinion respecting the propriety of a future Convention, with more enlarged powers, is founded; as it would be a useless intrusion of facts and observations, most of which have been frequently the subject of public discussion, and none of which can have escaped the penetration of those to whom they would in this instance be addressed. They are, however, of a nature so serious, as, in the view of your Commissioners, to render the situation of the United States delicate and critical, calling for an exertion of the untied virtue and wisdom of all the members of the Confederacy.

Under this impression, Your Commissioners, with the most respectful deference, beg leave to suggest their unanimous conviction that it may essentially tend to advance the interests of the union if the States, by whom they have been respectively delegated, would themselves concur, and use their endeavors to procure the concurrence of the other States, in the appointment of Commissioners, to meet at Philadelphia on the second Monday in May next, to take into consideration the situation of the United States, to devise such further provisions as shall appear to them necessary to render the constitution of

"They are, however, of a nature so serious, as, in the view of your Commissioners, to render the situation of the United States delicate and critical, calling for an exertion of the untied virtue and wisdom of all the members of the Confederacy."

The delegates called for a broader convention to meet at a specific time and place with authority to examine a broad range of issues. They further anticipated that the delegates to that convention would report their findings to Congress, which would, in turn, send proposals to existing state legislatures for ratification. The Convention would later decide to send the proposed constitution not to existing state legislatures but to special state conventions called specifically for the purpose of deciding whether or not to ratify.

the Federal Government adequate to the exigencies of the Union; and to report such an Act for that purpose to the United States in Congress assembled, as when agreed to, by them, and afterwards confirmed by the Legislatures of every State, will effectually provide for the same.

Though your Commissioners could not with propriety address these observations and sentiments to any but the States they have the honor to represent, they have nevertheless concluded from motives of respect, to transmit copies of the Report to the United States in Congress assembled, and to the executives of the other States.

Source: Proceedings of Commissioners to Remedy Defects of the Federal Government (Annapolis Convention Resolution), September 11, 1786. *Documents Illustrative of the Formation of the Union of the American States.* Washington, DC: Government Printing Office, 1927. Avalon Project database. Accessed January 15, 2015. http://avalon.law.yale.edu/18th_century/annapoli.asp.

As a Mean to Remedy

Congressional Endorsement of Annapolis Convention Resolution

February 21, 1787

INTRODUCTION

In the 18th century, conventions sometimes responded to needs that existing legislative bodies or other established institutions ignored, but it was not clear that the call from the Annapolis Convention would have succeeded without congressional approval, which the Convention sought by requesting Congress to endorse its call. The Congress accordingly adopted the following resolution, offered by the Massachusetts delegation, on February 21, 1787. One impetus for congressional action was widespread concern that Congress had not adequately been able to respond to a taxpayer rebellion that winter in Massachusetts known as Shays' Rebellion.

Whereas there is provision in the Articles of Confederation & perpetual Union for making alterations therein by the assent of a Congress of the United States and of the legislatures of the several States; And whereas experience hath evinced that there are defects in the present Confederation, as a mean to remedy which several of the States and particularly the State of New York by express instructions to their delegates in Congress have suggested a convention for the purposes expressed in the following resolution and such convention appearing to be the most probable mean of establishing in these states a firm national government.

Resolved that in the opinion of Congress it is expedient that on the second Monday in May next a Convention of delegates who shall have been appointed by the several states be held at Philadelphia for the sole and express

This resolution pointed to the provision in the Articles for adopting amendments without calling attention to the fact that such amendments would require unanimous state consent. Although giving its blessings to such a convention, the Congress indicated that it anticipated that both it and the states would subsequently approve. Curiously, it was similar to the Articles of Confederation in that it did not specifically refer to state legislatures as a vehicle for passing amendments.

> *"[R]evising the Articles of Confederation and reporting to Congress and the several legislatures such alterations and provisions therein as shall when agreed to in Congress and confirmed by the states render the federal constitution adequate to the exigencies of Government & the preservation of the Union."*

purpose of revising the Articles of Confederation and reporting to Congress and the several legislatures such alterations and provisions therein as shall when agreed to in Congress and confirmed by the states render the federal constitution adequate to the exigencies of Government & the preservation of the Union.

Source: Report of Proceedings in Congress, February 21, 1787. *Documents Illustrative of the Formation of the Union of the American States.* Washington, DC: Government Printing Office, 1927. Avalon Project database. Accessed January 15, 2015. http://avalon.law.yale.edu/18th_century/const04.asp.

An Aggregate View
James Madison Discusses Vices of the Political System of the United States
April 1787

> **INTRODUCTION**
>
> No one worked harder or longer preparing for the Constitutional Convention of 1787 than did James Madison, who had served both in Congress and in the Virginia state legislature. His friend Thomas Jefferson, who was serving as an ambassador to France, sent him crates of books on political issues. Based on this reading and on his experience at both the state and national level, Madison identified the "vices," or ills, in the existing political system. In another unpublished essay, he examined the difficulties of earlier confederacies. These diagnoses served largely as the foundation for the Virginia Plan, which Governor Edmund Randolph introduced at the Constitutional Convention.

1. Failure of the States to comply with the Constitutional requisitions.

This evil has been so fully experienced both during the war and since the peace, results so naturally from the number and independent authority of the States and has been so uniformly examplified in every similar Confederacy, that it may be considered as not less radically and permanently inherent in, than it is fatal to the object of, the present System.

Confederal systems like that of the Articles of Confederation do not have authority to act directly upon individuals. Under the Articles, as in earlier confederations, states sometimes refused to comply with congressional requests.

2. Encroachments by the States on the federal authority.

Examples of this are numerous and repetitions may be foreseen in almost every case where any favorite object of a State shall present a temptation. Among these examples are the wars and Treaties of Georgia with the Indians—The unlicensed compacts between Virginia and Maryland, and between Pena. & N. Jersey—the troops raised and to be kept up by Massts.

3. Violations of the law of nations and of treaties.

From the number of Legislatures, the sphere of life from which most of their members are taken, and the circumstances under which their legislative business is carried on, irregularities of this kind must frequently happen. Accordingly not a year has passed without instances of them in some one or other of the States. The Treaty of peace—the treaty with France—the treaty with Holland have each been violated. The causes of these irregularities must necessarily produce frequent violations of the law of nations in other respects.

As yet foreign powers have not been rigorous in animadverting on us. This moderation however cannot be mistaken for a permanent partiality to our faults, or a permanent security agst. those disputes with other nations, which being among the greatest of public calamities, it ought to be least in the power of any part of the Community to bring on the whole.

4. Trespasses of the States on the rights of each other.

These are alarming symptoms, and may be daily apprehended as we are admonished by daily experience. See the law of Virginia restricting foreign vessels to certain ports—of Maryland in favor of vessels belonging to her own citizens—of N. York in favor of the same.

Paper money, instalments of debts, occlusion of Courts, making property a legal tender, may likewise be deemed aggressions on the rights of other States. As the Citizens

of every State aggregately taken stand more or less in the relation of Creditors or debtors, to the Citizens of every other States, Acts of the debtor State in favor of debtors, affect the Creditor State, in the same manner, as they do its own citizens who are relatively creditors towards other citizens. This remark may be extended to foreign nations. If the exclusive regulation of the value and alloy of coin was properly delegated to the federal authority, the policy of it equally requires a controul on the States in the cases above mentioned. It must have been meant 1. to preserve uniformity in the circulating medium throughout the nation. 2. to prevent those frauds on the citizens of other States, and the subjects of foreign powers, which might disturb the tranquility at home, or involve the Union in foreign contests.

The practice of many States in restricting the commercial intercourse with other States, and putting their productions and manufactures on the same footing with those of foreign nations, though not contrary to the federal articles, is certainly adverse to the spirit of the Union, and tends to beget retaliating regulations, not less expensive & vexatious in themselves, than they are destructive of the general harmony.

> Congress under the Articles of Confederation had no power to control interstate or foreign commerce, and states thus taxed one another, robbing the nation of the economic advantages that it would have otherwise derived from a national market. States also had the power to coin their own money, which made doing business from one state to another much like that of doing business with other countries and allowed some states to pursue inflationary policies while others were exercising fiscal restraint.

5. want of concert in matters where common interest requires it.

This defect is strongly illustrated in the state of our commercial affairs. How much has the national dignity, interest, and revenue suffered from this cause? Instances of inferior moment are the want of uniformity in the laws concerning naturalization & literary property; of provision for national seminaries, for grants of incorporation for national purposes, for canals and other works of general utility, wch. may at present be defeated by the perverseness of particular States whose concurrence is necessary.

6. want of guaranty to the States of their Constitutions & laws against internal violence.

Madison's thoughts were undoubtedly influenced on this subject in part by the weak congressional response to Shays' Rebellion in Massachusetts. At a time when many southerners were also concerned about enlisting national help in the case of slave rebellions, Madison appeared more concerned about the impact of slavery on republican institutions.

The confederation is silent on this point and therefore by the second article the hands of the federal authority are tied. According to Republican Theory, Right and power being both vested in the majority, are held to be synonimous. According to fact and experience a minority may in an appeal to force, be an overmatch for the majority. 1. If the minority happen to include all such as possess the skill and habits of military life, & such as possess the great pecuniary resources, one third only may conquer the remaining two thirds. 2. One third of those who participate in the choice of the rulers, may be rendered a majority by the accession of those whose poverty excludes them from a right of suffrage, and who for obvious reasons will be more likely to join the standard of sedition than that of the established Government. 3. Where slavery exists the republican Theory becomes still more fallacious.

7. want of sanction to the laws, and of coercion in the Government of the Confederacy.

> "A sanction is essential to the idea of law, as coercion is to that of Government. The federal system being destitute of both, wants the great vital principles of a Political Cons[ti]tution."

A sanction is essential to the idea of law, as coercion is to that of Government. The federal system being destitute of both, wants the great vital principles of a Political Cons[ti]tution. Under the form of such a Constitution, it is in fact nothing more than a treaty of amity of commerce and of alliance, between so many independent and Sovereign States.

From what cause could so fatal an omission have happened in the articles of Confederation? from a mistaken confidence that the justice, the good faith, the honor, the sound policy, of the several legislative assemblies would render superfluous any appeal to the ordinary motives by which the laws secure the obedience of individuals: a confidence which does honor to the enthusiastic virtue of the compilers, as much as the inexperience of the crisis apologizes for their errors. The time which has since elapsed has had the double effect, of increasing the light, and tempering the warmth, with which the arduous work may be revised. It is no longer doubted that a unanimous and punctual obedience of 13 independent bodies, to the acts of the federal Government, ought not be calculated on. Even during the war, when external danger supplied in some degree the defect of legal & coercive sanctions, how imperfectly did the States fulfil their obligations to the Union? In time of peace, we see already what is to be expected. How indeed could it be otherwise? In the first place, Every general act of the Union must necessarily bear unequally hard on some particular member or members of it. Secondly the partiality of the members to their own interests and rights, a partiality which will be fostered by the Courtiers of popularity, will naturally exaggerate the inequality where it exists, and even suspect it where it has no existence. Thirdly a distrust of the voluntary compliance of each other may prevent the compliance of any, although it should be the latent disposition of all. Here are causes & pretexts which will never fail to render federal measures abortive. If the laws of the States, were merely recommendatory to their citizens, or if they were to be rejudged by County authorities, what security, what probability would exist, that they would be carried into execution? Is the security or probability greater in favor of the acts of Congs. which depending for their execution on the will of the state legislatures, wch. are tho' nominally authoritative, in fact recommendatory only.

> *"It is no longer doubted that a unanimous and punctual obedience of 13 independent bodies, to the acts of the federal Government, ought not be calculated on. Even during the war, when external danger supplied in some degree the defect of legal & coercive sanctions, how imperfectly did the States fulfil their obligations to the Union? In time of peace, we see already what is to be expected."*

8. want of ratification by the people of the articles of Confederation.

> Madison believed that a national constitution needed a firmer foundation than mere state legislative approval. He pointed out that when states saw fellow states refuse to comply with congressional demands, they were likely to conclude that it gave them the right to do likewise. He may have further been suggesting that existing state violations were sufficient to void the agreement under the Articles of Confederation.

In some of the States the Confederation is recognized by, and forms a part of the constitution. In others however it has received no other sanction than that of the Legislative authority. From this defect two evils result: 1. Whenever a law of a State happens to be repugnant to an act of Congress, particularly when the latter is of posterior date to the former, it will be at least questionable whether the latter must not prevail; and as the question must be decided by the Tribunals of the State, they will be most likely to lean on the side of the State. 2. As far as the Union of the States is to be regarded as a league of sovereign powers, and not as a political Constitution by virtue of which they are become one sovereign power, so far it seems to follow from the doctrine of compacts, that a breach of any of the articles of the confederation by any of the parties to it, absolves the other parties from their respective obligations, and gives them a right if they chuse to exert it, of dissolving the Union altogether.

9. Multiplicity of laws in the several States.

In developing the evils which viciate the political system of the U. S. it is proper to include those which are found within the States individually, as well as those which directly affect the States collectively, since the former class have an indirect influence on the general malady and must not be overlooked in forming a compleat remedy. Among the evils then of our situation may well be ranked the multiplicity of laws from which no State is exempt. As far as laws are necessary, to mark with precision the duties of those who are to obey them, and to take from those who are to administer them a discretion, which might be abused, their number is the price of liberty. As far as the laws exceed this limit, they are a nusance: a nusance of the most pestilent kind. Try the Codes of the several States by this test, and what a luxuriancy of legislation do they present. The short period of independency has filled as many pages as the century which preceded it. Every year, almost every session, adds a new volume. This may be the effect in part, but it can only be in part, of the situation in which the revolution has placed us. A review of the several codes will shew that every necessary and useful part of the least voluminous of them might be compressed into one tenth of the compass, and at the same time be rendered tenfold as perspicuous.

10. mutability of the laws of the States.

This evil is intimately connected with the former yet deserves a distinct notice as it emphatically denotes a vicious legislation. We daily see laws repealed or superseded, before any trial can have been made of their merits: and even before a knowledge of them can have reached the remoter districts within which they were to operate. In the regulations of trade this instability becomes a snare not only to our citizens but to foreigners also.

11. Injustice of the laws of States.

If the multiplicity and mutability of laws prove a want of wisdom, their injustice betrays a defect still more alarming: more alarming not merely because it is a greater evil in itself, but because it brings more into question the fundamental principle of republican Government, that the majority who rule in such Governments, are the safest Guardians both of public Good and of private rights. To what causes is this evil to be ascribed?

> *"A review of the several codes will shew that every necessary and useful part of the least voluminous of them might be compressed into one tenth of the compass, and at the same time be rendered tenfold as perspicuous."*

> *"If the multiplicity and mutability of laws prove a want of wisdom, their injustice betrays a defect still more alarming: more alarming not merely because it is a greater evil in itself, but because it brings more into question the fundamental principle of republican Government, that the majority who rule in such Governments, are the safest Guardians both of public Good and of private rights."*

These causes lie 1. in the Representative bodies.
2. in the people themselves.

> *"Representative appointments are sought from 3 motives. 1. ambition 2. personal interest. 3. public good. Unhappily the two first are proved by experience to be most prevalent. Hence the candidates who feel them, particularly, the second, are most industrious, and most successful in pursuing their object: and forming often a majority in the legislative Councils, with interested views, contrary to the interest, and views, of their Constituents, join in a perfidious sacrifice of the latter to the former."*

1. Representative appointments are sought from 3 motives. 1. ambition 2. personal interest. 3. public good. Unhappily the two first are proved by experience to be most prevalent. Hence the candidates who feel them, particularly, the second, are most industrious, and most successful in pursuing their object: and forming often a majority in the legislative Councils, with interested views, contrary to the interest, and views, of their Constituents, join in a perfidious sacrifice of the latter to the former. A succeeding election it might be supposed, would displace the offenders, and repair the mischief. But how easily are base and selfish measures, masked by pretexts of public good and apparent expediency? How frequently will a repetition of the same arts and industry which succeeded in the first instance, again prevail on the unwary to misplace their confidence?

How frequently too will the honest but unenlightened representative be the dupe of a favorite leader, veiling his selfish views under the professions of public good, and varnishing his sophistical arguments with the glowing colours of popular eloquence?

2. A still more fatal if not more frequent cause lies among the people themselves. All civilized societies are divided into different interests and factions, as they happen to be creditors or debtors—Rich or poor—husbandmen, merchants or manufacturers—members of different religious sects—followers of different political leaders—inhabitants of different districts—owners of different kinds of property &c &c. In republican Government the majority however composed, ultimately give the law. Whenever

therefore an apparent interest or common passion unites a majority what is to restrain them from unjust violations of the rights and interests of the minority, or of individuals? Three motives only 1. a prudent regard to their own good as involved in the general and permanent good of the Community. This consideration although of decisive weight in itself, is found by experience to be too often unheeded. It is too often forgotten, by nations as well as by individuals that honesty is the best policy. 2dly. respect for character. However strong this motive may be in individuals, it is considered as very insufficient to restrain them from injustice. In a multitude its efficacy is diminished in proportion to the number which is to share the praise or the blame. Besides, as it has reference to public opinion, which within a particular Society, is the opinion of the majority, the standard is fixed by those whose conduct is to be measured by it. The public opinion without the Society, will be little respected by the people at large of any Country. Individuals of extended views, and of national pride, may bring the public proceedings to this standard, but the example will never be followed by the multitude. Is it to be imagined that an ordinary citizen or even an assemblyman of R. Island in estimating the policy of paper money, ever considered or cared in what light the measure would be viewed in France or Holland; or even in Massts or Connect.? It was a sufficient temptation to both that it was for their interest: it was a sufficient sanction to the latter that it was popular in the State; to the former that it was so in the neighbourhood. 3dly. will Religion the only remaining motive be a sufficient restraint? It is not pretended to be such on men individually considered. Will its effect be greater on them considered in an aggregate view? quite the reverse. The conduct of every popular assembly acting on oath, the strongest of religious Ties, proves that individuals join without remorse in acts, against which their consciences would revolt if proposed to them

"[R]espect for character. However strong this motive may be in individuals, it is considered as very insufficient to restrain them from injustice. In a multitude its efficacy is diminished in proportion to the number which is to share the praise or the blame."

under the like sanction, separately in their closets. When indeed Religion is kindled into enthusiasm, its force like that of other passions, is increased by the sympathy of a multitude. But enthusiasm is only a temporary state of religion, and while it lasts will hardly be seen with pleasure at the helm of Government. Besides as religion in its coolest state, is not infallible, it may become a motive to oppression as well as a restraint from injustice. Place three individuals in a situation wherein the interest of each depends on the voice of the others, and give to two of them an interest opposed to the rights of the third?

Will the latter be secure? The prudence of every man would shun the danger. The rules & forms of justice suppose & guard against it. Will two thousand in a like situation be less likely to encroach on the rights of one thousand? The contrary is witnessed by the notorious factions & oppressions which take place in corporate towns limited as the opportunities are, and in little republics when uncontrouled by apprehensions of external danger. If an enlargement of the sphere is found to lessen the insecurity of private rights, it is not because the impulse of a common interest or passion is less predominant in this case with the majority; but because a common interest or passion is less apt to be felt and the requisite combinations less easy to be formed by a great than by a small number. The Society becomes broken into a greater variety of interests, of pursuits, of passions, which check each other, whilst those who may feel a common sentiment have less opportunity of communication and concert. It may be inferred that the inconveniences of popular States contrary to the prevailing Theory, are in proportion not to the extent, but to the narrowness of their limits.

"If an enlargement of the sphere is found to lessen the insecurity of private rights, it is not because the impulse of a common interest or passion is less predominant in this case with the majority; but because a common interest or passion is less apt to be felt and the requisite combinations less easy to be formed by a great than by a small number."

The great desideratum in Government is such a modification of the Sovereignty as will render it sufficiently neutral between the different interests and factions, to controul one part of the Society from invading the rights of another, and at the same time sufficiently controuled itself, from setting up an interest adverse to that of the whole Society. In absolute Monarchies, the prince is sufficiently, neutral towards his subjects, but frequently sacrifices their happiness to his ambition or his avarice. In small Republics, the sovereign will is sufficiently controuled from such a Sacrifice of the entire Society, but is not sufficiently neutral towards the parts composing it. As a limited Monarchy tempers the evils of an absolute one; so an extensive Republic meliorates the administration of a small Republic.

> Madison would return to these themes in speeches to the Constitutional Convention and in Federalist No. 10, where he identified the problem as factionalism. The solution, according to Madison, was to build a system of representatives and create a government that spanned so many interests that no one was likely to dominate. In Federalist No. 51, Madison would further argue for the advantages of a system that separated powers, so that each individual officeholder's self-interest would be tied to the interest of his institution.

An auxiliary desideratum for the melioration of the Republican form is such a process of elections as will most certainly extract from the mass of the Society the purest and noblest characters which it contains; such as will at once feel most strongly the proper motives to pursue the end of their appointment, and be most capable to devise the proper means of attaining it.

12. Impotence of the laws of the States

Source: James Madison. Vices of the Political System of the United States, April 1787. *The Writings of James Madison*. Vol. 2. Edited by Gaillard Hunt. New York: G. P. Putnam's Sons, 1901.

A House to Do Business

Rules for the Constitutional Convention

May 28, 1787

INTRODUCTION

One clear indication that a body intends to proceed in a deliberative fashion is that it outlines a set of rules intended to encourage such deliberation. Almost immediately after the Constitutional Convention delegates selected George Washington to preside over the Convention on its first day (May 25), Charles Pinckney of South Carolina proposed that the Convention establish a committee to draft rules for the proceedings. The committee was composed of George Wythe, a professor of law from Virginia's College of William and Mary; Alexander Hamilton of New York; and Charles Pinckney. It made its report the following Monday, undoubtedly drawing from the delegates' wide experience in other assemblies.

Mr. WYTHE from the Committee for preparing rules made a report which employed the deliberations of this day.

As under the Articles of Confederation, delegates to the Constitutional Convention voted by states. Rufus King of Massachusetts indicated that he opposed recording votes under the names of individual delegates, whom he feared might be embarrassed to change recorded votes if, on fuller information or on the basis of persuasion, they thought it wise to do so. This is another indication of how seriously the Convention took the idea of adopting a government through calm deliberation.

Mr. KING objected to one of the rules in the Report authorising any member to call for the yeas & nays and have them entered on the minutes. He urged that as the acts of the Convention were not to bind the Constituents, it was unnecessary to exhibit this evidence of the votes; and improper as changes of opinion would be frequent in the course of the business & would fill the minutes with contradictions.

Col. MASON seconded the objection; adding that such a record of the opinions of members would be an obstacle to a change of them on conviction; and in case of its being hereafter promulged must furnish handles to the adversaries of the Result of the Meeting. The proposed rule was rejected nem. contradicente. The standing rules agreed to were as follow:

Rules to be observed as the standing Orders of the Convention.

A House to do business shall consist of the Deputies of not less than seven States; and all questions shall be decided by the greater number of these which shall be fully represented: but a less number than seven may adjourn from day to day.

> Almost every collective body establishes a quorum consisting of the minimum number of members needed to conduct business. The Convention set this number at 7, a majority of the 13 states, not all of which were present (and, in the case of Rhode Island, one of which would never send delegates) during the opening days.

Immediately after the President shall have taken the chair, and the members their seats, the minutes of the preceding day shall be read by the Secretary.

Every member, rising to speak, shall address the President; and whilst he shall be speaking, none shall pass between them, or hold discourse with another, or read a book, pamphlet or paper, printed or manuscript-and of two members rising at the same time, the President shall name him who shall be first heard.

> Most of these are fairly sensible rules. They were designed to introduce a degree of formality into the proceedings (something the election of George Washington had already done), to keep the delegates focused on the proceedings at hand, and to provide for an orderly way to recognize speakers. During the early weeks of the Convention, the delegates often acted as a Committee of the Whole, which allowed for more informal procedures to prevail.

A member shall not speak oftener than twice, without special leave, upon the same question; and not the second time, before every other, who had been silent, shall have been heard, if he choose to speak upon the subject.

A motion made and seconded, shall be repeated, and if written, as it shall be when any member shall so require, read aloud by the Secretary, before it shall be debated; and may be withdrawn at any time, before the vote upon it shall have been declared.

Rules for the Constitutional Convention

> *"That Committees shall be appointed by ballot; and the members who have the greatest number of ballots, altho' not a majority of the votes present, shall be the Committee- When two or more members have an equal number of votes, the member standing first on the list in the order of taking down the ballots, shall be preferred."*

Orders of the day shall be read next after the minutes, and either discussed or postponed, before any other business shall be introduced.

When a debate shall arise upon a question, no motion, other than to amend the question, to commit it, or to postpone the debate shall be received.

A question which is complicated, shall, at the request of any member, be divided, and put separately on the propositions, of which it is compounded.

The determination of a question, altho' fully debated, shall be postponed, if the deputies of any State desire it until the next day.

A writing which contains any matter brought on to be considered, shall be read once throughout for information, then by paragraphs to be debated, and again, with the amendments, if any, made on the second reading; and afterwards, the question shall be put on the whole, amended, or approved in its original form, as the case shall be.

That Committees shall be appointed by ballot; and the members who have the greatest number of ballots, altho' not a majority of the votes present, shall be the Committee- When two or more members have an equal number of votes, the member standing first on the list in the order of taking down the ballots, shall be preferred.

A member may be called to order by any other member, as well as by the President; and may be allowed to explain his conduct or expressions supposed to be reprehensible.- And all questions of order shall be decided by the President without appeal or debate.

Upon a question to adjourn for the day, which may be made at any time, if it be seconded, the question shall be put without a debate.

When the House shall adjourn, every member shall stand in his place, until the President pass him. . . .

Mr. BUTLER moved that the House provide agst. interruption of business by absence of members, and against licentious publications of their proceedings-to which was added by-Mr. SPAIGHT-a motion to provide that on the one hand the House might not be precluded by a vote upon any question, from revising the subject matter of it when they see cause, nor, on the other hand, be led too hastily to rescind a decision, which was the result of mature discussion.— Whereupon it was ordered that these motions be referred to the consideration of the Committee appointed to draw up the standing rules and that the Committee make report thereon.

Adjd. till tomorrow 10. OClock.
May 29, 1787

Tuesday May 29, 1787

John Dickenson, and Elbridge Gerry, the former from Delaware, the latter from Massts. took their seats. The following rules were added, on the report of Mr. Wythe from the Committee

Additional rules. That no member be absent from the House, so as to interrupt the representation of the State, without leave.

That Committees do not sit whilst the House shall be or ought to be, sitting.

*"**Mr. BUTLER** moved that the House provide agst. interruption of business by absence of members, and against licentious publications of their proceedings . . ."*

Rules for the Constitutional Convention

> It is difficult to imagine a modern meeting of similar consequence meeting in secret. Especially since the Progressive Era at the beginning of the 20th century, it is common to associate secrecy with cabals or coups. The delegates to the Constitutional Convention, however, wanted delegates to be able to discuss issues freely without worrying about street demonstrations or violence. They anticipated reporting the final product to the public for its approval and thought it more important to disclose the finished document than to provide Americans with a day-by-day account of its actual making. James Madison's extensive personal notes of the Convention were not released until 1840.

That no copy be taken of any entry on the journal during the sitting of the House without leave of the House.

That members only be permitted to inspect the journal.

That nothing spoken in the House be printed, or otherwise published or communicated without leave.

That a motion to reconsider a matter which had been determined by a majority, may be made, with leave unanimously given, on the same day on which the vote passed; but otherwise not without one day's previous notice: in which last case, if the House agree to the reconsideration, some future day shall be assigned for the purpose.

Source: *Records of the Federal Convention of 1787.* Vol. 1. Edited by Max Farrand. New Haven, CT: Yale University Press, 1911, pp. 1–19.

The Infancy of the Science of Constitutions
The Virginia Plan
May 29, 1787

INTRODUCTION

Although most delegates arrived in Philadelphia in May 1787 believing that they were there to amend the Articles of Confederation, members of the Virginia delegation, who spent time prior to obtaining a quorum at the Convention socializing and consulting with Pennsylvania delegates who were already in Philadelphia, had other plans. James Madison had been analyzing the perceived defects in the Articles of Confederation and in earlier confederations for months and appears to have been the intellectual leader behind the birth of the following plan. Edmund Randolph introduced the plan probably because he was the state governor and was known as a more powerful speaker. The Convention debated these proposals for the first two weeks, meaning that this plan served an agenda-setting function. Once the Convention considered such an alternative this seriously, it would have seemed timid had it simply enacted some minor changes to the Articles.

Mr. RANDOLPH then opened the main business. He expressed his regret, that it should fall to him, rather than those, who were of longer standing in life and political experience, to open the great subject of their mission. But, as the convention had originated from Virginia, and his colleagues supposed that some proposition was expected from them, they had imposed this task on him. He then commented on the difficulty of the crisis, and the necessity of preventing the fulfilment of the prophecies of the American downfal. He observed that in revising the foederal system we ought to inquire 1. into the properties, which such a government ought to possess, 2. the defects of the confederation, 3. the danger of our situation & 4. the remedy.

1. The Character of such a government ought to secure 1. against foreign invasion: 2. against dissentions between

"He observed that in revising the foederal system we ought to inquire 1. into the properties, which such a government ought to possess, 2. the defects of the confederation, 3. the danger of our situation & 4. the remedy."

These objectives focused on the need for greater central authority to combat both internal and external threats. They make for a fascinating comparison to the objectives that were later stated in the Preamble to the Constitution.

The Virginia Plan

members of the Union, or seditions in particular states: 3. to procure to the several States, various blessings, of which an isolated situation was incapable: 4. to be able to defend itself against incroachment: & 5. to be paramount to the state constitutions.

> The Virginians attributed most weaknesses of the Articles not to their authors' lack of wisdom but to their authors' lack of experience with specific problems that had arisen after the Articles had been adopted.

2. In speaking of the defects of the confederation he professed a high respect for its authors, and considered them, as having done all that patriots could do, in the then infancy of the science, of constitutions, & of confederacies,- when the inefficiency of requisitions was unknown- no commercial discord had arisen among any states-no rebellion had appeared as in Massts.-foreign debts had not become urgent-the havoc of paper money had not been foreseen-treaties had not been violated-and perhaps nothing better could be obtained from the jealousy of the states with regard to their sovereignty.

He then proceeded to enumerate the defects:

> *"[T]hat the confederation produced no security against foreign invasion; congress not being permitted to prevent a war nor to support it by their own authority . . ."*

1. that the confederation produced no security against foreign invasion; congress not being permitted to prevent a war nor to support it by their own authority-Of this he cited many examples; most of which tended to shew, that they could not cause infractions of treaties or of the law of nations, to be punished: that particular states might by their conduct provoke war without controul; and that neither militia nor draughts being fit for defence on such occasions, inlistments only could be successful, and these could not be executed without money.

2. that the foederal government could not check the quarrels between states, nor a rebellion in any, not having constitutional power nor means to interpose according to the exigency:

3. that there were many advantages, which the U. S. might acquire, which were not attainable under the confederation-such as a productive impost- counteraction of the commercial regulations of other nations-pushing of commerce ad libitum-&c &c.

4. that the foederal government could not defend itself against the incroachments from the states.

> The terminology is somewhat confusing, but prior to the writing of the U.S. Constitution, the Articles of Confederation (what we today call a confederal government) was called a foederal, or federal, government).

5. that it was not even paramount to the state constitutions, ratified, as it was in may of the states.

> These concerns can be fruitfully compared to the problems that James Madison had identified in his essay "Vices of the Political System of the United States."

3. He next reviewed the danger of our situation, appealed to the sense of the best friends of the U. S.-the prospect of anarchy from the laxity of government every where; and to other considerations. He proposed as conformable to his ideas the following resolutions, which he explained one by one.

Resolutions proposed by Mr. Randolph in Convention May 29, 1787.

1. Resolved that the articles of Confederation ought to be so corrected & enlarged as to accomplish the objects proposed by their institution; namely, "common defence, security of liberty and general welfare."

> As delegates would soon point out, this resolution appeared to downplay the novelty of the proposals that followed.

2. Resd. therefore that the rights of suffrage in the National Legislature ought to be proportioned to the Quotas of contribution, or to the number of free inhabitants, as the one or the other rule may seem best in different cases.

> It is often difficult to separate principles from the self-interests of the delegates. Regardless of their populations or wealth, states were equally represented under the Articles of Confederation. As residents of the most populous and one of the wealthiest states, it is not surprising that Virginians wanted to modify this system so that states would be represented according to wealth and/or population.

The Virginia Plan

> The relatively weak Congress under the Articles of Confederation had one house; this proposed two. The British Parliament may have provided a model, but the general thinking seemed to be that if the Congress were to have increased powers, it needed to have greater safeguards. Bicameralism thus shared a common objective with the doctrine of separation of powers.

3. Resd. that the National Legislature ought to consist of two branches.

4. Resd. that the members of the first branch of the National Legislature ought to be elected by the people of the several States every———- for the term of———-; to be of the age of———- years at least, to receive liberal stipends by with they may be compensated for the devotion of their time to public service; to be ineligible to any office established by a particular State, or under the authority of the United States, except those peculiarly belonging to the functions of the first branch, during the term of service, and for the space of———- after its expiration; to be incapable of reelection for the space of———- after the expiration of their term of service, and to be subject to recall.

> The Convention eventually altered this provision to allow state legislatures to choose their states' senators. In turn, the Seventeenth Amendment (1913) altered this provision to provide for direct election of U.S. senators.

5. Resold. that the members of the second branch of the National Legislature ought to be elected by those of the first, out of a proper number of persons nominated by the individual Legislatures, to be of the age of———- years at least; to hold their offices for a term sufficient to ensure their independency; to receive liberal stipends, by which they may be compensated for the devotion of their time to public service; and to be ineligible to any office established by a particular State, or under the authority of the United States, except those peculiarly belonging to the functions of the second branch, during the term of service, and for the space of———- after the expiration thereof.

> This proposal anticipated a relatively broad expansion of congressional powers, including the power to nullify state laws and to use force against individual states. Ultimately, the nation would settle instead on allowing courts to invalidate unconstitutional state and federal legislation and on giving the Congress the power to act directly upon individual citizens rather than have to exert physical force on individual states.

6. Resolved that each branch ought to possess the right of originating Acts; that the National Legislature ought to be impowered to enjoy the Legislative Rights vested in Congress by the Confederation & moreover to legislate in all cases to which the separate States are incompetent, or

in which the harmony of the United States may be interrupted by the exercise of individual Legislation; to negative all laws passed by the several States, contravening in the opinion of the National Legislature the articles of Union; and to call forth the force of the Union agst. any member of the Union failing to fulfill its duty under the articles thereof.

7. Resd. that a National Executive be instituted; to be chosen by the National Legislature for the term of———- years, to receive punctually at stated times, a fixed compensation for the services rendered, in which no increase or diminution shall be made so as to affect the Magistracy, existing at the time of increase or diminution, and to be ineligible a second time; and that besides a general authority to execute the National laws, it ought to enjoy the Executive rights vested in Congress by the Confederation.

> The closest the Articles of Confederation came to a chief executive was a committee of congressmen who met together when Congress was not in session. The idea of creating a separate executive embodied the principle of separation of powers. The initial one-term limit was designed to prevent Congress, which was slated to select presidents, from exerting undue influence on a sitting executive.

8. Resd. that the Executive and a convenient number of the National Judiciary, ought to compose a Council of revision with authority to examine every act of the National Legislature before it shall operate, & every act of a particular Legislature before a Negative thereon shall be final; and that the dissent of the said Council shall amount to a rejection, unless the Act of the National Legislature be again passed, or that of a particular Legislature be again negatived by———- of the members of each branch.

> Although the convention rejected this proposal for a Council of Revision, it eventually settled both on a limited executive veto and on an independent judicial branch that would exercise the power to decide whether or not laws were constitutional.

9. Resd. that a National Judiciary be established to consist of one or more supreme tribunals, and of inferior tribunals to be chosen by the National Legislature, to hold their offices during good behaviour; and to receive punctually at stated times fixed compensation for their services, in which no increase or diminution shall be made so

> There had been no independent national judiciary under the Articles of Confederation. This would provide for at least one such national tribunal and others that Congress might later provide. This, too, was consistent with the doctrine of separation of powers.

The Virginia Plan

as to affect the persons actually in office at the time of such increase or diminution, that the jurisdiction of the inferior tribunals shall be to hear & determine in the first instance, and of the supreme tribunal to hear and determine in the dernier resort, all piracies & felonies on the high seas, captures from an enemy; cases in which foreigners or citizens of other States applying to such jurisdictions may be interested, or which respect the collection of the National revenue; impeachments of any National officers, and questions which may involve the national peace and harmony.

> No new states had been admitted under the Articles of Confederation, but a number of areas, including Vermont and western sections of existing states, anticipated forming new governments and entering the new union.

10. Resolvd. that provision ought to be made for the admission of States lawfully arising within the limits of the United States, whether from a voluntary junction of Government & Territory or otherwise, with the consent of a number of voices in the National legislature less than the whole.

> This provision, which would be largely incorporated in Article IV of the U.S. Constitution, was designed to ensure that each individual state continued to have a republican, or representative, government.

11. Resd. that a Republican Government & the territory of each State, except in the instance of a voluntary junction of Government & territory, ought to be guarantied by the United States to each State.

12. Resd. that provision ought to be made for the continuance of Congress and their authorities and privileges, until a given day after the reform of the articles of Union shall be adopted, and for the completion of all their engagements.

> As a preliminary proposal, the Virginia Plan sometimes pointed to the need for a provision to accomplish a goal, in this case the addition of future amendments, without specifying the specific machinery for doing so.

13. Resd. that provision ought to be made for the amendment of the Articles of Union whensoever it shall seem necessary, and that the assent of the National Legislature ought not to be required thereto.

14. Resd. that the Legislative Executive & Judiciary powers within the several States ought to be bound by oath to support the articles of Union

15. Resd. that the amendments which shall be offered to the Confederation, by the Convention ought at a proper time, or times, after the approbation of Congress to be submitted to an assembly or assemblies of Representatives, recommended by the several Legislatures to be expressly chosen by the people, to consider & decide thereon.

Source: The Virginia Plan, 1787. *Documents Illustrative of the Formation of the Union of the American States.* Washington, DC: Government Printing Office, 1927.

"Resd. that the amendments which shall be offered to the Confederation, by the Convention ought at a proper time, or times, after the approbation of Congress to be submitted to an assembly or assemblies of Representatives, recommended by the several Legislatures to be expressly chosen by the people, to consider & decide thereon."

Adequate to the Exigencies of Government

The New Jersey Plan

June 15, 1787

INTRODUCTION

Although the Virginia Plan set the stage for the first two weeks of debate, opposition began to emerge—especially after the arrival of delegates from some of the less populous states. These men wanted to keep the equal representation that they had enjoyed with the Articles of Confederation. There is still scholarly debate about the degree to which New Jersey statesman William Paterson, who introduced this rival plan, was really interested in proposing an alternative and the degree to which he was using an alternate plan as a means to obtain what he considered to be fairer representation for the less populous states.

Note that this wording is arguably more consistent with the original charge that the Convention had received than that of proposing a whole new plan.

1. Resd that the articles of Confederation ought to be so revised, corrected & enlarged, as to render the federal Constitution adequate to the exigencies of Government, & the preservation of the Union.

Whereas the Virginia Plan anticipated reorganizing Congress into two houses, both based on population, the New Jersey Plan favored keeping a unicameral Congress in which each state would continue to have a single vote, regardless of size. One of the ironies of the New Jersey Plan, which is generally understood to have favored a weaker central government than the Virginia Plan alternative, is that it sought an enumeration of congressional powers over the rather general phraseology of the Virginia Plan. These included a number of powers, including that of regulating commerce, which the Congress under the Articles of Confederation had no authority to exercise.

2. Resd that in addition to the powers vested in the U. States in Congress, by the present existing articles of Confederation, they be authorized to pass acts for raising a revenue, by levying a duty or duties on all goods or merchandises of foreign growth or manufacture, imported into any part of the U. States, by Stamps on paper, vellum or parchment, and by a postage on all letters or packages passing through the general post-office, to be applied to such federal purposes as they shall deem proper & expedient; to make rules & regulations for the collection thereof; and the same from time to time, to alter & amend in such manner as they shall think proper: to pass

Acts for the regulation of trade & commerce as well with foreign nations as with each other: provided that all punishments, fines, forfeitures & penalties to be incurred for contravening such acts rules and regulations shall be adjudged by the Common law Judiciaries of the State in which any offense contrary to the true intent & meaning of such Acts rules & regulations shall have been committed or perpetrated, with liberty of commencing in the first instance all suits & prosecutions for that purpose in the superior common law Judiciary in such State, subject nevertheless, for the correction of all errors, both in law & fact in rendering Judgment, to an appeal to the Judiciary of the U. States.

3. Resd that whenever requisitions shall be necessary, instead of the rule for making requisitions mentioned in the articles of Confederation, the United States in Congs be authorized to make such requisitions in proportion to the whole number of white & other free citizens & inhabitants of every age sex and condition including those bound to servitude for a term of years & three fifths of all other persons not comprehended in the foregoing description, except Indians not paying taxes; that if such requisitions be not complied with, in the time specified therein, to direct the collection thereof in the non complying States & for that purpose to devise and pass acts directing & authorizing the same; provided that none of the powers hereby vested in the U. States in Congs shall be exercised without the consent of at least States, and in that proportion if the number of Confederated States should hereafter be increased or diminished.

4. Resd that the U. States in Congs be authorized to elect a federal Executive to consist of persons, to continue in office for the term of years, to receive punctually at stated

> While most proponents of the Virginia Plan favored a single executive, advocates of the New Jersey Plan favored a plural executive. At this point, both plans still favored selection of the executive by Congress.

The New Jersey Plan

times a fixed compensation for their services, in which no increase or diminution shall be made so as to affect the persons composing the Executive at the time of such increase or diminution, to be paid out of the federal treasury; to be incapable of holding any other office or appointment during their time of service and for years thereafter; to be ineligible a second time, & removeable by Congs on application by a majority of the Executives of the several States; that the Executives besides their general authority to execute the federal acts ought to appoint all federal officers not otherwise provided for, & to direct all military operations; provided that none of the persons composing the federal Executive shall on any occasion take command of any troops, so as personally to conduct any enterprise as General or in other capacity.

> Whereas the Virginia Plan had proposed that Congress would select federal judges, the New Jersey Plan proposed that the president should select them. In time, the delegates would compromise by allowing the president to appoint with the advice and consent of the Senate.

5. Resd that a federal Judiciary be established to consist of a supreme Tribunal the Judges of which to be appointed by the Executive, & to hold their offices during good behaviour, to receive punctually at stated times a fixed compensation for their services in which no increase or diminution shall be made, so as to affect the persons actually in office at the time of such increase or diminution; that the Judiciary so established shall have authority to hear & determine in the first instance on all impeachments of federal officers, & by way of appeal in the dernier resort in all cases touchung the rights of Ambassadors, in all cases of captures from an enemy, in all cases of piracies & felonies on the high Seas, in all cases in which foreigners may be interested, in the construction of any treaty or treaties, or which may arise on any of the Acts for regulation of trade, or the collection of the

federal Revenue: that none of the Judiciary shall during the time they remain in office be capable of receiving or holding any other office or appointment during their time of service, or for thereafter.

6. Resd that all Acts of the U. States in Congs made by virtue & in pursuance of the powers hereby & by the articles of Confederation vested in them, and all Treaties made & ratified under the authority of the U. States shall be the supreme law of the respective States so far forth as those Acts or Treaties shall relate to the said States or their Citizens, and that the Judiciary of the several States shall be bound thereby in their decisions, any thing in the respective laws of the Individual States to the contrary notwithstanding; and that if any State, or any body of men in any State shall oppose or prevent ye carrying into execution such acts or treaties, the federal Executive shall be authorized to call forth ye power of the Confederated States, or so much thereof as may be necessary to enforce and compel an obedience to such Acts, or an observance of such Treaties.

7. Resd that provision be made for the admission of new States into the Union.

8. Resd the rule for naturalization ought to be the same in every State.

The New Jersey Plan included a number of provisions of the Virginia Plan, which the delegates had debated, and accepted, in the first two weeks of debate.

9. Resd a Citizen of one State committing an offense in another State of the Union, shall be deemed guilty of the same offense as if it had been committed by a Citizen of the State in which the offense was committed.

Source: The New Jersey Plan. *Debates in the Federal Convention of 1787 Reported by James Madison.* Edited by Gaillard Hunt and James B. Scott. New York: 1920, pp. 102–4.

Blessings on Our Deliberations

Debates over State Representation Lead to
a Call for Prayer

June 28, 1787

INTRODUCTION

Of all the issues at the Convention, none received more attention than state representation in Congress. The Virginia Plan had proposed that states be represented in both houses according to population, while the New Jersey Plan had proposed that that states continue to be represented equally, as under the Articles of Confederation. On June 11, Connecticut's Roger Sherman had proposed that states be represented according to population in one house and equally in the other, but both sides resisted this compromise until it was finally accepted on July 16.

IN CONVENTION

Mr. L. MARTIN resumed his discourse, contending that the Genl. Govt. ought to be formed for the States, not for individuals: that if the States were to have votes in proportion to their numbers of people, it would be the same thing whether their representatives were chosen by the Legislatures or the people; the smaller States would be equally enslaved; that if the large States have the same interest with the smaller as was urged, there could be no danger in giving them an equal vote; they would not injure themselves, and they could not injure the large ones on that supposition without injuring themselves and if the interests, were not the same, the inequality of suffrage wd. be dangerous to the smaller States: that it will be in vain to propose any plan offensive to the rulers of the States, whose influence over the people will certainly prevent their adopting it: that the large States were weak at present in proportion to their extent: & could only be made formidable to the small ones, by the weight of their votes; that in case a dissolution of the Union should take place, the small States would have nothing to fear from their power; that if in such a case the three great States should league themselves together, the other ten could do so too: & that he had rather see partial confederacies take place, than the plan on the table.

This was the substance of the residue of his discourse which was delivered with much diffuseness & considerable vehemence.

Mr. LANSING & Mr. DAYTON moved to strike out "not." so that the 7 art. might read that the rights of suffrage in the 1st. branch ought to be according to the rule established by the Confederation.

Mr. [JONATHAN] DAYTON expressed great anxiety that the question might not be put till tomorrow; Governr. Livingston being kept away by indisposition, and the representation of N. Jersey thereby suspended.

Mr. [HUGH] WILLIAMSON. thought that if any political truth could be grounded on mathematical demonstration, it was that if the States were equally sovereign now, and parted with equal proportions of sovereignty, that they would remain equally sovereign. He could not comprehend how the smaller States would be injured in the case, and wished some Gentleman would vouchsafe a solution of it. He observed that the small States, if they had a plurality of votes would have an interest in throwing the burdens off their own shoulders on those of the large ones. He begged that the expected addition of new

> Luther Martin of Maryland gave one of the longest speeches at the Convention (it had begun the previous day) in defense of states' rights. Many listeners recorded that it was disorganized and tedious, but there was little doubt of his passion and conviction, and it is not surprising that Martin would end up opposing ratification of the Constitution, even after the Convention adopted the Great Compromise.

> Although he represented a relatively small state (North Carolina), Hugh Williamson was concerned that without majority rule, small states, including those who would be added on an equal basis with the existing ones, might seek to gain favors at the expense of the more populous states. Smaller states had similar fears about the powers of the more populous states.

Debates over State Representation Lead to a Call for Prayer

States from the Westward might be kept in view. They would be small States, they would be poor States, they would be unable to pay in proportion to their numbers; their distance from market rendering the produce of their labour less valuable; they would consequently be tempted to combine for the purpose of laying burdens on commerce & consumption which would fall with greatest weight on the old States.

In a speech, which has been shortened here, Madison continued to plea for representation by population in both houses of Congress. In his speech, he responded to a suggestion by New Jersey's David Brearly proposing that state boundaries be redrawn so each would have equal population.

Mr. MADISON, Sd. he was much disposed to concur in any expedient not inconsistent with fundamental principles, that could remove the difficulty concerning the rule of representation. But he could neither be convinced that the rule contended for was just, nor necessary for the safety of the small States agst. the large States. That it was not just, had been conceded by Mr. Breerly & Mr. Patterson themselves. The expedient proposed by them was a new partition of the territory of the U. States. The fallacy of the reasoning drawn from the equality of Sovereign States in the formation of compacts, lay in confounding mere Treaties, in which were specified certain duties to which the parties were to be bound, and certain rules by which their subjects were to be reciprocally governed in their intercourse, with a compact by which an authority was created paramount to the parties, & making laws for the government of them....

Great Britain was widely known and criticized in the colonies for its system of "rotten buroughs," where scarcely populated districts got the same representation as more populous ones. Wilson was urging the delegates not to repeat this example in the United States. The U.S. Supreme Court would make similar arguments when it called for state legislative reapportionment based on the principle of "one-person-one-vote" in the 1960s.

Mr. WILSON. The leading argument of those who contend for equality of votes among the States is that the States as such being equal, and being represented not as districts of individuals, but in their political & corporate capacities, are entitled to an equality of suffrage. According to this mode of reasoning the representation of the boroughs in Engld which has been allowed on all hands to be the rotten part of the Constitution, is perfectly right & proper. They are like the States represented in their corporate capacity like the States therefore they are entitled to equal voices, old Sarum to as many as London. And instead of the injury supposed hitherto to be done to London, the true ground of complaint lies with old Sarum: for London instead of two which is her proper share, sends four representatives to Parliament.

Mr. SHERMAN. The question is not what rights naturally belong to men; but how they may be most equally & effectually guarded in Society. And if some give up more than others in order to attain this end, there can be no room for complaint. To do otherwise, to require an equal concession from all, if it would create danger to the rights of some, would be sacrificing the end to the means. The rich man who enters into Society along with the poor man, gives up more than the poor man, yet with an equal vote he is equally safe. Were he to have more votes than the poor man in proportion to his superior stake, the rights of the poor man would immediately cease to be secure. This consideration prevailed when the articles of Confederation were formed.

> Connecticut's Roger Sherman continued to argue that representation was not a purely abstract issue but one that should take existing arrangements into account.

The determination of the question from striking out the word "not" was put off till tomorrow at the request of the Deputies of N. York.

[Benjamin Franklin:]
Mr. President

The small progress we have made after 4 or five weeks close attendance & continual reasonings with each other-our different sentiments on almost every question, several of the last

Debates over State Representation Lead to a Call for Prayer

producing as many noes as ays, is methinks a melancholy proof of the imperfection of the Human Understanding. We indeed seem to feel our own want of political wisdom, since we have been running about in search of it. We have gone back to ancient history for models of Government, and examined the different forms of those Republics which having been formed with the seeds of their own dissolution now no longer exist. And we have viewed Modern States all round Europe, but find none of their Constitutions suitable to our circumstances.

> *"In this situation of this Assembly, groping as it were in the dark to find political truth, and scarce able to distinguish it when presented to us, how has it happened, Sir, that we have not hitherto once thought of humbly applying to the Father of lights to illuminate our understandings?"*

In this situation of this Assembly, groping as it were in the dark to find political truth, and scarce able to distinguish it when presented to us, how has it happened, Sir, that we have not hitherto once thought of humbly applying to the Father of lights to illuminate our understandings? In the beginning of the Contest with G. Britain, when we were sensible of danger we had daily prayer in this room for the divine protection.- Our prayers, Sir, were heard, & they were graciously answered. All of us who were engaged in the struggle must have observed frequent instances of a superintending providence in our favor. To that kind providence we owe this happy opportunity of consulting in peace on the means of establishing our future national felicity. And have we now forgotten that powerful friend? or do we imagine that we no longer need his assistance? I have lived, Sir, a long time, and the longer I live, the more convincing proofs I see of this truth- that God Governs in the affairs of men. And if a sparrow cannot fall to the ground without his notice, is it probable that an empire can rise without his aid? We have been assured, Sir, in the sacred writings, that "except the Lord build the House they labour in vain that build it." I firmly believe this; and I also believe that without his concurring aid we shall succeed in this political building no better, than the Builders of Babel: We shall be divided by our little partial local interests; our projects will be confounded, and we ourselves shall become a reproach and bye word down to future ages. And what is worse, mankind may hereafter from this unfortunate instance, despair of establishing Governments by Human wisdom and leave it to chance, war and conquest.

I therefore beg leave to move-that henceforth prayers imploring the assistance of Heaven, and its blessings on our deliberations, be held in this Assembly every morning before we proceed to business, and that one or more of the Clergy of this City be requested to officiate in that Service-

Mr. SHARMAN seconded the motion.

Mr. HAMILTON & several others expressed their apprehensions that however proper such a resolution might have been at the beginning of the convention, it might at this late day, I. bring on it some disagreeable animadversions. & 2. lead the public to believe that the embarrassments and dissensions within the Convention, had suggested this measure. It was answered by Docr. F. Mr. SHERMAN & others, that the past omission of a duty could not justify a further omission-that the rejection of such a proposition would expose the Convention to more unpleasant animadversions than the adoption of it: and that the alarm out of doors that might be excited for the state of things within, would at least be as likely to do good as ill.

Mr. WILLIAMSON, observed that the true cause of the omission could not be mistaken. The Convention had no funds.

Mr. RANDOLPH proposed in order to give a favorable aspect to ye. measure, that a sermon be preached at the

---

Few incidents at the Convention have been more frequently cited than this one. Amid rising tempers precipitated by the continuing stalemate over representation, Benjamin Franklin, who was not generally known for his piety but was widely known as a conciliator, suggested that the Convention should begin each session with prayer. Although the Convention did not adopt Franklin's suggestion, his motion must have had a sobering impact on delegates, many of whom may have doubted whether they could succeed without divine help.

"Mr. WILLIAMSON, observed that the true cause of the omission could not be mistaken. The Convention had no funds."

request of the convention on 4th of July, the anniversary of Independence; & thenceforward prayers be used in ye. Convention every morning. Dr. FRANKn. 2ded. this motion After several unsuccessful attempts for silently postponing the matter by adjourng. the adjournment was at length carried, without any vote on the motion.

Source: *The Debates in the Federal Convention of 1787.* Edited by Gaillard Hunt and James Brown Scott. Oxford University Press, 1920.

Articles of Compact
Northwest Ordinance
July 13, 1787

> **INTRODUCTION**
>
> Although it is far more common to describe the faults of the Articles of Confederation than to extoll its accomplishments, which included successfully pursuing the war against Great Britain, the government did adopt this ordinance, which was designed to provide for the temporary governance of territories that states gave up when they joined the Articles and to provide for the further division of this collective territory (the Northwest) into future states. The Northwest Ordinance was actually adopted at the time that the Constitutional Convention of 1787 was meeting in Philadelphia. It prepared the way for one of the unheralded but important provisions of the Constitution in Article IV, Section 3. This provision provided for the admission of new states on an equal basis with the original 13 states, thus removing the possibility of them being kept in colonial subjection, as the 13 colonies thought Britain had done to them. This provision would apply not only to the Northwest but to the Louisiana Territory, which the United States acquired from France in 1803, as well as subsequent land acquisitions.

An Ordinance for the government of the Territory of the United States northwest of the River Ohio.

Section 1. *Be it ordained by the United States in Congress assembled*, That the said territory, for the purposes of temporary government, be one district, subject, however, to be divided into two districts, as future circumstances may, in the opinion of Congress, make it expedient.

Sec 2. *[Omitted. Deals with division of property of individuals who die without wills].*

Sec. 3. *Be it ordained by the authority aforesaid*, That there shall be appointed from time to time by Congress, a governor, whose commission shall continue in force for the term of three years, unless sooner revoked by Congress; he shall reside in the district, and have a freehold estate therein in 1,000 acres of land, while in the exercise of his office.

Sec. 4. There shall be appointed from time to time by Congress, a secretary, whose commission shall continue in force for four years unless sooner revoked; he shall reside in the district, and have a freehold estate therein in 500 acres of land, while in the exercise of his office. It shall be his duty to keep and preserve the acts and laws passed by the legislature, and the public records of the district, and the proceedings of the governor in his executive department, and transmit authentic copies of such acts and proceedings, every six months, to the Secretary of Congress: There shall also be appointed a court to consist of three judges, any two of whom to form a court, who shall have a common law jurisdiction, and reside in the district, and have each therein a freehold estate in 500 acres of land while in the exercise of their offices; and their commissions shall continue in force during good behavior.

It is common to associate the U.S. Constitution with the doctrine of separation of powers, which divides the government into separate legislative, executive, and judicial branches. This document outlines similar principles for the governance of the Northwest Territory.

Sec. 5. The governor and judges, or a majority of them, shall adopt and publish in the district such laws of the original States, criminal and civil, as may be necessary and best suited to the circumstances of the district, and report them to Congress from time to time: which laws shall be in force in the district until the organization of the General Assembly therein, unless disapproved of by Congress; but afterwards the Legislature shall have authority to alter them as they shall think fit.

The term "commander in chief" is the same one used for the president in the U.S. Constitution.

Sec. 6. The governor, for the time being, shall be commander in chief of the militia, appoint and commission all officers in the same below the rank of general officers; all genera officers shall be appointed and commissioned by Congress.

Sec. 7. Previous to the organization of the general assembly, the governor shall appoint such magistrates and other civil officers in each county or township, as he shall find necessary for the preservation of the peace and good order in the same: After the general assembly shall be organized, the powers and duties of the magistrates and other civil officers shall be regulated and defined by the said assembly; but all magistrates and other civil officers not herein otherwise directed, shall during the continuance of this temporary government, be appointed by the governor.

Sec. 8. For the prevention of crimes and injuries, the laws to be adopted or made shall have force in all parts of the district, and for the execution of process, criminal and civil, the governor shall make proper divisions thereof; and he shall proceed from time to time as circumstances may require, to lay out the parts of the district in which the Indian titles shall have been extinguished, into counties and townships, subject, however, to such alterations as may thereafter be made by the legislature.

Sec. 9. So soon as there shall be five thousand free male inhabitants of full age in the district, upon giving proof thereof to the governor, they shall receive authority, with time and place, to elect a representative from their counties or townships to represent them in the general assembly: Provided, That, for every five hundred free male inhabitants, there shall be one representative, and so on progressively with the number of free male inhabitants shall the right of representation increase, until the number of representatives shall amount to twenty five; after which, the number and proportion of representatives shall be regulated by the

"So soon as there shall be five thousand free male inhabitants of full age in the district, upon giving proof thereof to the governor, they shall receive authority, with time and place, to elect a representative from their counties or townships to represent them in the general assembly..."

legislature: Provided, That no person be eligible or qualified to act as a representative unless he shall have been a citizen of one of the United States three years, and be a resident in the district, or unless he shall have resided in the district three years; and, in either case, shall likewise hold in his own right, in fee simple, two hundred acres of land within the same; Provided, also, That a freehold in fifty acres of land in the district, having been a citizen of one of the states, and being resident in the district, or the like freehold and two years residence in the district, shall be necessary to qualify a man as an elector of a representative.

> Two years is the same term that the U.S. Constitution would establish for members of the U.S. House of Representatives.

Sec. 10. The representatives thus elected, shall serve for the term of two years; and, in case of the death of a representative, or removal from office, the governor shall issue a writ to the county or township for which he was a member, to elect another in his stead, to serve for the residue of the term.

Sec. 11. The general assembly or legislature shall consist of the governor, legislative council, and a house of representatives. The Legislative Council shall consist of five members, to continue in office five years, unless sooner removed by Congress; any three of whom to be a quorum: and the members of the Council shall be nominated and appointed in the following manner, to wit: As soon as representatives shall be elected, the Governor shall appoint a time and place for them to meet together; and, when met, they shall nominate ten persons, residents in the district, and each possessed of a freehold in five hundred acres of land, and return their names to Congress; five of whom Congress shall appoint and commission to serve as aforesaid; and, whenever a vacancy shall happen in the council, by death or removal from office, the house of representatives shall nominate two persons, qualified as aforesaid, for each vacancy, and return their names to Congress;

one of whom congress shall appoint and commission for the residue of the term. And every five years, four months at least before the expiration of the time of service of the members of council, the said house shall nominate ten persons, qualified as aforesaid, and return their names to Congress; five of whom Congress shall appoint and commission to serve as members of the council five years, unless sooner removed. And the governor, legislative council, and house of representatives, shall have authority to make laws in all cases, for the good government of the district, not repugnant to the principles and articles in this ordinance established and declared. And all bills, having passed by a majority in the house, and by a majority in the council, shall be referred to the governor for his assent; but no bill, or legislative act whatever, shall be of any force without his assent. The governor shall have power to convene, prorogue, and dissolve the general assembly, when, in his opinion, it shall be expedient.

Sec. 12. The governor, judges, legislative council, secretary, and such other officers as Congress shall appoint in the district, shall take an oath or affirmation of fidelity and of office; the governor before the president of congress, and all other officers before the Governor. As soon as a legislature shall be formed in the district, the council and house assembled in one room, shall have authority, by joint ballot, to elect a delegate to Congress, who shall have a seat in Congress, with a right of debating but not voting during this temporary government.

Sec. 13. And, for extending the fundamental principles of civil and religious liberty, which form the basis whereon these republics, their laws and constitutions are erected; to fix and establish those principles as the basis of all laws, constitutions, and governments, which forever hereafter shall be formed in the said territory: to provide also for the establishment of States, and permanent government therein, and for

> *"And, for extending the fundamental principles of civil and religious liberty, which form the basis whereon these republics, their laws and constitutions are erected; to fix and establish those principles as the basis of all laws, constitutions, and governments, which forever hereafter shall be formed in the said territory: to provide also for the establishment of States, and permanent government therein, and for their admission to a share in the federal councils on an equal footing with the original States, at as early periods as may be consistent with the general interest . . ."*

their admission to a share in the federal councils on an equal footing with the original States, at as early periods as may be consistent with the general interest:

Sec. 14. It is hereby ordained and declared by the authority aforesaid, That the following articles shall be considered as articles of compact between the original States and the people and States in the said territory and forever remain unalterable, unless by common consent, to wit:

> Americans, many of whom had descended from individuals who had fled religious persecution in Europe, continued to view religious liberty as foremost. This attitude would continue with the adoption of the First Amendment to the new U.S. Constitution.

Art. 1. No person, demeaning himself in a peaceable and orderly manner, shall ever be molested on account of his mode of worship or religious sentiments, in the said territory.

> There is remarkable continuity between these guarantees of liberty and those that would find their way into the U.S. Constitution and the first 10 amendments to the U.S. Constitution, commonly known today as the Bill of Rights.

Art. 2. The inhabitants of the said territory shall always be entitled to the benefits of the writ of *habeas corpus*, and of the trial by jury; of a proportionate representation of the people in the legislature; and of judicial proceedings according to the course of the common law. All persons shall be bailable, unless for capital offenses, where the proof shall be evident or the presumption great. All fines shall be moderate; and no cruel or unusual punishments shall be inflicted. No man shall be deprived of his liberty or property, but by the judgment of his peers or the law of the land; and, should the public exigencies make it necessary, for the common preservation, to take any person's property, or to demand his particular services, full compensation shall be made for the same. And, in the just preservation of rights and property, it is understood and declared, that no law ought ever to be made, or have force in the said territory, that shall, in any manner whatever, interfere with or affect private contracts or engagements, *bona fide*, and without fraud, previously formed.

"No man shall be deprived of his liberty or property, but by the judgment of his peers or the law of the land . . ."

Art. 3. Religion, morality, and knowledge, being necessary to good government and the happiness of mankind, schools and the means of education shall forever be encouraged. The utmost good faith shall always be observed towards the Indians; their lands and property shall never be taken from them without their consent; and, in their property, rights, and liberty, they shall never be invaded or disturbed, unless in just and lawful wars authorized by Congress; but laws founded in justice and humanity, shall from time to time be made for preventing wrongs being done to them, and for preserving peace and friendship with them.

> In 1642, Puritan Massachusetts had adopted legislation requiring each district to set aside property for a school district to teach individuals literacy so that they could read the Bible and resist the wiles "of the Old Deluder Satan." Although the Northwest Ordinance guaranteed religious freedom, many Americans continued to believe that religion and morality were essential to the development of good citizenship. Since there were no organized states in the territories, the national government sought to guarantee through legislation the authority, including that over education, that states would otherwise assume under their police powers.

Art. 4. The said territory, and the States which may be formed therein, shall forever remain a part of this Confederacy of the United States of America, subject to the Articles of Confederation, and to such alterations therein as shall be constitutionally made; and to all the acts and ordinances of the United States in Congress assembled, conformable thereto. The inhabitants and settlers in the said territory shall be subject to pay a part of the federal debts contracted or to be contracted, and a proportional part of the expenses of government, to be apportioned on them by Congress according to the same common rule and measure by which apportionments thereof shall be made on the other States; and the taxes for paying their proportion shall be laid and levied by the authority and direction of the legislatures of the district or districts, or new States, as in the original States, within the time agreed upon by the United States in Congress assembled. The legislatures of those districts or new States, shall never interfere with the primary disposal of the soil by the United States in Congress assembled, nor with any regulations Congress may find necessary for securing the title in such soil to the *bona fide* purchasers. No tax shall be imposed on lands the property of the United States; and, in no case, shall nonresident proprietors be taxed higher than residents. The navigable waters leading into the Mississippi and St. Lawrence, and the carrying places between the same, shall be common highways and forever free, as well to the inhabitants of the said territory as to the citizens of the United States, and those of any other States that may be admitted into the confederacy, without any tax, impost, or duty therefor.

Art. 5. There shall be formed in the said territory, not less than three nor more than five States; and the boundaries of the States, as soon as Virginia shall alter her act of cession, and consent to the same, shall become fixed and established as follows. . . . [*this section continued to lay out boundaries of the states in the territories.*]

> This is perhaps the best-known provision of the law. The prohibition of slavery had been drafted by Thomas Jefferson and was taken from earlier Ordinances of 1784 and 1785. This provision shows that the framers did not want slavery to expand but that they also wanted to recognize the rights of slave owners. The U.S. Constitution would embody a similar fugitive clause. In the notorious Dred Scott decision (1857), the Supreme Court would later deny the right of the national government to exclude slavery from territories that had not yet been acquired when the Constitution was written. The Thirteenth (1865) and Fourteenth (1868) Amendments later invalidated this distinction.

Art. 6. There shall be neither slavery nor involuntary servitude in the said territory, otherwise than in the punishment of crimes whereof the party shall have been duly convicted: *Provided, always,* **That any person escaping into the same, from whom labor or service is lawfully claimed in any one of the original States, such fugitive may be lawfully reclaimed and conveyed to the person claiming his or her labor or service as aforesaid.**

Be it ordained by the authority aforesaid, That the resolutions of the 23rd of April, 1784, relative to the subject of this ordinance, be, and the same are hereby repealed and declared null and void.

Done by the United States, in Congress assembled, the 13th day of July, in the year of our Lord 1787, and of their sovereignty and independence the twelfth.

Source: The Northwest Ordinance. *Documents Illustrative of the Formation of the Union of the American States.* Edited by Charles C. Tansill. Washington, DC: Government Printing Office, 1927.

This Infernal Trafic
Debates at the Convention over Slavery
August 1787

> **INTRODUCTION**
>
> The key issue with regard to congressional representation at the Constitutional Convention centered on whether states should be represented equally (as under the Articles of Confederation, and as the New Jersey Plan had advocated) or on the basis of population, as the Virginia Plan had proposed. Although the Convention settled this issue on July 16 by deciding that states would be represented according to population in the House of Representatives and equally in the U.S. Senate, delegates still had to decide whether congressmen would be apportioned according to the free population or by also counting slaves, either in whole or in part. Eventually, delegates to the Convention settled on using a formula that had been proposed for taxation under the Articles of Confederation whereby each slave would be counted as three-fifths of a person for purposes of congressional representation.
>
> Not surprisingly, the delegates' opinions on this issue coincided to a large degree on whether they hailed from northern or southern states. In his speech, for example, delegate Gouverneur Morris of Pennsylvania expressed deep concern over providing any extra representation for slave states based on their slave population.

August 8, 1787.

Mr. Govr. MORRIS moved to insert "free" before the word inhabitants. Much he said would depend on this point. He never would concur in upholding domestic slavery. It was a nefarious institution. It was the curse of heaven on the States where it prevailed. Compare the free regions of the Middle States, where a rich & noble cultivation marks the prosperity & happiness of the people, with the misery & poverty which overspread the barren wastes of Va. Maryd. & the other States having slaves. Travel thro' ye. whole Continent & you behold the

In his speech, Morris pointed to the division of opinion as to whether slaves were legally considered to be persons or property. Although he questioned the morality of slavery, he focused on the deleterious effects that he thought the institution had on the economy and governance (he believed it led to aristocracy) of the slave states. Sadly, no one at the Convention appears to have seriously pursued Morris's proposal that the government pay slave owners to free the slaves, and it would take a bloody civil war before the institution was finally eliminated. Instead, the Convention agreed to allow slave states to count each slave as three-fifths of a person toward allocating their representatives within the House.

Debates at the Convention over Slavery

> "And What is the proposed compensation to the Northern States for a sacrifice of every principle of right, of every impulse of humanity. They are to bind themselves to march their militia for the defence of the S. States; for their defence agst. those very slaves of whom they complain."

prospect continually varying with the appearance & disappearance of slavery. The moment you leave ye. E. Sts. & enter N. York, the effects of the institution become visible, passing thro' the Jerseys & entering Pa. every criterion of superior improvement witnesses the change. Proceed south wdly & every step you take thro' ye. great region of slaves presents a desert increasing, with ye. increasing proportion of these wretched beings. Upon what principle is it that the slaves shall be computed in the representation? Are they men? Then make them Citizens and let them vote. Are they property? Why then is no other property included? The Houses in this city [Philada.] are worth more than all the wretched slaves which cover the rice swamps of South Carolina. The admission of slaves into the Representation when fairly explained comes to this: that the inhabitant of Georgia and S. C. who goes to the Coast of Africa, and in defiance of the most sacred laws of humanity tears away his fellow creatures from their dearest connections & damns them to the most cruel bondages, shall have more votes in a Govt. instituted for protection of the rights of mankind, than the Citizen of Pa. or N. Jersey who views with a laudable horror, so nefarious a practice. He would add that Domestic slavery is the most prominent feature in the aristocratic countenance of the proposed Constitution. The vassalage of the poor has ever been the favorite offspring of Aristocracy. And What is the proposed compensation to the Northern States for a sacrifice of every principle of right, of every impulse of humanity. They are to bind themselves to march their militia for the defence of the S. States; for their defence agst. those very slaves of whom they complain. They must supply vessels & seamen in case of foreign Attack. The Legislature will have indefinite power to tax them by excises, and duties on imports: both of which will fall heavier on them than on the Southern inhabitants; for the bohea tea used by a Northern freeman, will pay more tax than the whole consumption of the miserable slave, which consists of nothing more than his physical subsistence and the rag that covers his nakedness. On the other side the Southern States are not to be restrained from importing fresh supplies of wretched Africans, at once to increase the danger of attack, and the difficulty of defence; nay they are to be encouraged to it by an assurance of having their votes in the Natl. Govt. increased in proportion, and are at the same time to have their exports & their slaves exempt from all contributions for the public service. Let it not be said that direct taxation is to be proportioned to representation. It is idle to suppose that the Genl. Govt. can stretch its hand directly into the pockets of the people scattered over so vast a Country. They can only do it through the medium of exports imports & excises. For what then are all these sacrifices to be made? He would sooner submit himself to a tax for paying for all the negroes in the U. States, than saddle posterity with such a Constitution.

August 22, 1787

Art VII sect 4. resumed. Mr. SHERMAN was for leaving the clause as it stands. He disapproved of the slave trade; yet as the States were now possessed of the right to import slaves, as the public good did not require it to be taken from them, & as it was expedient to have as few objections as possible to the proposed scheme of Government, he thought it best to leave the matter as we find it. He observed that the abolition of Slavery seemed to be going on in the U. S. & that the good sense of the several States would probably by degrees compleat it. He urged on the Convention the necessity of despatching its business.

"On the other side the Southern States are not to be restrained from importing fresh supplies of wretched Africans, at once to increase the danger of attack, and the difficulty of defence; nay they are to be encouraged to it by an assurance of having their votes in the Natl. Govt. increased in proportion, and are at the same time to have their exports & their slaves exempt from all contributions for the public service."

On August 22, the Convention was debating whether to limit the slave trade. Although he was from a northern state, Connecticut's Roger Sherman, who was a major force behind the Great Compromise, saw little need to intervene. He believed that this was an issue for state regulation, in part because he believed that the institution of slavery was already in decline. But Sherman did not anticipate Eli Whitney's invention of the cotton gin, a machine that made cotton production—and thus slave labor—far more profitable.

Debates at the Convention over Slavery

Although he was from the South, Mason's sentiments (at least on the slave trade) were not far different from those that Gouverneur Morris had articulated earlier. Perhaps because he was himself a slaveholder, Mason blamed British and New England merchants for the trade rather than southern desires for cheap labor.

"Slavery discourages arts & manufactures. The poor despise labor when performed by slaves. They prevent the immigration of Whites, who really enrich & strengthen a Country. They produce the most pernicious effect on manners. Every master of slaves is born a petty tyrant. They bring the judgment of heaven on a Country. As nations can not be rewarded or punished in the next world they must be in this. By an inevitable chain of causes & effects providence punishes national sins, by national calamities."

Col. MASON. This infernal trafic originated in the avarice of British Merchants. The British Govt. constantly checked the attempts of Virginia to put a stop to it. The present question concerns not the importing States alone but the whole Union. The evil of having slaves was experienced during the late war. Had slaves been treated as they might have been by the Enemy, they would have proved dangerous instruments in their hands. But their folly dealt by the slaves, as it did by the Tories. He mentioned the dangerous insurrections of the slaves in Greece and Sicily; and the instructions given by Cromwell to the Commissioners sent to Virginia, to arm the servants & slaves, in case other means of obtaining its submission should fail. Maryland & Virginia he said had already prohibited the importation of slaves expressly. N. Carolina had done the same in substance. All this would be in vain if S. Carolina & Georgia be at liberty to import. The Western people are already calling out for slaves for their new lands, and will fill that Country with slaves if they can be got thro' S. Carolina & Georgia. Slavery discourages arts & manufactures. The poor despise labor when performed by slaves. They prevent the immigration of Whites, who really enrich & strengthen a Country. They produce the most pernicious effect on manners. Every master of slaves is born a petty tyrant. They bring the judgment of heaven on a Country. As nations can not be rewarded or punished in the next world they must be in this. By an inevitable chain of causes & effects providence punishes national sins, by national calamities. He lamented that some of our Eastern brethren had from a lust of gain embarked in this nefarious traffic. As to the States being in possession of the Right to import, this was the case with many other rights, now to be properly given up. He held it essential in every point of view that the Genl. Govt. should have power to prevent the increase of slavery.

Mr. ELSWORTH. As he had never owned a slave could not judge of the effects of slavery on character: He said however that if it was to be considered in a moral light we ought to go farther and free those already in the Country. -As slaves also multiply so fast in Virginia & Maryland that it is cheaper to raise than import them, whilst in the sickly rice swamps foreign supplies are necessary, if we go no farther than is urged, we shall be unjust towards S. Carolina & Georgia. Let us not intermeddle. As population increases poor laborers will be so plenty as to render slaves useless. Slavery in time will not be a speck in our Country. Provision is already made in Connecticut for abolishing it. And the abolition has already taken place in Massachusetts. As to the danger of insurrections from foreign influence, that will become a motive to kind treatment of the slaves.

> Connecticut's Oliver Ellsworth was taking a clear dig at Mason in his opening sentence and suggesting that if slavery were as nefarious as Mason suggested, the delegates should seek to eliminate it rather than simply eliminate the slave trade. Ultimately, however, he agreed with Sherman in believing that this was an issue for states to handle on their own.

Mr. PINKNEY. If slavery be wrong, it is justified by the example of all the world. He cited the case of Greece Rome & other ancient States; the sanction given by France England, Holland & other modern States. In all ages one half of mankind have been slaves. If the S. States were let alone they will probably of themselves stop importations. He wd. himself as a Citizen of S. Carolina vote for it. An attempt to take away the right as proposed will produce serious objections to the Constitution which he wished to see adopted.

"Mr. PINKNEY. If slavery be wrong, it is justified by the example of all the world."

General PINKNEY declared it to be his firm opinion that if himself & all his colleagues were to sign the Constitution & use their personal influence, it would be of no avail

> Charles Pinckney of South Carolina expressed the view of the Deep South (South Carolina and Georgia delegates) that slavery was sanctioned by the experience of history and that his state would be unlikely to join the union if further imports were prohibited. His cousin Charles Cotesworth Pinckney, a Revolutionary War general, concurred.

towards obtaining the assent of their Constituents. S. Carolina & Georgia cannot do without slaves. As to Virginia she will gain by stopping the importations. Her slaves will rise in value, & she has more than she wants. It would be unequal to require S. C. & Georgia to confederate on such unequal terms. He said the Royal assent before the Revolution had never been refused to S. Carolina as to Virginia. He contended that the importation of slaves would be for the interest of the whole Union. The more slaves, the more produce to employ the carrying trade; The more consumption also, and the more of this, the more of revenue for the common treasury. He admitted it to be reasonable that slaves should be dutied like other imports, but should consider a rejection of the clause as an exclusion of S. Carola. from the Union.

> *"Mr. BALDWIN had conceived national objects alone to be before the Convention, not such as like the present were of a local nature."*

Mr. BALDWIN had conceived national objects alone to be before the Convention, not such as like the present were of a local nature. Georgia was decided on this point. That State has always hitherto supposed a Genl. Governmt. to be the pursuit of the central States who wished to have a vortex for every thing- that her distance would preclude her from equal advantage-& that she could not prudently purchase it by yielding national powers. From this it might be understood in what light she would view an attempt to abridge one of her favorite prerogatives. If left to herself, she may probably put a stop to the evil. As one ground for this conjecture, he took notice of the sect of—————which he said was a respectable class of people, who carried their ethics beyond the mere equality of men, extending their humanity to the claims of the whole animal creation.

Mr. WILSON observed that if S. C. & Georgia were themselves disposed to get rid of the importation of slaves in a short time as had been suggested, they would never refuse to Unite because the importation might be prohibited. As the Section now stands all articles imported are to be taxed. Slaves alone are exempt. This is in fact a bounty on that article.

Mr. GERRY thought we had nothing to do with the conduct of the States as to Slaves, but ought to be careful not to give any sanction to it.

Mr. DICKENSON considered it as inadmissible on every principle of honor & safety that the importation of slaves should be authorised to the States by the Constitution. The true question was whether the national happiness would be promoted or impeded by the importation, and this question ought to be left to the National Govt. not to the States particularly interested. If Engd. & France permit slavery, slaves are at the same time excluded from both those Kingdoms. Greece and Rome were made unhappy by their slaves. He could not believe that the Southn. States would refuse to confederate on the account apprehended; especially as the power was not likely to be immediately exercised by the Genl. Government.

Mr. WILLIAMSON stated the law of N. Carolina on the subject, to wit that it did not directly prohibit the importation of slaves. It imposed a duty of 5. on each slave imported from Africa. 10 on each from elsewhere, & 50 on each from a State licensing manumission. He thought the S. States could not be members of the Union if the clause shd. be rejected, and that it was wrong to force any thing down, not absolutely necessary, and which any State must disagree to.

Mr. KING thought the subject should be considered in a political light only. If two States will not agree to the

"Mr. DICKENSON considered it as inadmissible on every principle of honor & safety that the importation of slaves should be authorised to the States by the Constitution."

Debates at the Convention over Slavery

Constitution as stated on one side, he could affirm with equal belief on the other, that great & equal opposition would be experienced from the other States. He remarked on the exemption of slaves from duty whilst every other import was subjected to it, as an inequality that could not fail to strike the commercial sagacity of the Northn. & middle States.

Mr. LANGDON was strenuous for giving the power to the Genl. Govt. He cd. not with a good conscience leave it with the States who could then go on with the traffic, without being restrained by the opinions here given that they will themselves cease to import slaves.

Genl. PINKNEY thought himself bound to declare candidly that he did not think S. Carolina would stop her importations of slaves in any short time, but only stop them occasionally as she now does. He moved to commit the clause that slaves might be made liable to an equal tax with other imports which he thought right & wch. wd. remove one difficulty that had been started.

> *"Mr. RUTLIDGE. If the Convention thinks that N. C. S. C. & Georgia will ever agree to the plan, unless their right to import slaves be untouched, the expectation is vain."*

Mr. RUTLIDGE. If the Convention thinks that N. C. S. C. & Georgia will ever agree to the plan, unless their right to import slaves be untouched, the expectation is vain. The people of those States will never be such fools as to give up so important an interest. He was strenuous agst. striking out the Section, and seconded the motion of Genl. Pinkney for a commitment.

Mr. Govr. MORRIS wished the whole subject to be committed including the clauses relating to taxes on exports & to a navigation act. These things may form a bargain among the Northern & Southern States.

Mr. BUTLER declared that he never would agree to the power of taxing exports.

Mr. SHERMAN said it was better to let the S. States import slaves than to part with them, if they made that a sine qua non. He was opposed to a tax on slaves imported as making the matter worse, because it implied they were property. He acknowledged that if the power of prohibiting the importation should be given to the Genl. Government that it would be exercised. He thought it would be its duty to exercise the power.

Mr. READ was for the commitment provided the clause concerning taxes on exports should also be committed.

Mr. SHERMAN observed that that clause had been agreed to & therefore could not committed.

Mr. RANDOLPH was for committing in order that some middle ground might, if possible, be found. He could never agree to the clause as it stands. He wd. sooner risk the constitution. He dwelt on the dilemma to which the Convention was exposed. By agreeing to the clause, it would revolt the Quakers, the Methodists, and many others in the States having no slaves. On the other hand, two States might be lost to the Union. Let us then, he said, try the chance of a commitment.

Source: *The Debates in the Federal Convention of 1787*. Edited by Gaillard Hunt and James Brown Scott. Oxford University Press, 1920.

*"**Mr. SHERMAN** said it was better to let the S. States import slaves than to part with them, if they made that a sine qua non. He was opposed to a tax on slaves imported as making the matter worse, because it implied they were property."*

Randolph was not the first delegate to suggest the need for compromise on this issue. The Convention would ultimately allow for the continuing importation of slaves (with a tax of up to $10 each) for the next 20 years, after which Congress adopted a law suppressing the trade.

Experience Must Be Our Only Guide

John Dickinson Emphasizes the Need for Experience in Governing

August 13, 1787

INTRODUCTION

In creating the Constitution, delegates had to make hundreds of important decisions on scores of major issues. This snippet of debate is from discussions on August 13 as to whether the Convention should continue with the part of the Great Compromise that promised that money bills would originate in the House of Representatives, where states would be represented according to population. James Madison, who had favored representation according to population in both houses of Congress, was among those who thought the provision would be relatively meaningless. By contrast, John Dickinson, a delegate of Delaware known as the "Penman of the Revolution" and chief author of the Articles of Confederation, thought that it might prove useful. Here Dickinson argued that the proposal for origination of money bills in the lower house had been successfully tried at the state level and that states would be more likely to favor a similar provision in the national constitution.

If there is a single characteristic that might best apply to the delegates to the Constitutional Convention, it is that almost all of them were experienced politicians who were willing to compromise. Although they were familiar with works of European political philosophy, which Dickinson identified with "reason," they were even more acquainted with the art of politics, which he identified with "experience." They also were familiar with numerous state constitutions.

Mr. DICKENSON. Experience must be our only guide. Reason may mislead us. It was not Reason that discovered the singular & admirable mechanism of the English Constitution. It was not Reason that discovered or ever could have discovered the odd & in the eye of those who are governed by reason, the absurd mode of trial by Jury. Accidents probably produced these discoveries, and experience has give a sanction to them. This is then our guide. And has not experience verified the utility of restraining money bills to the immediate representatives of the people. Whence the effect may have proceeded he could not say; whether from the respect with which this privilege inspired the other branches of Govt. to the H. of Commons, or from the turn of thinking it gave to the people at large with regard to their rights, but the effect was visible & could not be doubted-Shall we oppose to this long experience, the short experience of 11 Years which we had ourselves, on this subject. As to disputes, they could not be avoided any way. If both Houses should originate, each would have a different bill to which it would be attached, and for which it would contend.

He observed that all the prejudices of the people would be offended by refusing this exclusive privilege to the H. of Repress. and these prejudices shd. never be disregarded by us when no essential purpose was to be served. When this plan goes forth it will be attacked by the popular leaders. **Aristocracy will be the watchword; the Shibboleth among its adversaries.** Eight States have inserted in their Constitutions the exclusive right of originating money bills in favor of the popular branch of the Legislature. Most of them however allowed the other branch to amend. This he thought would be proper for us to do.

> A shibboleth is considered a magic word.

Mr. RANDOLPH regarded this point as of such consequence, that as he valued the peace of this Country, he would press the adoption of it. We had numerous & monstrous difficulties to combat. Surely we ought not to increase them. When the people behold in the Senate, the countenance of an aristocracy; and in the president, the form at least of a little monarch, will not their alarms be sufficiently raised without taking from their immediate representatives, a right which has been so long appropriated to them. -The Executive will have more influence over the Senate, than over the H. of Reps. Allow the Senate to originate in this case, & that influence will be sure to mix itself in their deliberations & plans. The Declaration of War he conceived ought not to be in the Senate

> Like Dickinson, Virginia Governor Edmund Randolph argued for the value of accepting relatively inconsequential provisions that might increase the likelihood that the states would ratify the new Constitution—even though some delegates had doubts about them. The Convention eventually agreed to do so. Randolph was one of three delegates who remained at the Convention on the last day and did not sign the document, but he later announced support for it during the Virginia Ratifying Convention.

composed of 26 men only, but rather in the other House. In the other House ought to be placed the origination of the means of war. As to Commercial regulations which may involve revenue, the difficulty may be avoided by restraining the definition to bills, for the mere or sole, purpose of raising revenue. The Senate will be more likely to be corrupt than the H. of Reps. and should therefore have less to do with money matters. His principal object however was to prevent popular objections against the plan, and to secure its adoption.

Source: *The Debates in the Federal Convention of 1787.* Edited by Gaillard Hunt and James Brown Scott. Oxford University Press, 1920.

Cabal and Corruption
Debates over the Presidency
September 4, 1787

INTRODUCTION

The Constitutional Convention handled much of its work through committees, which often proved to be more effective forums for compromise than the Convention as a whole. Commonly, the Convention chose a committee consisting of one delegate from each state. In this case, a Committee of Postponed Matters had been entrusted with a number of issues including presidential selection. The proposal in the original Virginia Plan, which had provided for legislative selection of the President, conflicted with the idea of separation of powers because it made the president dependent upon another body; the Virginia Plan had accordingly limited the president to a single term. Those who favored direct popular election had to contend both with those who thought that this was carrying democracy too far and those of a more practical bent who feared that it would be difficult to count votes throughout 13 states. They also worried that residents in the more populous states might always outvote those in the less populous ones. Despite modern-day criticisms that it is not sufficiently democratic, the Electoral College was one of the Convention's most brilliant compromises because it provided for an independent body (or series of bodies) to meet a single time and cast votes, which would then be counted within Congress. It further incorporated the Connecticut Compromise by assigning electors to states on the basis of their combined representation in the U.S. House and Senate. As the following excerpt from the *Notes on the Debates of the Federal Convention* makes clear, the question of how to elect the president elicited spirited debate.

Mr. [DAVID] BREARLY from the Committee of eleven made a further partial Report as follows

The Committee of Eleven to whom sundry resolutions &c were referred on the 31st. of August, report that in their opinion the following additions and alterations should be made to the Report before the Convention, viz

Debates over the Presidency

(1) The first clause of sect: 1. art. 7. to read as follow-'The Legislature shall have power to lay and collect taxes duties imposts & excises, to pay the debts and provide for the common defence & general welfare, of the U. S.'

(2) At the end of the 2d. clause of sect. 1. art. 7. add 'and with the Indian Tribes.'

(3) In the place of the 9th. art. Sect. 1. to be inserted 'The Senate of the U. S. shall have power to try all impeachments; but no person shall be convicted without the concurrence of two thirds of the members present.'

> Under this plan, which was largely incorporated in the Constitution, states would choose electors, equal to their total number of representatives, and senators, who met in their respective state legislatures to cast two votes (at least one for an out-of-state resident), which would then be sent to the U.S. Senate. The Senate would then count the votes. It would announce the winner president and the runner-up vice president or (if no candidate had a majority) cast votes among the top candidates. (This would later be modified so that members of the House, voting by state delegations, would vote for President, and members of the Senate would vote for vice president.)

(4) After the word 'Excellency' in sect. 1. art. 10. to be inserted. 'He shall hold his office during the term of four years, and together with the vice-President, chosen for the same term, be elected in the following manner, viz. Each State shall appoint in such manner as its Legislature may direct, a number of electors equal to the whole number of Senators and members of the House of Representatives to which the State may be entitled in the Legislature. The Electors shall meet in their respective States, and vote by ballot for two persons, of whom one at least shall not be an inhabitant of the same State with themselves; and they shall make a list of all the persons voted for, and of the number of votes for each, which list they shall sign and certify and transmit sealed to the Seat of the Genl. Government, directed to the President of the Senate-The President of the Senate shall in that House open all the certificates; and the votes shall be then & there counted. The Person having the greatest number of votes shall be the President, if such number be a majority of that of the electors; and if there be more than one who have such majority, and have an equal number of votes, then the Senate shall immediately choose by ballot one of

them for President: but if no person have a majority, then from the five highest on the list, the Senate shall choose by ballot the President. And in every case after the choice of the President, the person having the greatest number of votes shall be vice-president: but if there should remain two or more who have equal votes, the Senate shall choose from them the vice-President. The Legislature may determine the time of choosing and assembling the Electors, and the manner of certifying and transmitting their votes.'

(5) 'Sect. 2. No person except a natural born citizen or a Citizen of the U. S. at the time of the adoption of this Constitution shall be eligible to the office of President; nor shall any person be elected to that office, who shall be under the age of thirty five years, and who has not been in the whole, at least fourteen years a resident within the U. S.'

> This proposal, which continues to be controversial (the Constitution does not usually distinguish between the rights of natural-born and naturalized citizens), was chiefly designed to calm fears that the U.S. might seek a monarch from abroad.

(6) 'Sect. 3. The vice-president shall be ex officio President of the Senate, except when they sit to try the impeachment of the President, in which case the Chief Justice shall preside, and excepting also when he shall exercise the powers and duties of President, in which case & in case of his absence, the Senate shall chuse a President pro tempore-The vice President when acting as President of the Senate shall not have a vote unless the House be equally divided.'

> One arguable defect of the Electoral College was that it created a vice president largely as a consequence of its system of presidential selection, wherein each elector would cast two votes. Making the vice president the president of the Senate was not in strict accord with the doctrine of separation of powers but gave the officer something to do other than simply being available in case of a presidential vacancy.

(7) 'Sect. 4. The President by and with the advice and Consent of the Senate, shall have power to make Treaties; and he shall nominate and by and with the advice and consent of the Senate shall appoint ambassadors, and other public Ministers, Judges of the Supreme Court, and all other Officers of the U. S., whose appointments

> This represented another compromise between advocates of the Virginia Plan, which proposed allowing Congress to appoint ambassadors and judges, and advocates of the New Jersey Plan, which had proposed vesting this power within Congress.

are not otherwise herein provided for. But no Treaty shall be made without the consent of two thirds of the members present.'

(8) After the words–"into the service of the U. S." in sect. 2. art: 10. add 'and may require the opinion in writing of the principal officer in each of the Executive Departments, upon any subject relating to the duties of their respective offices.'

The latter part of Sect. 2. Art: 10. to read as follows.

(9) 'He shall be removed from his office on impeachment by the House of Representatives, and conviction by the Senate, for Treason, or bribery, and in case of his removal as aforesaid, death, absence, resignation or inability to discharge the powers or duties of his office, the vice-president shall exercise those powers and duties until another President be chosen, or until the inability of the President be removed.'

The (1st.) clause of the Report was agreed to, nem. con.

The (2) clause was also agreed to nem: con:

The (3) clause was postponed in order to decide previously on the mode of electing the President.

The (4) clause was accordingly taken up.

Mr. GORHAM disapproved of making the next highest after the President, the vice-President, without referring the decision to the Senate in case the next highest should have less than a majority of votes. As the regulation stands a very obscure man with very few votes may arrive at that appointment

Mr. SHERMAN said the object of this clause of the report of the Committee was to get rid of the ineligibility, which was attached to the mode of election by the Legislature, & to render the Executive independent of the Legislature. As the choice of the President was to be made out of the five highest, obscure characters were sufficiently guarded against in that case; and he had no objection to requiring the vice-President to be chosen in like manner, where the choice was not decided by a majority in the first instance

Mr. MADISON was apprehensive that by requiring both the President & vice President to be chosen out of the five highest candidates, the attention of the electors would be turned too much to making candidates instead of giving their votes in order to a definitive choice. Should this turn be given to the business, the election would, in fact be consigned to the Senate altogether. It would have the effect at the same time, he observed, of giving the nomination of the candidates to the largest States.

Mr. Govr. MORRIS concurred in, & enforced the remarks of Mr. Madison.

Mr. RANDOLPH & Mr. PINKNEY wished for a particular explanation & discussion of the reasons for changing the mode of electing the Executive.

Mr. Govr. MORRIS said he would give the reasons of the Committee and his own. The 1st. was the danger of intrigue & faction if the appointmt. should be made by the Legislature. 2. the inconveniency of an ineligibility required by that mode in order to lessen its evils. 3. The difficulty of establishing a Court of Impeachments, other than the Senate which would not be so proper for the trial

"Mr. SHERMAN said the object of this clause of the report of the Committee was to get rid of the ineligibility, which was attached to the mode of election by the Legislature . . ."

One of the most satisfying aspects of reading the debates of the Constitutional Convention is seeing how delegates offered arguments for their proposals. In a speech summarized here, Gouverneur Morris, the most loquacious member of the Convention, offered a number of points that motivated members of the Committee to adapt the Electoral College for selecting presidents.

Debates over the Presidency

nor the other branch for the impeachment of the President, if appointed by the Legislature, 4. No body had appeared to be satisfied with an appointment by the Legislature. 5. Many were anxious even for an immediate choice by the people. 6. the indispensible necessity of making the Executive independent of the Legislature. -As the Electors would vote at the same time throughout the U. S. and at so great a distance from each other, the great evil of cabal was avoided. It would be impossible also to corrupt them. A conclusive reason for making the Senate instead of the Supreme Court the Judge of impeachments, was that the latter was to try the President after the trial of the impeachment.

Col. MASON confessed that the plan of the Committee had removed some capital objections, particularly the danger of cabal and corruption. It was liable however to this strong objection, that nineteen times in twenty the President would be chosen by the Senate, an improper body for the purpose.

Mr. BUTLER thought the mode not free from objections, but much more so than an election by the Legislature, where as in elective monarchies, cabal faction & violence would be sure to prevail.

Mr. PINKNEY stated as objections to the mode 1. that it threw the whole appointment in fact into the hands of the Senate. 2. The Electors will be strangers to the several candidates and of course unable to decide on their comparative merits. 3. It makes the Executive reeligible which will endanger the public liberty. 4. It makes the same body of men which will in fact elect the President his Judges in case of an impeachment.

Delegates could not always forecast the consequences of their actions with certainty. Virginia's George Mason believed that the Electoral College would almost always result in ultimate legislative selection of the president. In point of fact, Congress has only directly made this decision twice—in the presidential elections of 1800 and 1824.

Mr. WILLIAMSON had great doubts whether the advantage of reeligibility would balance the objection to such a dependence of the President on the Senate for his reappointment. He thought at least the Senate ought to be restrained to the two highest on the list

Mr. Govr. MORRIS said the principal advantage aimed at was that of taking away the opportunity for cabal. The President may be made if thought necessary ineligible on this as well as on any other mode of election. Other inconveniences may be no less redressed on this plan than any other.

Mr. BALDWIN thought the plan not so objectionable when well considered, as at first view. The increasing intercourse among the people of the States, would render important characters less & less unknown; and the Senate would consequently be less & less likely to have the eventual appointment thrown into their hands.

Mr. WILSON. This subject has greatly divided the House, and will also divide people out of doors. It is in truth the most difficult of all on which we have had to decide. He had never made up an opinion on it entirely to his own satisfaction. He thought the plan on the whole a valuable improvement on the former. It gets rid of one great evil, that of cabal & corruption; & Continental Characters will multiply as we more & more coalesce, so as to enable the electors in every part of the Union to know & judge of them. It clears the way also for a discussion of the question of reeligibility on its own merits, which the former mode of election seems to forbid. He thought it might be better however to refer the eventual appointment to the Legislature than to the Senate, and to confine it to a smaller number than five of the Candidates. The eventual

"Mr. Govr. MORRIS said the principal advantage aimed at was that of taking away the opportunity for cabal."

Pennsylvania's James Wilson was a vigorous proponent of presidential power at the Convention (the belief that George Washington would be the first individual to occupy this position was a further spur to increasing its dignity and power). Although Wilson had favored direct election, he viewed the Electoral College as a worthy alternative. Notably, Wilson and other Federalist supporters of the Constitution shared widely held Anti-Federalist fears of cabal and corruption.

Debates over the Presidency

election by the Legislature wd. not open cabal anew, as it would be restrained to certain designated objects of choice, and as these must have had the previous sanction of a number of the States: and if the election be made as it ought as soon as the votes of the electors are opened & it is known that no one has a majority of the whole, there can be little danger of corruption. Another reason for preferring the Legislature to the Senate in this business, was that the House of Reps. will be so often changed as to be free from the influence & faction to which the permanence of the Senate may subject that branch.

> Randolph planted a seed of doubt about the plan that would eventuate in selection of the president by the House of Representatives rather than the Senate.

Mr. RANDOLPH preferred the former mode of constituting the Executive, but if the change was to be made, he wished to know why the eventual election was referred to the Senate and not to the Legislature? He saw no necessity for this and many objections to it. He was apprehensive also that the advantage of the eventual appointment would fall into the hands of the States near the Seat of Government.

Source: *The Debates in the Federal Convention of 1787.* Edited by Gaillard Hunt and James Brown Scott. Oxford University Press, 1920.

Make Manifest Our Unanimity
Benjamin Franklin's Final Speech at the Constitutional Convention
September 17, 1787

> **INTRODUCTION**
>
> The Constitutional Convention began officially meeting on May 25, 1787, and continued through September 17. Toward the end of the Convention, three delegates—George Mason and Edmund Randolph of Virginia and Elbridge Gerry of Massachusetts—indicated that they did not plan to sign the document. Throughout the Convention, Benjamin Franklin had served as a conciliator, suggesting compromises and at one point recommending that the Convention should begin each session with prayer. On the last day, he made yet another plea for unanimity. Federalist publicists would not only utilize his arguments but also use his support (and that of Washington) as arguments for ratifying the document.

Mr. President:

I confess that I do not entirely approve of this Constitution at present, but Sir, I am not sure I shall never approve it: For having lived long, I have experienced many Instances of being oblig'd, by better Information or fuller Consideration, to change Opinions even on important Subjects, which I once thought right, but found to be otherwise. It is therefore that the older I grow the more apt I am to doubt my own Judgment, and to pay more Respect to the Judgment of others. Most Men indeed as well as most Sects in Religion, think themselves in Possession of all Truth, and that wherever others differ from them it is so far Error. Steele, a Protestant in a Dedication tells the Pope, that the only Difference between our two Churches in their Opinions of the Certainty of their Doctrine, is, the

> Franklin was appealing to delegates to consider that none of them were likely to have been completely infallible on various subjects of governance, and to adopt a spirit of accommodation and compromise.

> *"It is therefore that the older I grow the more apt I am to doubt my own Judgment, and to pay more Respect to the Judgment of others."*

Benjamin Franklin's Final Speech at the Constitutional Convention

Romish Church is infallible, and the Church of England is never in the Wrong. But tho' many private Persons think almost as highly of their own Infallibility, as of that of their Sect, few express it so naturally as a certain French Lady, who in a little Dispute with her Sister, said, I don't know how it happens, Sister, but I meet with no body but myself that's always in the right. Il n'y a que moi qui a toujours raison.

In these Sentiments, Sir, I agree to this Constitution, with all its Faults, if they are such; because I think a General Government necessary for us, and there is no Form of Government but what may be a Blessing to the People if well administered; and I believe farther that this is likely to be well administered for a Course of Years, and can only end in Despotism as other Forms have done before it, when the People shall become so corrupted as to need Despotic Government, being incapable of any other.

I doubt too whether any other Convention we can obtain, may be able to make a better Constitution: For when you assemble a Number of Men to have the Advantage of their joint Wisdom, you inevitably assemble with those Men all their Prejudices, their Passions, their Errors of Opinion, their local Interests, and their selfish Views. From such an Assembly can a perfect Production be expected? It therefore astonishes me, Sir, to find this System approaching so near to Perfection as it does; and I think it will astonish our Enemies, who are waiting with Confidence to hear that our Councils are confounded, like those of the Builders of Babel, and that our States are on the Point of Separation, only to meet hereafter for the Purpose of cutting one another's throats. Thus I consent,

> *"In these Sentiments, Sir, I agree to this Constitution, with all its Faults, if they are such; because I think a General Government necessary for us, and there is no Form of Government but what may be a Blessing to the People if well administered . . ."*

James Madison is commonly described as the "father" of the Constitution, but Franklin emphasized that the Constitution was a collective product. Its compromises embodied not only the wisdom of a collective body but some of its errors as well. Franklin recognized that the Constitution was not intended to be a utopian ideal but a practical instrument of government.

Sir, to this Constitution because I expect no better, and because I am not sure that it is not the best.

The Opinions I have had of its Errors, I sacrifice to the Public Good. I have never whispered a Syllable of them abroad. Within these Walls they were born, and here they shall die. If every one of us in returning to our Constituents were to report the Objections he has had to it, and use his Influence to gain Partisan in support of them, we might prevent its being generally received, and thereby lose all the salutary Effects and great Advantages resulting naturally in our favour among foreign Nations, as well as among ourselves, from our real or apparent Unanimity. Much of the Strength and Efficiency of any Government, in procuring and securing Happiness to the People depends on Opinion, on the general Opinion of the Goodness of that Government as well as of the Wisdom and Integrity of its Governors. I hope therefore that for our own Sakes, as a Part of the People, and for the sake of our Posterity, we shall act heartily and unanimously in recommending this Constitution, wherever our Influence may extend, and turn our future Thoughts and Endeavours to the Means of having it well administered.

> *"The Opinions I have had of its Errors, I sacrifice to the Public Good."*

On the whole, Sir, I cannot help expressing a Wish, that every Member of the Convention, who may still have Objections to it, would with me on this Occasion doubt a little of his own Infallibility, and to make manifest our Unanimity, put his Name to this instrument.

Source: *The Debates in the Federal Convention of 1787.* Edited by Gaillard Hunt and James Brown Scott. Oxford University Press, 1920.

> As the oldest member of the Convention (81 years old), Franklin may have hoped to get the last word but his speech was followed by still others. He still had a story ready. Madison records that while the last delegates were signing the document, Franklin pointed to the large Chippendale chair on which President Washington was sitting (it and the inkwell into which delegates dipped their quill are the only two remaining artifacts from the room) and observed that it contained a painted picture of a sun on its crowning slat. Further observing that artists found it difficult to distinguish between a rising and setting sun, he expressed his conviction that the sun was indeed rising on a new and hopeful day for the nation.

We the People
The Constitution of the United States
1787

INTRODUCTION

The delegates to the Constitutional Convention of 1787 labored the entire summer to produce the following document, which is less than 5,000 words. The document was divided into seven articles (most of which are subdivided into sections), each of which addresses a different issue or institution. Underlined sections indicate provisions that have subsequently been changed or superseded by constitutional amendments.

This opening paragraph, known as the Preamble, was largely the work of Gouverneur Morris, who served on the Committee of Style, which put the finishing touches on the document. The Preamble states the purposes of the document and clearly grounds its authority in "the People." The reference to "a more perfect Union" is an indirect reference to the Articles of Confederation, which preceded the Constitution.

We the People of the United States, in Order to form a more perfect Union, establish Justice, insure domestic Tranquility, provide for the common defence, promote the general Welfare, and secure the Blessings of Liberty to ourselves and our Posterity, do ordain and establish this Constitution for the United States of America.

Article. I.

Section. 1.

The first three articles of the Constitution embody the doctrine of separation of powers by outlining the structures, powers, and limitations on the three branches of the national government. The framers began with Congress because they anticipated both that it would be the most powerful branch and that it would be closest to the people.

All legislative Powers herein granted shall be vested in a Congress of the United States, which shall consist of a Senate and House of Representatives.

Section. 2.

The House of Representatives shall be composed of Members chosen every second Year by the People of the several

States, and the Electors in each State shall have the Qualifications requisite for Electors of the most numerous Branch of the State Legislature.

No Person shall be a Representative who shall not have attained to the Age of twenty five Years, and been seven Years a Citizen of the United States, and who shall not, when elected, be an Inhabitant of that State in which he shall be chosen.

Representatives and direct Taxes shall be apportioned among the several States which may be included within this Union, according to their respective Numbers, which shall be determined by adding to the whole Number of free Persons, including those bound to Service for a Term of Years, and excluding Indians not taxed, three fifths of all other Persons. The actual Enumeration shall be made within three Years after the first Meeting of the Congress of the United States, and within every subsequent Term of ten Years, in such Manner as they shall by Law direct. The Number of Representatives shall not exceed one for every thirty Thousand, but each State shall have at Least one Representative; and until such enumeration shall be made, the State of New Hampshire shall be entitled to chuse three, Massachusetts eight, Rhode-Island and Providence Plantations one, Connecticut five, New-York six, New Jersey four, Pennsylvania eight, Delaware one, Maryland six, Virginia ten, North Carolina five, South Carolina five, and Georgia three.

The highlighted portion of this section, since invalidated by the Thirteenth (1865) and Fourteenth (1868) Amendments, is the notorious three-fifths clause, which provided representation in the House of Representatives to states based not only on the number of free inhabitants but also on the basis of three-fifths of "all other Persons," namely slaves. The fact that the framers did not use the term "slavery" undoubtedly indicates their embarrassment on this point.

When vacancies happen in the Representation from any State, the Executive Authority thereof shall issue Writs of Election to fill such Vacancies.

The House of Representatives shall chuse their Speaker and other Officers; and shall have the sole Power of Impeachment.

Section. 3.

> Prior to the ratification of the Seventeenth Amendment (1913), state legislatures selected members of the Senate.

The Senate of the United States shall be composed of two Senators from each State, chosen by the Legislature thereof, for six Years; and each Senator shall have one Vote.

Immediately after they shall be assembled in Consequence of the first Election, they shall be divided as equally as may be into three Classes. The Seats of the Senators of the first Class shall be vacated at the Expiration of the second Year, of the second Class at the Expiration of the fourth Year, and of the third Class at the Expiration of the sixth Year, so that one third may be chosen every second Year; and if Vacancies happen by Resignation, or otherwise, during the Recess of the Legislature of any State, the Executive thereof may make temporary Appointments until the next Meeting of the Legislature, which shall then fill such Vacancies.

No Person shall be a Senator who shall not have attained to the Age of thirty Years, and been nine Years a Citizen of the United States, and who shall not, when elected, be an Inhabitant of that State for which he shall be chosen.

The Vice President of the United States shall be President of the Senate, but shall have no Vote, unless they be equally divided.

The Senate shall chuse their other Officers, and also a President pro tempore, in the Absence of the Vice President, or when he shall exercise the Office of President of the United States.

The Senate shall have the sole Power to try all Impeachments. When sitting for that Purpose, they shall be on Oath or Affirmation. When the President of the United States is tried, the Chief Justice shall preside: And no Person shall be convicted without the Concurrence of two thirds of the Members present.

Judgment in Cases of Impeachment shall not extend further than to removal from Office, and disqualification to hold and enjoy any Office of honor, Trust or Profit under the United States: but the Party convicted shall nevertheless be liable and subject to Indictment, Trial, Judgment and Punishment, according to Law.

Section. 4.

The Times, Places and Manner of holding Elections for Senators and Representatives, shall be prescribed in each State by the Legislature thereof; but the Congress may at any time by Law make or alter such Regulations, except as to the Places of chusing Senators.

The Congress shall assemble at least once in every Year, and such Meeting shall be on the first Monday in December, unless they shall by Law appoint a different Day.

"The Congress shall assemble at least once in every Year..."

Section. 5.

Each House shall be the Judge of the Elections, Returns and Qualifications of its own Members, and a Majority of each shall constitute a Quorum to do Business; but a smaller Number may adjourn from day to day, and may be authorized to compel the Attendance of absent Members, in such Manner, and under such Penalties as each House may provide.

Each House may determine the Rules of its Proceedings, punish its Members for disorderly Behaviour, and, with the Concurrence of two thirds, expel a Member.

Each House shall keep a Journal of its Proceedings, and from time to time publish the same, excepting such Parts as may in their Judgment require Secrecy; and the Yeas and Nays of the Members of either House on any question shall, at the Desire of one fifth of those Present, be entered on the Journal.

Neither House, during the Session of Congress, shall, without the Consent of the other, adjourn for more than three days, nor to any other Place than that in which the two Houses shall be sitting.

Section. 6.

The Senators and Representatives shall receive a Compensation for their Services, to be ascertained by Law, and paid out of the Treasury of the United States. They shall in all Cases, except Treason, Felony and Breach of the Peace, be privileged from Arrest during their Attendance at the Session of their respective Houses, and in going to and returning from the same; and for any Speech or Debate in either House, they shall not be questioned in any other Place.

> Whereas the British government permits members of Parliament to serve as cabinet officers, the U.S. Constitution does not. This further emphasizes the Constitution's reliance on the doctrine of separation of powers.

No Senator or Representative shall, during the Time for which he was elected, be appointed to any civil Office under the Authority of the United States, which shall have been created, or the Emoluments whereof shall have been encreased during such time; and no Person holding any Office under the United States, shall be a Member of either House during his Continuance in Office.

Section. 7.

All Bills for raising Revenue shall originate in the House of Representatives; but the Senate may propose or concur with Amendments as on other Bills.

Every Bill which shall have passed the House of Representatives and the Senate, shall, before it become a Law, be presented to the President of the United States; If he approve he shall sign it, but if not he shall return it, with his Objections to that House in which it shall have originated, who shall enter the Objections at large on their Journal, and proceed to reconsider it. If after such Reconsideration two thirds of that House shall agree to pass the Bill, it shall be sent, together with the Objections, to the other House, by which it shall likewise be reconsidered, and if approved by two thirds of that House, it shall become a Law. But in all such Cases the Votes of both Houses shall be determined by yeas and Nays, and the Names of the Persons voting for and against the Bill shall be entered on the Journal of each House respectively. If any Bill shall not be returned by the President within ten Days (Sundays excepted) after it shall have been presented to him, the Same shall be a Law, in like Manner as if he had signed it, unless the Congress by their Adjournment prevent its Return, in which Case it shall not be a Law.

Every Order, Resolution, or Vote to which the Concurrence of the Senate and House of Representatives may be necessary (except on a question of Adjournment) shall be presented to the President of the United States; and before the Same shall take Effect, shall be approved by him, or being disapproved by him, shall be repassed by two thirds of the Senate and House of Representatives, according to the Rules and Limitations prescribed in the Case of a Bill.

"Every Bill which shall have passed the House of Representatives and the Senate, shall, before it become a Law, be presented to the President of the United States . . ."

The provisions outlined here for adopting legislation require the consent of both houses of Congress. The President is given a conditional veto, which may in turn be overridden by two-thirds majorities of both houses. Even thereafter, such laws may be challenged in courts that exercise the power to decide whether they are constitutional or unconstitutional.

The Constitution of the United States

Section. 8.

Consistent with the desire that there be no taxation without representation, the Constitution vests Congress with what is known as "the power of the purse," that is, the power to tax and spend. The framers expected these powers to be broad but limited, hence they enumerated them.

The Congress shall have Power To lay and collect Taxes, Duties, Imposts and Excises, to pay the Debts and provide for the common Defence and general Welfare of the United States; but all Duties, Imposts and Excises shall be uniform throughout the United States;

To borrow Money on the credit of the United States;

The Articles of Confederation had not vested Congress with this important power over interstate and foreign commerce, which allows the national economy to operate in a single market. As the economy has grown, and interconnections have increased, this power has become increasingly important.

To regulate Commerce with foreign Nations, and among the several States, and with the Indian Tribes;

To establish an uniform Rule of Naturalization, and uniform Laws on the subject of Bankruptcies throughout the United States;

To coin Money, regulate the Value thereof, and of foreign Coin, and fix the Standard of Weights and Measures;

To provide for the Punishment of counterfeiting the Securities and current Coin of the United States;

To establish Post Offices and post Roads;

To promote the Progress of Science and useful Arts, by securing for limited Times to Authors and Inventors the exclusive Right to their respective Writings and Discoveries;

Congress acted to implement this provision with the adoption of the Judiciary Act of 1789 and subsequent acts of legislation that fill in the relatively sparse language of Article III.

To constitute Tribunals inferior to the supreme Court;

To define and punish Piracies and Felonies committed on the high Seas, and Offences against the Law of Nations;

To declare War, grant Letters of Marque and Reprisal, and make Rules concerning Captures on Land and Water;

To raise and support Armies, but no Appropriation of Money to that Use shall be for a longer Term than two Years;

To provide and maintain a Navy;

To make Rules for the Government and Regulation of the land and naval Forces;

To provide for calling forth the Militia to execute the Laws of the Union, suppress Insurrections and repel Invasions;

To provide for organizing, arming, and disciplining, the Militia, and for governing such Part of them as may be employed in the Service of the United States, reserving to the States respectively, the Appointment of the Officers, and the Authority of training the Militia according to the discipline prescribed by Congress;

To exercise exclusive Legislation in all Cases whatsoever, over such District (not exceeding ten Miles square) as may, by Cession of particular States, and the Acceptance of Congress, become the Seat of the Government of the United States, and to exercise like Authority over all Places purchased by the Consent of the Legislature of the State in which the Same shall be, for the Erection of Forts, Magazines, Arsenals, dock-Yards, and other needful Buildings;—And

To make all Laws which shall be necessary and proper for carrying into Execution the foregoing Powers, and all

This clause vests the power to declare war in Congress along with the ancillary power to commission privateers (letters of marque and reprisal) to raid foreign shipping. Consistent with the idea of checks and balances, the congressional power to declare war, like the powers that immediately follow, is balanced against the president's power as commander in chief of the armed forces.

This provides authority for Congress to govern what is today called the District of Columbia. Because residents still do not have voting representatives in Congress, they continue to claim to be victims of "no taxation without representation."

The final clause in this section is sometimes called the "elastic," or "sweeping," clause, because it recognizes a potential host of subsidiary powers that Congress can exercise. In McCulloch v. Maryland *(1819), the U.S. Supreme Court used this provision to uphold the constitutionality of the national bank. Chief Justice John Marshall argued that Congress was not restricted to using those means that were "absolutely necessary," but had a broad choice of means, as long as they did not trespass on other constitutional provisions.*

other Powers vested by this Constitution in the Government of the United States, or in any Department or Officer thereof.

Section. 9.

> Whereas Article I, Section 8 outlines the powers of Congress, Section 9 outlines restrictions on such powers. The first such restriction, a compromise between the northern and southern states, allows for the continuing importation of slaves for an additional 20 years, after which Congress will make the trade illegal.

The Migration or Importation of such Persons as any of the States now existing shall think proper to admit, shall not be prohibited by the Congress prior to the Year one thousand eight hundred and eight, but a Tax or duty may be imposed on such Importation, not exceeding ten dollars for each Person.

> The term "habeas corpus" literally means "it is commanded that you have the body." The writ required the government to specify reasons for arresting and detaining a citizen. It thus prohibited the government from holding individuals without charges. Congress may, however, suspend this writ in specified emergencies.

The Privilege of the Writ of Habeas Corpus shall not be suspended, unless when in Cases of Rebellion or Invasion the public Safety may require it.

> Even before the adoption of the Bill of Rights, the framers sought to limit governmental powers over individual rights. A bill of attainder is a legislative judgment that condemns specific individuals to punishment without a trial; an ex post facto law is a retroactive criminal law.

No Bill of Attainder or ex post facto Law shall be passed.

> The underlined section was repealed by the Sixteenth Amendment (1913), which permits Congress to enact a national income tax.

No Capitation, or other direct, Tax shall be laid, unless in Proportion to the Census or enumeration herein before directed to be taken.

No Tax or Duty shall be laid on Articles exported from any State.

No Preference shall be given by any Regulation of Commerce or Revenue to the Ports of one State over those of another: nor shall Vessels bound to, or from, one State, be obliged to enter, clear, or pay Duties in another.

No Money shall be drawn from the Treasury, but in Consequence of Appropriations made by Law; and a regular

Statement and Account of the Receipts and Expenditures of all public Money shall be published from time to time.

No Title of Nobility shall be granted by the United States: And no Person holding any Office of Profit or Trust under them, shall, without the Consent of the Congress, accept of any present, Emolument, Office, or Title, of any kind whatever, from any King, Prince, or foreign State.

> This further indicates the founders' desire to prevent the establishment of nonrepublican institutions.

Section. 10.

No State shall enter into any Treaty, Alliance, or Confederation; grant Letters of Marque and Reprisal; coin Money; emit Bills of Credit; make any Thing but gold and silver Coin a Tender in Payment of Debts; pass any Bill of Attainder, ex post facto Law, or Law impairing the Obligation of Contracts, or grant any Title of Nobility.

> Whereas Article I, Section 9 limits Congress, this section limits the states. In addition to preventing states from exercising powers specifically entrusted to the national government, or from adopting unjust laws that were also prohibited to Congress, the Constitution prohibits states from interfering with the obligation of contracts, which many framers thought they had done under the Articles. The framers may have been following the theory that Madison had articulated in Federalist No. 10, that it would be less necessary to impose a similar limitation on the national government, which would embrace a far greater number of interests.

No State shall, without the Consent of the Congress, lay any Imposts or Duties on Imports or Exports, except what may be absolutely necessary for executing it's inspection Laws: and the net Produce of all Duties and Imposts, laid by any State on Imports or Exports, shall be for the Use of the Treasury of the United States; and all such Laws shall be subject to the Revision and Controul of the Congress.

No State shall, without the Consent of Congress, lay any Duty of Tonnage, keep Troops, or Ships of War in time of Peace, enter into any Agreement or Compact with another State, or with a foreign Power, or engage in War, unless actually invaded, or in such imminent Danger as will not admit of delay.

Article. II.

Section. 1.

> Whereas the Constitution divides the legislature into two houses, it provides for a single executive. This was designed to enhance what *The Federalist* described as the "energy" of the office. Alexander Hamilton argued that the language of this clause, which omits the term "herein granted" that is found in the corresponding provision of Article I, was designed to indicate that the Constitution expected the president to exercise broader prerogative powers.

The executive Power shall be vested in a President of the United States of America. He shall hold his Office during the Term of four Years, and, together with the Vice President, chosen for the same Term, be elected, as follows;

Each State shall appoint, in such Manner as the Legislature thereof may direct, a Number of Electors, equal to the whole Number of Senators and Representatives to which the State may be entitled in the Congress: but no Senator or Representative, or Person holding an Office of Trust or Profit under the United States, shall be appointed an Elector.

> This section, subsequently modified by the Twelfth Amendment, was designed to create an indirect method of electing the president through an Electoral College, where states would be represented by the same formula that dictated representation within the House of Representatives. As the presidential elections of 1800 and 2000 later demonstrated, it remains possible for an individual to win the presidency without garnering the greatest number of popular votes.

The Electors shall meet in their respective States, and vote by Ballot for two Persons, of whom one at least shall not be an Inhabitant of the same State with themselves. And they shall make a List of all the Persons voted for, and of the Number of Votes for each; which List they shall sign and certify, and transmit sealed to the Seat of the Government of the United States, directed to the President of the Senate. The President of the Senate shall, in the Presence of the Senate and House of Representatives, open all the Certificates, and the Votes shall then be counted. The Person having the greatest Number of Votes shall be the President, if such Number be a Majority of the whole Number of Electors appointed; and if there be more than one who have such Majority, and have an equal Number of Votes, then the House of Representatives shall immediately chuse by Ballot one of them for President; and if no Person have a Majority, then from the five highest on the List the said House shall in like Manner chuse the President.

But in chusing the President, the Votes shall be taken by States, the Representation from each State having one Vote; A quorum for this Purpose shall consist of a Member or Members from two thirds of the States, and a Majority of all the States shall be necessary to a Choice. In every Case, after the Choice of the President, the Person having the greatest Number of Votes of the Electors shall be the Vice President. But if there should remain two or more who have equal Votes, the Senate shall chuse from them by Ballot the Vice President.

The Congress may determine the Time of chusing the Electors, and the Day on which they shall give their Votes; which Day shall be the same throughout the United States.

No Person except a natural born Citizen, or a Citizen of the United States, at the time of the Adoption of this Constitution, shall be eligible to the Office of President; neither shall any Person be eligible to that Office who shall not have attained to the Age of thirty five Years, and been fourteen Years a Resident within the United States.

In Case of the Removal of the President from Office, or of his Death, Resignation, or Inability to discharge the Powers and Duties of the said Office, the Same shall devolve on the Vice President, and the Congress may by Law provide for the Case of Removal, Death, Resignation or Inability, both of the President and Vice President, declaring what Officer shall then act as President, and such Officer shall act accordingly, until the Disability be removed, or a President shall be elected.

The President shall, at stated Times, receive for his Services, a Compensation, which shall neither be encreased nor

"No Person except a natural born Citizen, or a Citizen of the United States, at the time of the Adoption of this Constitution, shall be eligible to the Office of President . . ."

This provision was subsequently refined by the adoption of the Twenty-Fifth Amendment (1967).

diminished during the Period for which he shall have been elected, and he shall not receive within that Period any other Emolument from the United States, or any of them.

Before he enter on the Execution of his Office, he shall take the following Oath or Affirmation:—"I do solemnly swear (or affirm) that I will faithfully execute the Office of President of the United States, and will to the best of my Ability, preserve, protect and defend the Constitution of the United States."

Section. 2.

> The Constitution establishes civilian control over the military by granting Congress the power to declare war and by vesting the president with the power of serving as commander in chief of the armed forces. It also entrusts the president with broad power to issue reprieves and pardons.

The President shall be Commander in Chief of the Army and Navy of the United States, and of the Militia of the several States, when called into the actual Service of the United States; he may require the Opinion, in writing, of the principal Officer in each of the executive Departments, upon any Subject relating to the Duties of their respective Offices, and he shall have Power to grant Reprieves and Pardons for Offences against the United States, except in Cases of Impeachment.

> The President exercises the power to appoint key officials, including ambassadors, judges, and justices, with the advice and consent (approval) of the U.S. Senate. Following a decision made by the first Congress, which was designed to increase executive accountability, Supreme Court decisions have subsequently given the president the power to fire cabinet members and others who are not holding judicial, or quasi-judicial, positions.

He shall have Power, by and with the Advice and Consent of the Senate, to make Treaties, provided two thirds of the Senators present concur; and he shall nominate, and by and with the Advice and Consent of the Senate, shall appoint Ambassadors, other public Ministers and Consuls, Judges of the supreme Court, and all other Officers of the United States, whose Appointments are not herein otherwise provided for, and which shall be established by Law: but the Congress may by Law vest the Appointment of such inferior Officers, as they think proper, in the President alone, in the Courts of Law, or in the Heads of Departments.

The President shall have Power to fill up all Vacancies that may happen during the Recess of the Senate, by granting Commissions which shall expire at the End of their next Session.

Section. 3.

He shall from time to time give to the Congress Information of the State of the Union, and recommend to their Consideration such Measures as he shall judge necessary and expedient; he may, on extraordinary Occasions, convene both Houses, or either of them, and in Case of Disagreement between them, with Respect to the Time of Adjournment, he may adjourn them to such Time as he shall think proper; he shall receive Ambassadors and other public Ministers; he shall take Care that the Laws be faithfully executed, and shall Commission all the Officers of the United States.

> *"He shall from time to time give to the Congress Information of the State of the Union, and recommend to their Consideration such Measures as he shall judge necessary and expedient . . ."*

Section. 4.

The President, Vice President and all civil Officers of the United States, shall be removed from Office on Impeachment for, and Conviction of, Treason, Bribery, or other high Crimes and Misdemeanors.

Impeachment is designed as a check against illegal executive or judicial actions. The Constitution limits the definition of impeachable offenses to prevent the mechanism from being used for purely partisan purposes.

Article. III.

Section. 1.

The judicial Power of the United States, shall be vested in one supreme Court, and in such inferior Courts as the Congress may from time to time ordain and establish. The Judges, both of the supreme and inferior Courts, shall hold their Offices during good Behaviour, and shall,

Members of the judicial branch are appointed and confirmed by the two previous branches. Only the U.S. Supreme Court is mentioned by name. Judges serve "during good Behavior" or for life, unless they are impeached by the House of Representatives and found guilty of an impeachable offense in a trial by the U.S. Senate.

at stated Times, receive for their Services, a Compensation, which shall not be diminished during their Continuance in Office.

Section. 2.

> Whereas the two elected branches can initiate legislation, the judiciary serves a more passive role, waiting for issues to come to it for resolution in the form of cases. Not every issue is justiciable, or subject to judicial scrutiny. This section outlines the central kinds of cases over which federal courts have jurisdiction. Jurisdiction over cases described in the underlined portion was withdrawn by the early adoption of the Eleventh Amendment.

The judicial Power shall extend to all Cases, in Law and Equity, arising under this Constitution, the Laws of the United States, and Treaties made, or which shall be made, under their Authority;—to all Cases affecting Ambassadors, other public Ministers and Consuls;—to all Cases of admiralty and maritime Jurisdiction;—to Controversies to which the United States shall be a Party;—to Controversies between two or more States;—between a State and Citizens of another State,—between Citizens of different States,—between Citizens of the same State claiming Lands under Grants of different States, and between a State, or the Citizens thereof, and foreign States, Citizens or Subjects.

> The Judiciary Act of 1789 created a federal judicial system consisting of three tiers. U.S. district courts hear most, albeit not all, cases in the first instance (cases of original jurisdiction), whereas the circuit courts of appeal and the U.S. Supreme Court chiefly hear cases on appeal.

In all Cases affecting Ambassadors, other public Ministers and Consuls, and those in which a State shall be Party, the supreme Court shall have original Jurisdiction. In all the other Cases before mentioned, the supreme Court shall have appellate Jurisdiction, both as to Law and Fact, with such Exceptions, and under such Regulations as the Congress shall make.

The Trial of all Crimes, except in Cases of Impeachment, shall be by Jury; and such Trial shall be held in the State where the said Crimes shall have been committed; but when not committed within any State, the Trial shall be at such Place or Places as the Congress may by Law have directed.

Section. 3.

Treason against the United States, shall consist only in levying War against them, or in adhering to their Enemies, giving them Aid and Comfort. No Person shall be convicted of Treason unless on the Testimony of two Witnesses to the same overt Act, or on Confession in open Court.

The Congress shall have Power to declare the Punishment of Treason, but no Attainder of Treason shall work Corruption of Blood, or Forfeiture except during the Life of the Person attainted.

> The Constitution offers a narrow definition of treason and provides strict standards of proof. In Great Britain, punishments sometimes extended from one generation to another. This provision was designed to prohibit this.

Article. IV.

Section. 1.

Full Faith and Credit shall be given in each State to the public Acts, Records, and judicial Proceedings of every other State. And the Congress may by general Laws prescribe the Manner in which such Acts, Records and Proceedings shall be proved, and the Effect thereof.

> Having outlined the powers of the three branches of the national government, the Constitution proceeds to describe the relationship between the national government and the states and among each other. It created what is today called a federal system, with a national government and a set of state governments—each with its own constitution, and each with power to act directly on its individual citizens.

Section. 2.

The Citizens of each State shall be entitled to all Privileges and Immunities of Citizens in the several States.

> This provision, which was designed to extend the benefits of citizenship to individuals when they travel out of state, did not define citizenship; that task was left undone until the adoption of the Fourteenth Amendment in 1868, which extended such citizenship to "all persons born or naturalized in the United States" and thus included African Americans.

A Person charged in any State with Treason, Felony, or other Crime, who shall flee from Justice, and be found in another State, shall on Demand of the executive Authority of the State from which he fled, be delivered up, to be removed to the State having Jurisdiction of the Crime.

The Constitution of the United States

> This is the notorious fugitive slave clause, one of the compromises at the Convention between northern and southern states. This clause became irrelevant with the Thirteenth Amendment's elimination of slavery in 1865.

No Person held to Service or Labour in one State, under the Laws thereof, escaping into another, shall, in Consequence of any Law or Regulation therein, be discharged from such Service or Labour, but shall be delivered up on Claim of the Party to whom such Service or Labour may be due.

Section. 3.

New States may be admitted by the Congress into this Union; but no new State shall be formed or erected within the Jurisdiction of any other State; nor any State be formed by the Junction of two or more States, or Parts of States, without the Consent of the Legislatures of the States concerned as well as of the Congress.

> Without providing for the entry of new states, the United States could have ended up as a colonial power on its own continent. This power was balanced by requiring that new states would not, without state consent, be formed from among existing entities.

The Congress shall have Power to dispose of and make all needful Rules and Regulations respecting the Territory or other Property belonging to the United States; and nothing in this Constitution shall be so construed as to Prejudice any Claims of the United States, or of any particular State.

Section. 4.

> A republican form of government is representative. Congress acknowledges the republican nature of state governments when it seats their representatives. The provision relative to domestic rebellions was in part a response to Shays' Rebellion.

The United States shall guarantee to every State in this Union a Republican Form of Government, and shall protect each of them against Invasion; and on Application of the Legislature, or of the Executive (when the Legislature cannot be convened), against domestic Violence.

Article. V.

The Congress, whenever two thirds of both Houses shall deem it necessary, shall propose Amendments to this Constitution, or, on the Application of the Legislatures of two thirds of the several States, shall call a Convention for proposing Amendments, which, in either Case, shall be valid to all Intents and Purposes, as Part of this Constitution, when ratified by the Legislatures of three fourths of the several States, or by Conventions in three fourths thereof, as the one or the other Mode of Ratification may be proposed by the Congress; Provided that no Amendment which may be made prior to the Year One thousand eight hundred and eight shall in any Manner affect the first and fourth Clauses in the Ninth Section of the first Article; and that no State, without its Consent, shall be deprived of its equal Suffrage in the Senate.

> The framers of the Constitution thought that the provisions requiring unanimous state consent under the Articles of Confederation had been too onerous, and they crafted provisions that they thought would be easier. Amendments may be proposed either by two-thirds of both houses of Congress or (in a still-unused mechanism) by a convention called by Congress at the request of two-thirds of the states. Congress specifies whether either kind of proposal will be ratified by state legislatures or by special state conventions called for this purpose, as in the case of the Twenty-First Amendment repealing national alcoholic prohibition.

Article. VI.

All Debts contracted and Engagements entered into, before the Adoption of this Constitution, shall be as valid against the United States under this Constitution, as under the Confederation.

This Constitution, and the Laws of the United States which shall be made in Pursuance thereof; and all Treaties made, or which shall be made, under the Authority of the United States, shall be the supreme Law of the Land; and the Judges in every State shall be bound thereby, any Thing in the Constitution or Laws of any State to the Contrary notwithstanding.

> This paragraph, which originated with the New Jersey Plan, is called the supremacy clause because it provides that judges throughout the nation must give the national Constitution supremacy over any conflicting state or local laws. Courts exercise this power when they exercise judicial review.

The Senators and Representatives before mentioned, and the Members of the several State Legislatures, and all executive and judicial Officers, both of the United States and of the several States, shall be bound by Oath or Affirmation, to support this Constitution; but no religious Test shall ever be required as a Qualification to any Office or public Trust under the United States.

Article. VII.

The Ratification of the Conventions of nine States, shall be sufficient for the Establishment of this Constitution between the States so ratifying the Same.

> Whereas the Articles of Confederation required unanimous consent of state legislatures to constitutional amendments, the Constitution provided that it would go into effect when ratified by special conventions in two-thirds of the states, albeit only among those that agreed to it.

The Word, "the," being interlined between the seventh and eighth Lines of the first Page, The Word "Thirty" being partly written on an Erazure in the fifteenth Line of the first Page, The Words "is tried" being interlined between the thirty second and thirty third Lines of the first Page and the Word "the" being interlined between the forty third and forty fourth Lines of the second Page.

Attest William Jackson Secretary done in Convention by the Unanimous Consent of the States present the Seventeenth Day of September in the Year of our Lord one thousand seven hundred and Eighty seven and of the Independance of the United States of America the Twelfth In witness whereof We have hereunto subscribed our Names,

G°. Washington
Presidt and deputy from Virginia

> *"[D]one in Convention by the Unanimous Consent of the States present the Seventeenth Day of September in the Year of our Lord one thousand seven hundred and Eighty seven and of the Independance of the United States of America the Twelfth..."*

Delaware
Geo: Read
Gunning Bedford jun
John Dickinson
Richard Bassett
Jaco: Broom

Maryland
James McHenry
Dan of St Thos. Jenifer
Danl. Carroll

Virginia
John Blair
James Madison Jr.

North Carolina
Wm. Blount
Richd. Dobbs Spaight
Hu Williamson

South Carolina
J. Rutledge
Charles Cotesworth Pinckney
Charles Pinckney
Pierce Butler

Georgia
William Few
Abr Baldwin

New Hampshire
John Langdon
Nicholas Gilman

Massachusetts
Nathaniel Gorham
Rufus King

Connecticut
Wm. Saml. Johnson
Roger Sherman

The Constitution of the United States

New York
Alexander Hamilton

New Jersey
Wil: Livingston
David Brearley
Wm. Paterson
Jona: Dayton

Pensylvania
B Franklin
Thomas Mifflin
Robt. Morris
Geo. Clymer
Thos. FitzSimons
Jared Ingersoll
James Wilson
Gouv Morris

> At the Constitutional Convention, votes were cast by states from North to South. Apparently, the delegates signed in similar fashion, beginning with New Hampshire but ran out of room and started a new column to the left. Of the 42 delegates who remained on September 17, all but 3 signed.

Source: Constitution of the United States, 1787. National Archives website. Accessed January 15, 2015. http://www.archives.gov/exhibits/charters/constitution_transcript.html.

The Consolidation of Our Union
George Washington Transmits the Constitution to Congress
September 17, 1787

> **INTRODUCTION**
>
> Since the delegates were proposing a substantially new document, they sought to improve its chances of receiving a warm reception in Congress. They aimed to do this by capitalizing on the reputation of George Washington, the Revolutionary War hero who had served as president of the Convention and whom a majority of delegates correctly anticipated would also be elected as the first president of the nation. Washington obliged by signing this letter, largely composed by Gouverneur Morris, which accompanied the transmittal of the proposed Constitution to Congress.

Sir:

We have now the honor to submit to the consideration of the United States in Congress assembled, that Constitution which has appeared to us the most advisable.

The friends of our country have long seen and desired, that the power of making war, peace and treaties, that of levying money and regulating commerce, and the correspondent executive and judicial authorities should be fully and effectually vested in the general government of the Union: but the impropriety of delegating such extensive trust to one body of men is evident—Hence results the necessity of a different organization.

These objectives are similar to those that Washington had outlined in his circular letter to governors on June 8, 1783.

It is obviously impracticable in the federal government of these States, to secure all rights of independent sovereignty to each, and yet provide for the interest and safety

Each state's delegation had engaged in extensive give-and-take at the Convention. Washington stressed the difficulty of knowing how to divide powers between the people and the government, and the nation and the states.

of all—Individuals entering into society, must give up a share of liberty to preserve the rest. The magnitude of the sacrifice must depend as well on situation and circumstance, as on the object to be obtained. It is at all times difficult to draw with precision the line between those rights which must be surrendered, and those which may be reserved; and on the present occasion this difficulty was increased by a difference among the several States as to their situation, extent, habits, and particular interests.

> As Franklin had indicated during his closing speech to the Convention, no individual or state had emerged from the Convention completely satisfied with the results. But Washington's letter indicates that delegates had compromised on minor points in order to reach their key objectives.

In all our deliberations on this subject we kept steadily in our view, that which appears to us the greatest interest of every true American, the consolidation of our Union, in which is involved our prosperity, felicity, safety, perhaps our national existence. This important consideration, seriously and deeply impressed on our minds, led each State in the Convention to be less rigid on points of inferior magnitude, than might have been otherwise expected; and thus the Constitution, which we now present, is the result of a spirit of amity, and of that mutual deference and concession which the peculiarity of our political situation rendered indispensable.

"[T]hat it is liable to as few exceptions as could reasonably have been expected, we hope and believe; that it may promote the lasting welfare of that country so dear to us all, and secure her freedom and happiness, is our most ardent wish."

That it will meet the full and entire approbation of every State is not perhaps to be expected; but each will doubtless consider, that had her interests been alone consulted, the consequences might have been particularly disagreeable or injurious to others; that it is liable to as few exceptions as could reasonably have been expected, we hope and believe; that it may promote the lasting welfare of that country so dear to us all, and secure her freedom and happiness, is our most ardent wish.

With great respect, We have the honor to be, Sir, Your Excellency's most Obedient and humble Servants,

George Washington, President
By unanimous Order of the Convention

Source: *Documents Illustrative of the Formation of the Union of the American States.* Selected. Arranged and indexed by Charles C. Tansill. Washington, DC: Government Printing Office, 1927. House Document No. 398.

In Conformity to the Resolves

Resolution of Congress Submitting the Constitution to the Several States

September 28, 1787

INTRODUCTION

Once the delegates submitted their report to Congress, its members, some of whom had attended the Convention, had a number of choices. They could reject the proposals, endorse the proposals and send them to the state legislators for the unanimous consent required for amendments under the Articles of Confederation, or send them with or without endorsement to the states to ratify in conventions, as Article VII of the proposed document specified. Although an affirmative vote might have helped, it appears that Federalist supporters of the new Constitution preferred for Congress to just pass it along rather than take the chance that a vote might instead reveal opposition. Congress did send the document to the states, arguably further legitimizing the method that the convention delegates had chosen for ratifying the document.

Congress having received the report of the Convention lately assembled in Philadelphia

This resolution accepted the method of constitutional ratification that the Convention had proposed, thus assuring that if the states did ratify the new document, it would be on even sounder democratic footing than the Articles of Confederation had been.

Resolved Unanimously that the said Report with the resolutions and letter accompanying the same be transmitted to the several legislatures in Order to be submitted to a convention of Delegates chosen in each state by the people thereof in conformity to the resolves of the Convention made and provided in that case.

Source: *Documentary History of The Constitution.* Vol. 2 (1894), Washington, DC: Department of State, p. 22.

Section IV: Debating, Ratifying, Implementing, and Amending the New Constitution

The Instrument of the Union

James Wilson Comments on Ratifying the Proposed Constitution

October 6, 1787

INTRODUCTION

James Wilson of Pennsylvania, a law professor who had immigrated from Scotland and who would later serve as a justice of the U.S. Supreme Court, was among the most influential delegates at the Constitutional Convention of 1787. He was particularly known for advocating a strong presidency. The following is an excerpt from a speech that Wilson gave on October 6 to a meeting held at Independence Hall to nominate individuals to the state nominating convention.

By October, Anti-Federalist opposition to the proposed Constitution was crystalizing around a number of points, the most important of which centered on the lack of a bill of rights—a concern that George Mason had raised in the final days of the Convention. Using arguments that might have been more convincing to his law school students than the general public, Wilson argued that such a bill was unnecessary because Congress could only exercise delegated powers, and such powers did not give Congress authority to impede or interfere with rights like those that would later be articulated within the first 10 amendments. Alexander Hamilton would later use similar arguments in *The Federalist*, where he argued that the entire Constitution served as a bill of rights. In time, however, Federalists recognized that they were unlikely to receive approval for the Constitution without a distinct enumeration not only of governmental powers but also of individual rights.

Mr. Chairman and Fellow Citizens:

Having received the honor of an appointment to represent you in the late convention, it is perhaps my duty to comply with the request of many gentlemen whose characters and judgements I sincerely respect, and who have urged that this would be a proper occasion to lay before you any information which will serve to explain and elucidate the principles and arrangements of the constitution that has been submitted to the consideration of the United States. . . .

It will be proper . . . to mark the leading discrimination between the State constitutions and the constitution of the United States. When the people established the powers of legislation under their separate governments, they invested their representatives with every right and authority which they did not in explicit terms reserve; and therefore upon every question respecting the jurisdiction of the House of Assembly, if the frame

of government is silent, the jurisdiction is efficient and complete. But in delegating federal powers, another criterion was necessarily introduced, and the congressional power is to be collected, not from tacit implication, but from the positive grant expressed in the instrument of the union. Hence, it is evident, that in the former case everything which is not reserved is given; but in the latter the reverse of the proposition prevails, and everything which is not given is reserved.

This distinction being recognized, will furnish an answer to those who think the omission of a bill of rights a defect in the proposed constitution; for it would have been superfluous and absurd to have stipulated with a federal body of our own creation, that we should enjoy those privileges of which we are not divested, either by the intention or the act that has brought the body into existence. For instance, the liberty of the press, which has been a copious source of declamation and opposition—what control can proceed from the Federal government to shackle or destroy that sacred palladium of national freedom? If, indeed, a power similar to that which has been granted for the regulation of commerce had been granted to regulate literary publications, it would have been as necessary to stipulate that the liberty of the press should be preserved inviolate, as that the impost should be general in its operation. With respect likewise to the particular district of ten miles, which is to be made the seat of federal government, it will undoubtedly be proper to observe this salutary precaution, as there the legislative power will be exclusively lodged in the President, Senate, and House of Representatives of the United States. But this could not be an object with the Convention, for it must naturally depend upon a future compact to which the citizens immediately interested will, and ought to be, parties; and there is no reason to suspect that

> *"This distinction being recognized, will furnish an answer to those who think the omission of a bill of rights a defect in the proposed constitution; for it would have been superfluous and absurd to have stipulated with a federal body of our own creation, that we should enjoy those privileges of which we are not divested, either by the intention or the act that has brought the body into existence."*

so popular a privilege will in that case be neglected. In truth, then, the proposed system possesses no influence whatever upon the press, and it would have been merely nugatory to have introduced a formal declaration upon the subject—nay, that very declaration might have been construed to imply that some degree of power was given, since we undertook to define its extent.

Source: *Pennsylvania and the Federal Constitution, 1787–1788.* Edited by John Bach McMaster and Frederick D. Stone. Lancaster, PA: Historical Society of Pennsylvania, 1888, p. 143.

Our Freedom We've Won
"The Grand Constitution" Song
October 1787

> **INTRODUCTION**
>
> Although it is common to stress the intellectual origins of the U.S. Constitution, proponents of ratification also used emotional appeals to rally support for the document. One such example was "The Grand Constitution; Or, The Palladium of Columbia," the lyrics of which were published in the *Massachusetts Centinel* newspaper on October 6, 1787.

From scenes of affliction—Columbia opprest—Of credit expiring—and commerce distrest, Of nothing to do—and of nothing to pay—From such dismal scenes let us hasten away.

Our Freedom we've won, and the prize let's maintain
Our hearts *are all right—*
Unite, Boys, Unite,
And our EMPIRE *in glory shall ever remain.*

The Muses no longer the cypress shall wear—For we turn our glad eyes to a prospect more fair: The soldier return'd to his small cultur'd farm, Enjoys the reward of his conquering arm.

"*Our Freedom we've won,*" &c.

Our trade and our commerce shall reach far and wide, And riches and honour flow in with each tide, *Kamschatka* and *China* with wonder shall stare, That the *Federal Stripes* should wave gracefully there.

"Columbia," derived from the name of Christopher Columbus, was a name frequently applied at the time to the United States ("Hail Columbia" was an early national patriotic song). This stanza highlights the commercial problems under the Articles of Confederation. It sought to tie the ratification of the Constitution to the earlier fight for liberty in the Revolution.

"The Grand Constitution" Song

"Our Freedom we've won," &c.

> Federalists frequently evoked the names of Benjamin Franklin and George Washington, the two most prominent individuals who had attended the Constitutional Convention, to garner support for the Constitution.

With gratitude let us acknowledge the worth, Of what the CONVENTION has call'd into birth, And the Continent wisely confirm what is done By FRANKLIN the sage, and by brave WASHINGTON.

"Our Freedom we've won," &c.

The wise CONSTITUTION let's truly revere, It points out the course for our EMPIRE to steer, For oceans of bliss do they hoist the broad sail, And *peace* is the current, and *plenty* the gale.

"Our Freedom we've won," &c.

> Republicanism stressed the virtues of representative democracy and of enlightened citizens willing to come to the aid of their country. Although Anti-Federalists thought that such republican virtue would only be possible in small areas, this song sought to tie the Constitution itself to republican values.

With gratitude fill'd—let the great Commonweal Pass round the full glass to Republican zeal—From ruin—their judgment and wisdom well aim'd, Our liberties, laws, and our credit reclaim'd.

"Our Freedom we've won," &c.

> Daniel Shays and Luke Day had been associated with Shays' Rebellion, which had closed down courts in some Massachusetts towns in the winter of 1787 and 1788 and raised fears that governments were disintegrating under the Articles of Confederation.

Here Plenty and Order and Freedom shall dwell, And your *Shayses* and *Dayses* won't dare to rebel—Independence and culture shall graciously smile, And the *Husbandman* reap the full fruit of his toil.

"Our Freedom we've won," &c.

That these are the blessings, Columbia knows— The blessings the Fed'ral CONVENTION bestows. O! then let the People confirm what

is done By **FRANKLIN** the sage, and by brave **WASHINGTON**.

Our freedom we've won, and the prize will maintain
By Jove we'll Unite,
Approve and Unite—
And huzza for **Convention** *again and again.*

Source: "The Grand Constitution; or, the Palladium of Columbia." William McCarty. *The American National Song Book.* Philadelpha, PA, 1842.

> The Preamble to the Constitution stressed the "blessings of liberty," which this passage highlights, along with the need for national unity.

The Destruction of Your Liberties

Brutus Issues His Anti-Federalist Essay
1787

> **INTRODUCTION**
>
> Among the Anti-Federalists who opposed ratification of the new Constitution, few were more articulate than the critic known as "Brutus." This moniker is believed to have been a pen name for Robert Yates, a delegate who had attended the Constitutional Convention from New York but left before the document was signed. His central concern about the proposed Constitution, expressed in this essay, was the absence of a bill of rights.

II
1 November 1787
To the Citizens of the State of New-York.

I flatter myself that my last address established this position, that to reduce the Thirteen States into one government, would prove the destruction of your liberties.

Anti-Federalists tended to favor states' rights and were opponents of excessive consolidation at the national level.

But lest this truth should be doubted by some, I will now proceed to consider its merits.

Though it should be admitted, that the argument[s] against reducing all the states into one consolidated government, are not sufficient fully to establish this point; yet they will, at least, justify this conclusion, that in forming a constitution for such a country, great care should be taken to limit and define its powers, adjust its parts, and guard against an abuse of authority. How far attention has been paid to these objects, shall be the subject of future enquiry. When a

"[I]n forming a constitution for such a country, great care should be taken to limit and define its powers, adjust its parts, and guard against an abuse of authority."

building is to be erected which is intended to stand for ages, the foundation should be firmly laid. **The constitution proposed to your acceptance, is designed not for yourselves alone, but for generations yet unborn. The principles, therefore, upon which the social compact is founded, ought to have been clearly and precisely stated, and the most express and full declaration of rights to have been made—But on this subject there is almost an entire silence.**

> One of the measures of statesmanship is a concern for the future. This concern was expressed in the Preamble to the Constitution as a concern to pass the blessings of liberty on to posterity. Brutus demonstrated that Anti-Federalists shared a similar concern.

If we may collect the sentiments of the people of America, from their own most solemn declarations, they hold this truth as self evident, that all men are by nature free. No one man, therefore, or any class of men, have a right, by the law of nature, or of God, to assume or exercise authority over their fellows. The origin of society then is to be sought, not in any natural right which one man has to exercise authority over another, but in the united consent of those who associate. The mutual wants of men, at first dictated the propriety of forming societies; and when they were established, protection and defence pointed out the necessity of instituting government. In a state of nature every individual pursues his own interest; in this pursuit it frequently happened, that the possessions or enjoyments of one were sacrificed to the views and designs of another; thus the weak were a prey to the strong, the simple and unwary were subject to impositions from those who were more crafty and designing. In this state of things, every individual was insecure; common interest therefore directed, that government should be established, in which the force of the whole community should be collected, and under such directions, as to protect and defend every one who composed it. The common good, therefore, is the end of

> This is a classic exposition of Lockean natural-rights philosophy, complete with a reference to the state of nature. Brutus argued for a government that not only protected people from one another but also offered them protections against their rulers.

> "From these observations it appears, that in forming a government on its true principles, the foundation should be laid in the manner I before stated, by expressly reserving to the people such of their essential natural rights, as are not necessary to be parted with."

civil government, and common consent, the foundation on which it is established. To effect this end, it was necessary that a certain portion of natural liberty should be surrendered, in order, that what remained should be preserved: how great a proportion of natural freedom is necessary to be yielded by individuals, when they submit to government, I shall not now enquire. So much, however, must be given up, as will be sufficient to enable those, to whom the administration of the government is committed, to establish laws for the promoting the happiness of the community, and to carry those laws into effect. But it is not necessary, for this purpose, that individuals should relinquish all their natural rights. Some are of such a nature that they cannot be surrendered. Of this kind are the rights of conscience, the right of enjoying and defending life, etc. Others are not necessary to be resigned, in order to attain the end for which government is instituted, these therefore ought not to be given up. To surrender them, would counteract the very end of government, to wit, the common good. From these observations it appears, that in forming a government on its true principles, the foundation should be laid in the manner I before stated, by expressly reserving to the people such of their essential natural rights, as are not necessary to be parted with. The same reasons which at first induced mankind to associate and institute government, will operate to influence them to observe this precaution. If they had been disposed to conform themselves to the rule of immutable righteousness, government would not have been requisite. It was because one part exercised fraud, oppression, and violence on the other, that men came together, and agreed that certain rules should be formed, to regulate the conduct of all, and the power of the whole community lodged in the hands of rulers to enforce an obedience to them. But rulers have the same propensities as other men; they are as likely to use the power with which they are vested for private purposes, and to the injury and oppression of those over whom they are placed, as individuals in a state of nature are to injure and oppress one another. It is therefore as proper that bounds should be set to their authority, as that government should have at first been instituted to restrain private injuries.

This principle, which seems so evidently founded in the reason and nature of things, is confirmed by universal experience. Those who have governed, have been found in all ages ever active to enlarge their powers and abridge the public liberty. This has induced the people in all countries, where any sense of freedom remained, to fix barriers against the encroachments of their rulers. The country from which we have derived our origin, is an eminent example of this. Their magna charta and bill of rights have long been the boast, as well as the security, of that nation. I need say no more, I presume, to an American, than, that this principle is a fundamental one, in all the constitutions of our own states; there is not one of them but what is either founded on a declaration or bill of rights, or has certain express reservation of rights interwoven in the body of them. From this it appears, that at a time when the pulse of liberty beat high and when an appeal was made to the people to form constitutions for the government of themselves, it was their universal sense, that such declarations should make a part of their frames of government. It is therefore the more astonishing, that this grand security, to the rights of the people, is not to be found in this constitution.

> Even though Britain did not have a single written constitution that could be changed by ordinary legislative means, Brutus pointed to key documents in both British and American history that were designed to secure individual rights. Brutus further drew from the experiences of the states to argue for the necessity of a bill, or declaration, of rights.

It has been said, in answer to this objection, that such declaration[s] of rights, however requisite they might be in the constitutions of the states, are not necessary in the

> Brutus was clearly responding to the arguments of James Wilson and other defenders of the Constitution, who had argued that the national government would only be able to exercise enumerated powers. Here, Brutus expresses his belief in the need for additional security.

Brutus Issues His Anti-Federalist Essay

> *"The powers, rights, and authority, granted to the general government by this constitution, are as complete, with respect to every object to which they extend, as that of any state government—It reaches to every thing which concerns human happiness—Life, liberty, and property, are under its controul. There is the same reason, therefore, that the exercise of power, in this case, should be restrained within proper limits, as in that of the state governments."*

Most of the specific protections that Brutus sought were already found in state bills, or declarations, of rights and were eventually incorporated into the Fourth through Eighth Amendments to the U.S. Constitution.

general constitution, because, "in the former case, every thing which is not reserved is given, but in the latter the reverse of the proposition prevails, and every thing which is not given is reserved." It requires but little attention to discover, that this mode of reasoning is rather specious than solid. The powers, rights, and authority, granted to the general government by this constitution, are as complete, with respect to every object to which they extend, as that of any state government—It reaches to every thing which concerns human happiness—Life, liberty, and property, are under its controul. There is the same reason, therefore, that the exercise of power, in this case, should be restrained within proper limits, as in that of the state governments. To set this matter in a clear light, permit me to instance some of the articles of the bills of rights of the individual states, and apply them to the case in question.

For the security of life, in criminal prosecutions, the bills of rights of most of the states have declared, that no man shall be held to answer for a crime until he is made fully acquainted with the charge brought against him; he shall not be compelled to accuse, or furnish evidence against himself—The witnesses against him shall be brought face to face, and he shall be fully heard by himself or counsel. That it is essential to the security of life and liberty, that trial of facts be in the vicinity where they happen.

Are not provisions of this kind as necessary in the general government, as in that of a particular state? The powers vested in the new Congress extend in many cases to life; they are authorised to provide for the punishment of a variety of capital crimes, and no restraint is laid upon them in its exercise, save only, that "the trial of all crimes, except in cases of impeachment, shall be by jury; and such trial shall be in the state where the said crimes shall have been committed." No man is secure of a trial in the county where he is charged to have committed a crime; he may be brought from Niagara to New-York, or carried from Kentucky to Richmond for trial for an offence, supposed to be committed. What security is there, that a man shall be furnished with a full and plain description of the charges against him? That he shall be allowed to produce all proof he can in his favor? That he shall see the witnesses against him face to face, or that he shall be fully heard in his own defence by himself or counsel?

For the security of liberty it has been declared, "that excessive bail should not be required, nor excessive fines imposed, nor cruel or unusual punishments inflicted—That all warrants, without oath or affirmation, to search suspected places, or seize any person, his papers or property, are grievous and oppressive."

These provisions are as necessary under the general government as under that of the individual states; for the power of the former is as complete to the purpose of requiring bail. imposing fines, inflicting punishments, granting search warrants, and seizing persons, papers, or property, in certain cases, as the other.

"These provisions are as necessary under the general government as under that of the individual states . . ."

For the purpose of securing the property of the citizens, it is declared by all the states, "that in all controversies at law, respecting property, the ancient mode of trial by jury is one of the best securities of the rights of the people, and ought to remain sacred and inviolable."

Does not the same necessity exist of reserving this right, under this national compact, as in that of these states? Yet nothing is said respecting it. In the bills of rights of the states it is declared, that a well regulated militia is the

Although the U.S. Bill of Rights did not include a prohibition of standing armies, it did provide in the Second Amendment for further protections for state militia.

proper and natural defence of a free government—That as standing armies in time of peace are dangerous, they are not to be kept up, and that the military should be kept under strict subordination to, and controuled by the civil power.

The same security is as necessary in this constitution, and much more so; for the general government will have the sole power to raise and to pay armies, and are under no controul in the exercise of it; yet nothing of this is to be found in this new system.

> Brutus discovered another hole in the Federalist arguments. Although they had argued that no such bill was necessary, they had included a limited number of such rights in Article I, Sections 9 and 10. If they thought them to be appropriate there, why not provide additional rights within a bill of rights?

I might proceed to instance a number of other rights, which were as necessary to be reserved, such as, that elections should be free, that the liberty of the press should be held sacred; but the instances adduced, are sufficient to prove, that this argument is without foundation.—Besides, it is evident, that the reason here assigned was not the true one, why the framers of this constitution omitted a bill of rights; if it had been, they would not have made certain reservations, while they totally omitted others of more importance. We find they have, in the 9th section of the 1st article, declared, that the writ of habeas corpus shall not be suspended, unless in cases of rebellion—that no bill of attainder, or expost facto law, shall be passed—that no title of nobility shall be granted by the United States, &c. If every thing which is not given is reserved, what propriety is there in these exceptions? Does this constitution any where grant the power of suspending the habeas corpus, to make expost facto laws, pass bills of attainder, or grant titles of nobility? It certainly does not in express terms. The only answer that can be given is, that these are implied in the general powers granted. With equal truth it may be said, that all the powers, which the bills of right, guard against the abuse of,

are contained or implied in the general ones granted by this constitution.

So far it is from being true, that a bill of rights is less necessary in the general constitution than in those of the states, the contrary is evidently the fact.—This system, if it is possible for the people of America to accede to it, will be an original compact: and being the last, will, in the nature of things, vacate every former agreement inconsistent with it. For it being a plan of government received and ratified by the whole people, all other forms, which are in existence at the time of its adoption, must yield to it. This is expressed in positive and unequivocal terms, in the 6th article, "That this constitution and the laws of the United States, which shall be made in pursuance thereof, and all treaties made, or which shall be made, under the authority of the United States, shall be the supreme law of the land; and the judges in every state shall be bound thereby, any thing in the constitution, or laws of any state, to the contrary notwithstanding.

"The senators and representatives before-mentioned, and the members of the several state legislatures, and all executive and judicial officers, both of the United States, and of the several states, shall be bound, by oath or affirmation, to support this constitution."

It is therefore not only necessarily implied thereby, but positively expressed. that the different state constitutions are repealed and entirely done away. so far as they are inconsistent with this, with the laws which shall be made in pursuance thereof, or with treaties made. or which shall be made, under the authority of the United States; of what avail will the constitutions of the respective states be to preserve the rights of its citizens? should they be plead, the answer would

> *"This system, if it is possible for the people of America to accede to it, will be an original compact: and being the last, will, in the nature of things, vacate every former agreement inconsistent with it."*

be. the constitution of the United States, and the laws made in pursuance thereof, is the supreme law, and all legislatures and judicial officers, whether of the general or state governments, are bound by oath to support it. No priviledge, reserved by the bills of rights, or secured by the state government, can limit the power granted by this, or restrain any laws made in pursuance of it. It stands therefore on its own bottom, and must receive a construction by itself without any reference to any other—And hence it was of the highest importance, that the most precise and express declarations and reservations of rights should have been made.

> Brutus's concern that the supremacy clause in Article VI of the Constitution could be used to adopt a treaty that would negate constitutional protections was resurrected at other times in American history. For example, it was one of the driving forces in the 1950s behind the so-called Bricker Amendment, which was specifically crafted to limit this power.

This will appear the more necessary, when it is considered, that not only the constitution and laws made in pursuance thereof, but all treaties made, or which shall be made, under the authority of the United States, are the supreme law of the land, and supersede the constitutions of all the states. The power to make treaties, is vested in the president, by and with the advice and consent of two thirds of the senate. I do not find any limitation, or restriction, to the exercise of this power. The most important article in any constitution may therefore be repealed, even without a legislative act. Ought not a government, vested with such extensive and indefinite authority to have been restricted by a declaration of rights? It certainly ought.

So clear a point is this, that I cannot help suspecting, that persons who attempt to persuade people, that such reservations were less necessary under this constitution than under those of the states, are wilfully endeavouring to deceive, and to lead you into an absolute state of vassalage.

Source: Brutus. "To the Citizens of the State of New-York." November 1, 1787. *Debates and Proceedings in the Convention of the Commonwealth of Massachusetts, Held in the Year 1788.* Boston: William White, 1856, pp. 378–384.

The Mischiefs of Faction
Federalist Papers, No. 10 & No. 51
1787–1788

INTRODUCTION

Although there were hundreds of essays published in defense of, and in opposition to, the proposed Constitution, few such writings are better remembered than *The Federalist*. This collection of 85 essays was originally published in New York newspapers in 1787–1788 and subsequently published in book form. This work, which is often assigned in introductory American government classes today, was published under the pen name of Publius. In reality, it was the joint work of Alexander Hamilton, James Madison, and John Jay. Jay wrote only a few of the pieces, chiefly dealing with foreign affairs. Hamilton was the most prolific contributor, but it is Madison who is often considered to have made the most profound contributions to the collection.

Madison wrote Federalist No. 10 to combat the idea, propounded most prominently by the Baron of Montesquieu (with whom delegates agreed on the need for separation of powers), that democratic government was only possible within a small nation. Madison presented the argument that democracy, at least the representative version, could thrive even on a vast continent like America. The argument could also be used for still further territorial expansion.

Madison's Federalist No. 51 concerned the distribution of power among the three branches of government. Whereas most of the power that was given to national authorities (and it was not much) under the Articles of Confederation was concentrated in Congress, the new Constitution divided powers among national legislative, executive, and judicial branches. Some undoubtedly thought such a division was unnecessary, while others thought it did not extend far enough. Madison sought to steer a middle course in defending the route taken by the Constitution.

The Federalist No. 10

The Same Subject Continued: The Union as a Safeguard Against Domestic Faction and Insurrection

AMONG the numerous advantages promised by a well constructed Union, none deserves to be more accurately developed than its tendency to break and control the violence of

> *"The instability, injustice, and confusion introduced into the public councils, have, in truth, been the mortal diseases under which popular governments have everywhere perished; as they continue to be the favorite and fruitful topics from which the adversaries to liberty derive their most specious declamations."*

faction. The friend of popular governments never finds himself so much alarmed for their character and fate, as when he contemplates their propensity to this dangerous vice. He will not fail, therefore, to set a due value on any plan which, without violating the principles to which he is attached, provides a proper cure for it. The instability, injustice, and confusion introduced into the public councils, have, in truth, been the mortal diseases under which popular governments have everywhere perished; as they continue to be the favorite and fruitful topics from which the adversaries to liberty derive their most specious declamations. The valuable improvements made by the American constitutions on the popular models, both ancient and modern, cannot certainly be too much admired; but it would be an unwarrantable partiality, to contend that they have as effectually obviated the danger on this side, as was wished and expected. Complaints are everywhere heard from our most considerate and virtuous citizens, equally the friends of public and private faith, and of public and personal liberty, that our governments are too unstable, that the public good is disregarded in the conflicts of rival parties, and that measures are too often decided, not according to the rules of justice and the rights of the minor party, but by the superior force of an interested and overbearing majority. However anxiously we may wish that these complaints had no foundation, the evidence, of known facts will not permit us to deny that they are in some degree true. It will be found, indeed, on a candid review of our situation, that some of the distresses under which we labor have been erroneously charged on the operation of our governments; but it will be found, at the same time, that other causes will not alone account for many of our heaviest misfortunes; and, particularly, for that prevailing and increasing distrust of public engagements, and alarm for private rights, which are echoed from one end of the continent to the other. These must be chiefly, if not wholly, effects of the unsteadiness and injustice with which a factious spirit has tainted our public administrations.

By a faction, I understand a number of citizens, whether amounting to a majority or a minority of the whole, who are united and actuated by some common impulse of passion, or of interest, adverse to the rights of other citizens, or to the permanent and aggregate interests of the community.

> Madison identified the chief problem with government as that of controlling factions, or what modern thinkers might be more likely to refer to as interest groups or parties. Madison recognized that even a majority can have interests that are adverse to the common good, or what he calls the "aggregate interests of the community." This means that democratic institutions alone might be inadequate to protecting the public.

There are two methods of curing the mischiefs of faction: the one, by removing its causes; the other, by controlling its effects.

There are again two methods of removing the causes of faction: the one, by destroying the liberty which is essential to its existence; the other, by giving to every citizen the same opinions, the same passions, and the same interests.

It could never be more truly said than of the first remedy, that it was worse than the disease. Liberty is to faction what air is to fire, an aliment without which it instantly expires. But it could not be less folly to abolish liberty, which is essential to political life, because it nourishes faction, than it would be to wish the annihilation of air, which is essential to animal life, because it imparts to fire its destructive agency.

> True to the framers' desire to secure the "blessings of liberty," Madison emphatically rejected the idea of suppressing liberty in order to combat faction. In his mind this would have been equivalent to burning down a barn to roast the pigs.

The second expedient is as impracticable as the first would be unwise. As long as the reason of man continues fallible, and he is at liberty to exercise it, different opinions will be formed. As long as the connection subsists between his reason and his self-love, his opinions and his passions will have a reciprocal influence on each other; and the former will be objects to which the latter will attach themselves. The

"As long as the connection subsists between his reason and his self-love, his opinions and his passions will have a reciprocal influence on each other; and the former will be objects to which the latter will attach themselves."

Madison traced differences of opinion, and the factions that result from them, to human nature. Long before Karl Marx pointed to the influence of property on public opinion, Madison believed that differing types and degrees of property were especially likely to lead to political differences. But, unlike Marx, he did not think that it was therefore necessary to destroy private property.

"But the most common and durable source of factions has been the various and unequal distribution of property. Those who hold and those who are without property have ever formed distinct interests in society. Those who are creditors, and those who are debtors, fall under a like discrimination."

diversity in the faculties of men, from which the rights of property originate, is not less an insuperable obstacle to a uniformity of interests. The protection of these faculties is the first object of government. From the protection of different and unequal faculties of acquiring property, the possession of different degrees and kinds of property immediately results; and from the influence of these on the sentiments and views of the respective proprietors, ensues a division of the society into different interests and parties.

The latent causes of faction are thus sown in the nature of man; and we see them everywhere brought into different degrees of activity, according to the different circumstances of civil society. A zeal for different opinions concerning religion, concerning government, and many other points, as well of speculation as of practice; an attachment to different leaders ambitiously contending for pre-eminence and power; or to persons of other descriptions whose fortunes have been interesting to the human passions, have, in turn, divided mankind into parties, inflamed them with mutual animosity, and rendered them much more disposed to vex and oppress each other than to co-operate for their common good. So strong is this propensity of mankind to fall into mutual animosities, that where no substantial occasion presents itself, the most frivolous and fanciful distinctions have been sufficient to kindle their unfriendly passions and excite their most violent conflicts. But the most common and durable source of factions has been the various and unequal distribution of property. Those who hold and those who are without property have ever formed distinct interests in society. Those who are creditors, and those who are debtors, fall under a like discrimination. A landed interest, a manufacturing interest, a mercantile interest, a moneyed interest, with many lesser interests,

grow up of necessity in civilized nations, and divide them into different classes, actuated by different sentiments and views. The regulation of these various and interfering interests forms the principal task of modern legislation, and involves the spirit of party and faction in the necessary and ordinary operations of the government.

No man is allowed to be a judge in his own cause, because his interest would certainly bias his judgment, and, not improbably, corrupt his integrity. With equal, nay with greater reason, a body of men are unfit to be both judges and parties at the same time; yet what are many of the most important acts of legislation, but so many judicial determinations, not indeed concerning the rights of single persons, but concerning the rights of large bodies of citizens? And what are the different classes of legislators but advocates and parties to the causes which they determine? Is a law proposed concerning private debts? It is a question to which the creditors are parties on one side and the debtors on the other. Justice ought to hold the balance between them. Yet the parties are, and must be, themselves the judges; and the most numerous party, or, in other words, the most powerful faction must be expected to prevail. Shall domestic manufactures be encouraged, and in what degree, by restrictions on foreign manufactures? are questions which would be differently decided by the landed and the manufacturing classes, and probably by neither with a sole regard to justice and the public good. The apportionment of taxes on the various descriptions of property is an act which seems to require the most exact impartiality; yet there is, perhaps, no legislative act in which greater opportunity and temptation are given to a predominant party to trample on the rules of justice. Every shilling with which they overburden the inferior number, is a shilling saved to their own pockets.

"And what are the different classes of legislators but advocates and parties to the causes which they determine?"

> In referring to "enlightened statesmen," Madison was likely thinking of individuals, like himself, who had spent most of the summer at the Constitutional Convention in Philadelphia. He argued that controlling factions would require more than simply electing the right individuals to office.

It is in vain to say that enlightened statesmen will be able to adjust these clashing interests, and render them all subservient to the public good. Enlightened statesmen will not always be at the helm. Nor, in many cases, can such an adjustment be made at all without taking into view indirect and remote considerations, which will rarely prevail over the immediate interest which one party may find in disregarding the rights of another or the good of the whole.

The inference to which we are brought is, that the CAUSES of faction cannot be removed, and that relief is only to be sought in the means of controlling its EFFECTS.

> Madison argued that democratic rule will take care of minority factions, but he recognized that it was also necessary to take precaution against majority factions as well.

If a faction consists of less than a majority, relief is supplied by the republican principle, which enables the majority to defeat its sinister views by regular vote. It may clog the administration, it may convulse the society; but it will be unable to execute and mask its violence under the forms of the Constitution. When a majority is included in a faction, the form of popular government, on the other hand, enables it to sacrifice to its ruling passion or interest both the public good and the rights of other citizens. To secure the public good and private rights against the danger of such a faction, and at the same time to preserve the spirit and the form of popular government, is then the great object to which our inquiries are directed. Let me add that it is the great desideratum by which this form of government can be rescued from the opprobrium under which it has so long labored, and be recommended to the esteem and adoption of mankind.

"To secure the public good and private rights against the danger of such a faction, and at the same time to preserve the spirit and the form of popular government, is then the great object to which our inquiries are directed."

By what means is this object attainable? Evidently by one of two only. Either the existence of the same passion or interest in a majority at the same time must be prevented, or the majority, having such coexistent passion or interest, must be rendered, by their number and local situation, unable to concert and carry into effect schemes of oppression. If the impulse and the opportunity be suffered to coincide, we well know that neither moral nor religious motives can be relied on as an adequate control. They are not found to be such on the injustice and violence of individuals, and lose their efficacy in proportion to the number combined together, that is, in proportion as their efficacy becomes needful.

From this view of the subject it may be concluded that a pure democracy, by which I mean a society consisting of a small number of citizens, who assemble and administer the government in person, can admit of no cure for the mischiefs of faction. A common passion or interest will, in almost every case, be felt by a majority of the whole; a communication and concert result from the form of government itself; and there is nothing to check the inducements to sacrifice the weaker party or an obnoxious individual. Hence it is that such democracies have ever been spectacles of turbulence and contention; have ever been found incompatible with personal security or the rights of property; and have in general been as short in their lives as they have been violent in their deaths. Theoretic politicians, who have patronized this species of government, have erroneously supposed that by reducing mankind to a perfect equality in their political rights, they would, at the same time, be perfectly equalized and assimilated in their possessions, their opinions, and their passions.

"From this view of the subject it may be concluded that a pure democracy, by which I mean a society consisting of a small number of citizens, who assemble and administer the government in person, can admit of no cure for the mischiefs of faction."

A republic, by which I mean a government in which the scheme of representation takes place, opens a different prospect, and promises the cure for which we are seeking. Let us examine the points in which it varies from pure democracy, and we shall comprehend both the nature of the cure and the efficacy which it must derive from the Union.

> The idea of democracy appears to have been born in small Greek city-states. Madison recognized that such cities were often torn by factional disputes, but he distinguished such "pure democracies" from modern republics, which are based on representative institutions covering larger districts.

The two great points of difference between a democracy and a republic are: first, the delegation of the government, in the latter, to a small number of citizens elected by the rest; secondly, the greater number of citizens, and greater sphere of country, over which the latter may be extended.

> Madison was essentially arguing that representatives can recognize and advance the best interests of the public better than the people can do in person.

The effect of the first difference is, on the one hand, to refine and enlarge the public views, by passing them through the medium of a chosen body of citizens, whose wisdom may best discern the true interest of their country, and whose patriotism and love of justice will be least likely to sacrifice it to temporary or partial considerations. Under such a regulation, it may well happen that the public voice, pronounced by the representatives of the people, will be more consonant to the public good than if pronounced by the people themselves, convened for the purpose. On the other hand, the effect may be inverted. Men of factious tempers, of local prejudices, or of sinister designs, may, by intrigue, by corruption, or by other means, first obtain the suffrages, and then betray the interests, of the people. The question resulting is, whether small or extensive republics are more favorable to the election of proper guardians of the public weal; and it is clearly decided in favor of the latter by two obvious considerations:

"Under such a regulation, it may well happen that the public voice, pronounced by the representatives of the people, will be more consonant to the public good than if pronounced by the people themselves, convened for the purpose."

In the first place, it is to be remarked that, however small the republic may be, the representatives must be raised to a certain number, in order to guard against the cabals of a few; and that, however large it may be, they must be limited to a certain number, in order to guard against the confusion of a multitude. Hence, the number of representatives in the two cases not being in proportion to that of the two constituents, and being proportionally greater in the small republic, it follows that, if the proportion of fit characters be not less in the large than in the small republic, the former will present a greater option, and consequently a greater probability of a fit choice.

In the next place, as each representative will be chosen by a greater number of citizens in the large than in the small republic, it will be more difficult for unworthy candidates to practice with success the vicious arts by which elections are too often carried; and the suffrages of the people being more free, will be more likely to centre in men who possess the most attractive merit and the most diffusive and established characters.

It must be confessed that in this, as in most other cases, there is a mean, on both sides of which inconveniences will be found to lie. By enlarging too much the number of electors, you render the representatives too little acquainted with all their local circumstances and lesser interests; as by reducing it too much, you render him unduly attached to these, and too little fit to comprehend and pursue great and national objects. The federal Constitution forms a happy combination in this respect; the great and aggregate interests being referred to the national, the local and particular to the State legislatures.

The other point of difference is, the greater number of citizens and extent of territory which may be brought within the compass of republican than of democratic

> *"[H]owever small the republic may be, the representatives must be raised to a certain number, in order to guard against the cabals of a few; and that, however large it may be, they must be limited to a certain number, in order to guard against the confusion of a multitude."*

This is the very heart of Madison's argument and his response to Montesquieu. Madison argues that the larger the nation, the more factions it will embrace, and the more factions it encompasses, the less likelihood there will be that any one will dominate. This suggests that Madison would have been quite comfortable with the expansion of the United States from 13 original states to 50.

government; and it is this circumstance principally which renders factious combinations less to be dreaded in the former than in the latter. The smaller the society, the fewer probably will be the distinct parties and interests composing it; the fewer the distinct parties and interests, the more frequently will a majority be found of the same party; and the smaller the number of individuals composing a majority, and the smaller the compass within which they are placed, the more easily will they concert and execute their plans of oppression. Extend the sphere, and you take in a greater variety of parties and interests; you make it less probable that a majority of the whole will have a common motive to invade the rights of other citizens; or if such a common motive exists, it will be more difficult for all who feel it to discover their own strength, and to act in unison with each other. Besides other impediments, it may be remarked that, where there is a consciousness of unjust or dishonorable purposes, communication is always checked by distrust in proportion to the number whose concurrence is necessary

"Hence, it clearly appears, that the same advantage which a republic has over a democracy, in controlling the effects of faction, is enjoyed by a large over a small republic,—is enjoyed by the Union over the States composing it."

Hence, it clearly appears, that the same advantage which a republic has over a democracy, in controlling the effects of faction, is enjoyed by a large over a small republic,—is enjoyed by the Union over the States composing it. Does the advantage consist in the substitution of representatives whose enlightened views and virtuous sentiments render them superior to local prejudices and schemes of injustice? It will not be denied that the representation of the Union will be most likely to possess these requisite endowments. Does it consist in the greater security afforded by a greater variety of parties, against the event of any one party being able to outnumber and oppress the rest? In an equal degree does the increased variety of parties comprised within the Union, increase this security. Does it, in fine, consist in the greater obstacles opposed to the concert and accomplishment of the secret wishes of an unjust and interested majority? Here, again, the extent of the Union gives it the most palpable advantage.

The influence of factious leaders may kindle a flame within their particular States, but will be unable to spread a general conflagration through the other States. A religious sect may degenerate into a political faction in a part of the Confederacy; but the variety of sects dispersed over the entire face of it must secure the national councils against any danger from that source. A rage for paper money, for an abolition of debts, for an equal division of property, or for any other improper or wicked project, will be less apt to pervade the whole body of the Union than a particular member of it; in the same proportion as such a malady is more likely to taint a particular county or district, than an entire State.

> *"The influence of factious leaders may kindle a flame within their particular States, but will be unable to spread a general conflagration through the other States."*

In the extent and proper structure of the Union, therefore, we behold a republican remedy for the diseases most incident to republican government. And according to the degree of pleasure and pride we feel in being republicans, ought to be our zeal in cherishing the spirit and supporting the character of Federalists.

> *"In the extent and proper structure of the Union, therefore, we behold a republican remedy for the diseases most incident to republican government."*

PUBLIUS.

The Federalist No. 51

The Structure of the Government Must Furnish the Proper Checks and Balances Between the Different Departments

TO WHAT expedient, then, shall we finally resort, for maintaining in practice the necessary partition of power among the several departments, as laid down in the Constitution? The only answer that can be given is, that as all

> The doctrine of separation of powers is often associated with that of checks and balances, which is, in turn, often employed in the area of international affairs. The framers aimed to design government so that it would work even when the wisest statesmen were not at the helm. One might further argue that the system is akin to free enterprise, which attempts to harness private desire for public good.

these exterior provisions are found to be inadequate, the defect must be supplied, by so contriving the interior structure of the government as that its several constituent parts may, by their mutual relations, be the means of keeping each other in their proper places. Without presuming to undertake a full development of this important idea, I will hazard a few general observations, which may perhaps place it in a clearer light, and enable us to form a more correct judgment of the principles and structure of the government planned by the convention.

> The Virginia Plan originally proposed that Congress would select the president, but because its authors feared that an executive would attempt to corrupt the legislature to gain re-election, it originally limited the executive to one term (a limit no longer needed when the Convention formulated an independent Electoral College). Madison lauded the Constitution for providing independent means of congressional and presidential election, but acknowledged that the system did not fully apply to members of the judiciary, who, because of the need for special expertise (which Hamilton stressed in Federalist No. 78), are appointed by the president with the "advice and consent" of the U.S. Senate.

In order to lay a due foundation for that separate and distinct exercise of the different powers of government, which to a certain extent is admitted on all hands to be essential to the preservation of liberty, it is evident that each department should have a will of its own; and consequently should be so constituted that the members of each should have as little agency as possible in the appointment of the members of the others. Were this principle rigorously adhered to, it would require that all the appointments for the supreme executive, legislative, and judiciary magistracies should be drawn from the same fountain of authority, the people, through channels having no communication whatever with one another. Perhaps such a plan of constructing the several departments would be less difficult in practice than it may in contemplation appear. Some difficulties, however, and some additional expense would attend the execution of it. Some deviations, therefore, from the principle must be admitted. In the constitution of the judiciary department in particular, it might be inexpedient to insist rigorously on the principle: first, because peculiar qualifications being essential in the members, the primary consideration ought to be to select that mode of choice which best

secures these qualifications; secondly, because the permanent tenure by which the appointments are held in that department, must soon destroy all sense of dependence on the authority conferring them.

It is equally evident, that the members of each department should be as little dependent as possible on those of the others, for the emoluments annexed to their offices. Were the executive magistrate, or the judges, not independent of the legislature in this particular, their independence in every other would be merely nominal. But the great security against a gradual concentration of the several powers in the same department, consists in giving to those who administer each department the necessary constitutional means and personal motives to resist encroachments of the others. The provision for defense must in this, as in all other cases, be made commensurate to the danger of attack. **Ambition must be made to counteract ambition. The interest of the man must be connected with the constitutional rights of the place. It may be a reflection on human nature, that such devices should be necessary to control the abuses of government. But what is government itself, but the greatest of all reflections on human nature? If men were angels, no government would be necessary. If angels were to govern men, neither external nor internal controls on government would be necessary. In framing a government which is to be administered by men over men, the great difficulty lies in this: you must first enable the government to control the governed; and in the next place oblige it to control itself.**

A dependence on the people is, no doubt, the primary control on the government; but experience has taught mankind the necessity of auxiliary precautions. This

> Whereas demagogues often flatter their constituents by praising their judgment, Madison presented a far dimmer view of the public by pointing out that they are not angels, and that government was needed not only to provide rules for the people but also to restrain the actions of elected leaders.

> Madison argued that, however valuable elections may be, they do not provide complete security for citizen liberties. Madison further argued that the legislative branch, likely to be the most powerful—and the first members of which were elected directly by the people—would need to be further checked. The framers did this by dividing it into two chambers, or houses (the principle of bicameralism). Although critics might argue that this contributes to unnecessary gridlock, Madison believed it to be essential to the preservation of liberty.

> *"[T]he constant aim is to divide and arrange the several offices in such a manner as that each may be a check on the other that the private interest of every individual may be a sentinel over the public rights."*

policy of supplying, by opposite and rival interests, the defect of better motives, might be traced through the whole system of human affairs, private as well as public. We see it particularly displayed in all the subordinate distributions of power, where the constant aim is to divide and arrange the several offices in such a manner as that each may be a check on the other that the private interest of every individual may be a sentinel over the public rights. These inventions of prudence cannot be less requisite in the distribution of the supreme powers of the State. But it is not possible to give to each department an equal power of self-defense. In republican government, the legislative authority necessarily predominates. The remedy for this inconveniency is to divide the legislature into different branches; and to render them, by different modes of election and different principles of action, as little connected with each other as the nature of their common functions and their common dependence on the society will admit. It may even be necessary to guard against dangerous encroachments by still further precautions. As the weight of the legislative authority requires that it should be thus divided, the weakness of the executive may require, on the other hand, that it should be fortified.

An absolute negative on the legislature appears, at first view, to be the natural defense with which the executive magistrate should be armed. But perhaps it would be neither altogether safe nor alone sufficient. On ordinary occasions it might not be exerted with the requisite firmness, and on extraordinary occasions it might be perfidiously abused. May not this defect of an absolute negative be supplied by some qualified connection between this weaker department and the weaker branch of the stronger department, by which the latter may be led to support the constitutional rights of the former, without being too much detached from the rights of its own department? If the principles on which these observations are founded be just, as I persuade myself they are, and they be applied as a criterion to the several State constitutions, and to the federal Constitution it will be found that if the latter does not perfectly correspond with them, the former are infinitely less able to bear such a test.

There are, moreover, two considerations particularly applicable to the federal system of America, which place that system in a very interesting point of view. First. In a single republic, all the power surrendered by the people is submitted to the administration of a single government; and the usurpations are guarded against by a division of the government into distinct and separate departments. In the compound republic of America, the power surrendered by the people is first divided between two distinct governments, and then the portion allotted to each subdivided among distinct and separate departments. Hence a double security arises to the rights of the people. The different governments will control each other, at the same time that each will be controlled by itself. Second. It is of great importance in a republic not only to guard the society against the oppression of its rulers, but to guard one part of the society against the injustice of the other part. Different interests necessarily exist in different classes of citizens. If a majority be united by a common interest, the rights of the minority will be insecure.

> In addition to dividing national powers among three branches, the Constitution also divides powers between the nation and the states in a system known as federalism. Madison argued that this system provided what he calls a "double security" for liberty.

There are but two methods of providing against this evil: the one by creating a will in the community independent of the majority that is, of the society itself; the other, by comprehending in the society so many separate descriptions of citizens as will render an unjust combination of a majority

> Madison returned to the theme of Federalist No. 10 by contrasting the installation of a hereditary monarch (which he considered inadequate) to guard the people with that of a territory so broad, with so many factions, that no faction would likely dominate to the disadvantage of others.

of the whole very improbable, if not impracticable. The first method prevails in all governments possessing an hereditary or self-appointed authority. This, at best, is but a precarious security; because a power independent of the society may as well espouse the unjust views of the major, as the rightful interests of the minor party, and may possibly be turned against both parties. The second method will be exemplified in the federal republic of the United States. Whilst all authority in it will be derived from and dependent on the society, the society itself will be broken into so many parts, interests, and classes of citizens, that the rights of individuals, or of the minority, will be in little danger from interested combinations of the majority.

In a free government the security for civil rights must be the same as that for religious rights. It consists in the one case in the multiplicity of interests, and in the other in the multiplicity of sects. The degree of security in both cases will depend on the number of interests and sects; and this may be presumed to depend on the extent of country and number of people comprehended under the same government. This view of the subject must particularly recommend a proper federal system to all the sincere and considerate friends of republican government, since it shows that in exact proportion as the territory of the Union may be formed into more circumscribed Confederacies, or States oppressive combinations of a majority will be facilitated: the best security, under the republican forms, for the rights of every class of citizens, will be diminished: and consequently the stability and independence of some member of the government, the only other security, must be proportionately increased. Justice is the end of government. It is the end of civil society. It ever has been and ever will be pursued until it be obtained, or until liberty be lost in the pursuit. In a society under the forms of which the stronger faction can readily unite and oppress the weaker,

> *"In a free government the security for civil rights must be the same as that for religious rights. It consists in the one case in the multiplicity of interests, and in the other in the multiplicity of sects."*

anarchy may as truly be said to reign as in a state of nature, where the weaker individual is not secured against the violence of the stronger; and as, in the latter state, even the stronger individuals are prompted, by the uncertainty of their condition, to submit to a government which may protect the weak as well as themselves; so, in the former state, will the more powerful factions or parties be gradually induced, by a like motive, to wish for a government which will protect all parties, the weaker as well as the more powerful.

It can be little doubted that if the State of Rhode Island was separated from the Confederacy and left to itself, the insecurity of rights under the popular form of government within such narrow limits would be displayed by such reiterated oppressions of factious majorities that some power altogether independent of the people would soon be called for by the voice of the very factions whose misrule had proved the necessity of it. In the extended republic of the United States, and among the great variety of interests, parties, and sects which it embraces, a coalition of a majority of the whole society could seldom take place on any other principles than those of justice and the general good; whilst there being thus less danger to a minor from the will of a major party, there must be less pretext, also, to provide for the security of the former, by introducing into the government a will not dependent on the latter, or, in other words, a will independent of the society itself. It is no less certain than it is important, notwithstanding the contrary opinions which have been entertained, that the larger the society, provided it lie within a practical sphere, the more duly capable it will be of self-government. And happily for the REPUBLICAN CAUSE, the practicable sphere may be carried to a very great extent, by a judicious modification and mixture of the FEDERAL PRINCIPLE.

The last paragraph provides a reminder that Rhode Island had not sent delegates to the Constitutional Convention. Madison argued that, as a smaller state, it was more likely than others to be dominated by a single faction or set of factions and that it would thus have even more to gain by joining. Article VII of the Constitution provided that it would go into effect when ratified by nine or more states, and neither Rhode Island or North Carolina ratified the document until it had already gone into effect among the others.

"[T]he larger the society, provided it lie within a practical sphere, the more duly capable it will be of self-government. And happily for the REPUBLICAN CAUSE, the practicable sphere may be carried to a very great extent, by a judicious modification and mixture of the FEDERAL PRINCIPLE"

PUBLIUS.

Sources:

James Madison. Federalist No. 10: "The Same Subject Continued: The Union as a Safeguard Against Domestic Faction and Insurrection." *New York Daily Advertiser,* November 22, 1787.

Alexander Hamilton or James Madison. Federalist No. 51: "The Structure of the Government Must Furnish the Proper Checks and Balances Between the Different Departments." *New York Packet,* February 8, 1788.

The Tyranny of Rulers

Patrick Henry's Speech at Virginia's Ratifying Convention

June 5, 1788

> **INTRODUCTION**
>
> However important Federalist and Anti-Federalist writings may have been in persuading the American people to support or oppose the new Constitution, the fight for ratification was ultimately won during the debates at the state ratifying conventions. No state was more important to ratification than that of Virginia, the most populous state, and no foe of ratification was more formidable than Patrick Henry. One of the "firebrands" of the Revolution (he had delivered the famous "Give Me Liberty or Give Me Death" speech at St. John's Church in Richmond on March 23, 1775), Henry was a staunch supporter of states' rights. It is doubtful that anyone was able to match his oratory, but in time delegates like James Madison and John Marshall refuted his arguments with systematic article-by-article defenses of the Constitution.

Mr. HENRY. Mr. Chairman, I am much obliged to the very worthy gentleman for his encomium. I wish I was possessed with talents, or possessed of any thing that might enable me to elucidate this great subject. I am not free from suspicion: I am apt to entertain doubts. I rose yesterday to ask a question which arose in my own mind. When I asked that question, I thought the meaning of my interrogation was obvious. **The fate of this question and of America may depend on this. Have they said, We, the states? Have they made a proposal of a compact between states? If they had, this would be a confederation. It is otherwise most clearly a consolidated government. The question turns, sir, on that poor little thing—the expression, We, the *people*, instead of the *states*, of America. I need not take much pains to show that the principles of this system are extremely pernicious, impolitic, and dangerous.**

> The federal system created by the new Constitution was truly something new under the sun. Contemporaries were familiar with unitary (what Henry called "consolidated") governments, like those of England and France, and with confederations, like that under the Articles, but not with federal governments in which both national and state governments had the power to act directly on the individual. Henry tapped into the fear of novelty and questioned the authority of convention delegates to speak on behalf of the people rather than on behalf of the states.

Patrick Henry's Speech at Virginia's Ratifying Convention

> *"It is radical in this transition; our rights and privileges are endangered, and the sovereignty of the states will be relinquished: and cannot we plainly see that this is actually the case? The rights of conscience, trial by jury, liberty of the press, all your immunities and franchises, all pretensions to human rights and privileges, are rendered insecure, if not lost, by this change, so loudly talked of by some, and inconsiderately by others."*

Is this a monarchy, like England—a compact between prince and people, with checks on the former to secure the liberty of the latter? Is this a confederacy, like Holland—an association of a number of independent states, each of which retains its individual sovereignty? It is not a democracy, wherein the people retain all their rights securely. Had these principles been adhered to, we should not have been brought to this alarming transition, from a confederacy to a consolidated government. We have no detail of these great consideration, which, in my opinion, ought to have abounded before we should recur to a government of this kind. Here is a resolution as radical as that which separated us from Great Britain. It is radical in this transition; our rights and privileges are endangered, and the sovereignty of the states will be relinquished: and cannot we plainly see that this is actually the case? The rights of conscience, trial by jury, liberty of the press, all your immunities and franchises, all pretensions to human rights and privileges, are rendered insecure, if not lost, by this change, so loudly talked of by some, and inconsiderately by others. Is this tame relinquishment of rights worthy of freemen? Is it worthy of that manly fortitude that ought to characterize republicans? It is said eight states have adopted this plan. I declare that if twelve states and a half had adopted it, I would, with manly firmness, and in spite of an erring world, reject it. You are not to inquire how your trade may be increased, nor how you are to become a great and powerful people, but how your liberties can be secured; for liberty ought to be the direct end of your government.

Having premised these things, I shall, with the aid of my judgment and information, which, I confess, are not extensive, go into the discussion of this system more minutely. **Is it necessary for your liberty that you should abandon those great rights by the adoption of this system? Is the relinquishment of the trial by jury and the liberty of the**

Much like other Anti-Federalists and counter to the arguments of James Wilson, Henry concluded that liberties that were not listed would be forfeited.

press necessary for your liberty? Will the abandonment of your most sacred rights tend to the security of your liberty? Liberty, the greatest of all earthly blessing—give us that precious jewel, and you may take every thing else!

But I am fearful I have lived long enough to become an old-fashioned fellow. Perhaps an invincible attachment to the dearest rights of man may, in these refined, enlightened days, be deemed old-fashioned; if so, I am contented to be so. I say, the time has been when every pulse of my heart beat for American liberty, and which, I believe, had a counterpart in the breast of every true American; but suspicions have gone forth—suspicions of my integrity—publicly reported that my professions are not real. Twenty-three years ago was I supposed a traitor to my country? I was then said to be the bane of sedition, because I supported the rights of my country. I may be thought suspicious when I say our privileges and rights are in danger. But, sir, a number of the people of this country are weak enough to think these things are too true. I am happy to find that the gentleman on the other side declares they are groundless. But, sir, suspicion is a virtue as long as its object is the preservation of the public good, and as long as it stays within proper bounds: should it fall on me, I am contented: conscious rectitude is a powerful consolation. I trust there are many who think my professions for the public good to be real. Let your suspicion look to both sides. There are many on the other side, who possibly may have been persuaded to the necessity of these measures, which I conceive to be dangerous to your liberty. Guard with jealous attention the public liberty. Suspect every one who approaches that jewel. Unfortunately, nothing will preserve it but downright force. Whenever you give up that force, you are inevitably ruined. I am answered by gentlemen, that, though I might speak of terrors, yet the fact was, that we were surrounded by none of the dangers I apprehended. I conceive this new

"Twenty-three years ago was I supposed a traitor to my country? I was then said to be the bane of sedition, because I supported the rights of my country. I may be thought suspicious when I say our privileges and rights are in danger. But, sir, a number of the people of this country are weak enough to think these things are too true."

> Henry recognized the achievements under the Articles and was unwilling to consider its government to be a failure. Moreover, he feared that the move to replace it would undermine civil rights and liberties.

government to be one of those dangers: it has produced those horrors which distress many of our best citizens. We are come hither to preserve the poor commonwealth of Virginia, if it can be possibly done: something must be done to preserve your liberty and mine. **The Confederation, this same despised government, merits, in my opinion, the highest encomium: it carried us through a long and dangerous war; it rendered us victorious in that bloody conflict with a powerful nation; it has secured us a territory greater than any European monarch possesses: and shall a government which has been thus strong and vigorous, be accused of imbecility, and abandoned for want of energy? Consider what you are about to do before you part with the government. Take longer time in reckoning things; revolutions like this have happened in almost every country in Europe; similar examples are to be found in ancient Greece and ancient Rome—instances of the people losing their liberty by their own carelessness and the ambition of a few. We are cautioned by the honorable gentleman, who presides, against faction and turbulence. I acknowledge that licentiousness is dangerous, and that it ought to be provided against: I acknowledge, also, the new form of government may effectually prevent it: yet there is another thing it will as effectually do—it will oppress and ruin the people.**

There are sufficient guards placed against sedition and licentiousness; for, when power is given to this government to suppress these, or for any other purpose, the language it assumes is clear, express, and unequivocal; but when this Constitution speaks of privileges, there is an ambiguity, sir, a fatal ambiguity—an ambiguity which is very astonishing. In the clause under consideration, there is the strangest language that I can conceive. I mean, when it says that there shall not be more representatives than one for every thirty thousand. Now, sir, how easy is it to evade this privilege! "The number shall not exceed one for every thirty thousand." This may be satisfied by one representative from each state. Let our numbers be ever so great, this immense continent may, by this artful expression, be reduced to have but thirteen representatives. I confess this construction is not natural; but the ambiguity of the expression lays a good ground for a quarrel. Why was it not clearly and unequivocally expressed, that they should be entitled to have one for every thirty thousand? This would have obviated all disputes; and was this difficult to be done? What is the inference? When population increases, and a state shall send representatives in this proportion, Congress may remand them, because the right of having one for every thirty thousand is not clearly expressed. This possibility of reducing the number to one for each state approximates to probability by that other expression—"but each state shall at least have one representative." Now, is it not clear that, from the first expression, the number might be reduced so much that some states should have no representatives at all, were it not for the insertion of this last expression? And as this is the only restriction upon them, we may fairly conclude that they may restrain the number to one from each state. Perhaps the same horrors may hang over my mind again. I shall be told I am continually afraid: but, sir, I have strong cause of apprehension. In some parts of the plan before you, the great rights of freemen are endangered; in other parts, absolutely taken away. How does your trial by jury stand? In civil cases gone—not sufficiently secured in criminal—this best privilege is gone. But we are told that we need not fear; because those in power, being our representatives, will not abuse the powers we put in their hands. **I am not well versed in history, but I will submit to your recollection, whether liberty has been destroyed most often by the licentiousness of the people, or by the tyranny of rulers.**

Whereas Madison and other defenders of the Constitution emphasized the weakness of the government and how it was torn by faction, Henry was more concerned about the dangers of entrusting governments with additional powers. The authors of the Constitution had, of course, attempted to guard against this by separating and dividing powers. The term "licentiousness" is a reference to lack of moral restraint, particularly with regard to sexual matters.

Patrick Henry's Speech at Virginia's Ratifying Convention

> "My great objection to this government is, that it does not leave us the means of defending our rights, or of waging war against tyrants."

I imagine, sir, you will find the balance on the side of tyranny. Happy will you be if you miss the fate of those nations, who, omitting to resist their oppressors, or negligently suffering their liberty to be wrested from them, have groaned under intolerable despotism! Most of the human race are now in this deplorable condition; and those nations who have gone in search of grandeur, power, and splendor, have also fallen a sacrifice, and been the victims of their own folly. While they acquired those visionary blessings, they lost their freedom. My great objection to this government is, that it does not leave us the means of defending our rights, or of waging war against tyrants. It is urged by some gentlemen, that this new plan will bring us an acquisition of strength—an army, and the militia of the states. This is an idea extremely ridiculous: gentlemen cannot be earnest. This acquisition will trample on our fallen liberty. Let my beloved Americans guard against that fatal lethargy that has pervaded the universe. Have we the means of resisting disciplined armies, when our only defence, the militia, is put into the hands of Congress? The honorable gentleman said that great danger would ensue if the Convention rose without adopting this system. I ask, Where is that danger? I see none. Other gentlemen have told us, within these walls, that the union is gone, or that the union will be gone. Is not this trifling with the judgment of their fellow-citizens? Till they tell us the grounds of their fears, I will consider them as imaginary. I rose to make inquiry where those dangers were; they could make no answer: I believe I never shall have that answer. Is there a disposition in the people of this country to revolt against the dominion of laws? Has there been a single tumult in Virginia? Have not the people of Virginia, when laboring under the severest pressure of accumulated distresses, manifested the most cordial acquiescence in the execution of the laws? **What could be more awful than their unanimous acquiescence under general distresses? Is there any revolution in Virginia? Whither is**

Whereas defenders of the Constitution portrayed it as the fruition of the Revolution, Henry feared that it was its betrayal.

the spirit of America gone? Whither is the genius of America fled? It was but yesterday, when our enemies marched in triumph through our country. Yet the people of this country could not be appalled by their pompous armaments: they stopped their carer, and victoriously captured them. Where is the peril, now, compared to that? Some minds are agitated by foreign alarms. Happily for us, there is no real danger from Europe; that country is engaged in more arduous business: from that quarter there is no cause of fear: you may sleep in safety forever for them.

Where is the danger? If, sir, there was any, I would recur to the American spirit to defend us; that spirit which has enabled us to surmount the greatest difficulties: to that illustrious spirit I address my most fervent prayer to prevent our adopting a system destructive to liberty. Let not gentlemen be told that it is not safe to reject this government. Wherefore is it not safe? We are told there are dangers, but those dangers are ideal; they cannot be demonstrated. To encourage us to adopt it, they tell us that there is a plain, easy way of getting amendments. When I come to contemplate this part, I suppose that I am mad, or that my countrymen are so. The way to amendment is, in my conception, shut. Let us consider this plain, easy way. "The Congress, whenever two thirds of both houses shall deem it necessary, shall propose amendments to this Constitution, or, on the application of the legislatures of two thirds of the several states, shall call a Convention for proposing amendments, which, in either case, shall be valid to all intents and purposes, as part of this Constitution, when ratified by the legislatures of three fourths of the several states, or by the Conventions in three fourths thereof, as the one or the other mode of ratification may be proposed by the Congress. Provided, that no amendment which may be made prior to the year 1808, shall in any manner affect the 1st and

"Let not gentlemen be told that it is not safe to reject this government. Wherefore is it not safe? We are told there are dangers, but those dangers are ideal; they cannot be demonstrated."

4th clauses in the 9th section of the 1st article; and that no state, without its consent, shall be deprived of its equal suffrage in the Senate."

Hence it appears that three fourths of the states must ultimately agree to any amendments that may be necessary. Let us consider the consequence of this. However uncharitable it may appear, yet I must tell my opinion—that the most unworthy characters may get into power, and prevent the introduction of amendments. Let us suppose—for the case is supposable, possible, and probable—that you happen to deal those powers to unworthy hands; will they relinquish powers already in their possession, or agree to amendments? Two thirds of the Congress, or of the state legislatures, are necessary even to propose amendments. If one third of these be unworthy men, they may prevent the application for amendments; but what is destructive and mischievous, is, that three fourths of the state legislatures, or of the state conventions, must concur in the amendments when proposed! In such numerous bodies, there must necessarily be some designing, bad men. To suppose that so large a number as three fourths of the states will concur, is to suppose that they will possess genius, intelligence, and integrity, approaching to miraculous. It would indeed be miraculous that they should concur in the same amendments, or even in such as would bear some likeness to one another; for four of the smallest states, that do not collectively contain one tenth part of the population of the United States, may obstruct the most salutary and necessary amendments. **Nay, in these four states, six tenths of the people may reject these amendments; and suppose that amendments shall be opposed to amendments, which is highly probable,—is it possible that three fourths can ever agree to the same amendments? A bare majority in these four small states may hinder the adoption of amendments; so that we may fairly and justly conclude that one**

> Whereas Federalists argued that governmental defects could be remedied by amendments, Henry suggested that the process would be too difficult. What Henry failed to mention was that allowing one fourth of the states to block additional changes was consistent with his own support for states' rights. Moreover, the new document would be much easier to amend than the existing Articles, which required unanimous state consent.

twentieth part of the American people may prevent the removal of the most grievous inconveniences and oppression, by refusing to accede to amendments. A trifling minority may reject the most salutary amendments. Is this an easy mode of securing the public liberty? It is, sir, a most fearful situation, when the most contemptible minority can prevent the alteration of the most oppressive government; for it may, in many respects, prove to be such. Is this the spirit of republicanism?

What, sir, is the genius of democracy? Let me read that clause of the bill of rights of Virginia which relates to this: 3d clause:—that government is, or ought to be, instituted for the common benefit, protection, and security of the people, nation, or community. Of all the various modes and forms of government, that is best, which is capable of producing the greatest degree of happiness and safety, and is most effectually secured against the danger of mal-administration; and that whenever any government shall be found inadequate, or contrary to those purposes, a majority of the community hath an indubitable, unalienable, and indefeasible right to reform, alter, or abolish it, in such manner as shall be judged most conducive to the public weal. . . .

A standing army we shall have, also, to execute the execrable commands of tyranny; and how are you to punish them? Will you order them to be punished? Who shall obey these orders? Will your mace-bearer be a match for a disciplined regiment? In what situation are we to be? The clause before you gives a power of direct taxation, unbounded and unlimited, exclusive power of legislation, in all cases whatsoever, for ten miles square, and over all places purchased for the erection of forts, magazines, arsenals, dockyards, &c. What resistance could be made? The attempt would be madness. You will find all the

---

"Of all the various modes and forms of government, that is best, which is capable of producing the greatest degree of happiness and safety, and is most effectually secured against the danger of mal-administration . . ."

Henry and other Anti-Federalists feared a "standing army," which they further associated with governmental oppression. The Second Amendment, which provides for the right to bear arms, was devised in part to respond to this fear.

Patrick Henry's Speech at Virginia's Ratifying Convention

strength of this country in the hands of your enemies; their garrisons will naturally be the strongest places in the country. Your militia is given up to Congress, also, in another part of this plan: they will therefore act as they think proper: all power will be in their own possession. You cannot force them to receive their punishment: of what service would militia be to you, when, most probably, you will not have a single musket in the state? for, as arms are to be provided by Congress, they may or may not furnish them....

> Henry capitalized on the fear of excessive taxation by emphasizing that under the proposed Constitution two sets of governments would now have the authority to enact taxes.

In this scheme of energetic government, the people will find two sets of tax-gatherers—the state and the federal sheriffs. This, it seems to me, will produce such dreadful oppression as the people cannot possibly bear. The federal sheriff may commit what oppression, make what distresses, he pleases, and ruin you with impunity; for how are you to tie his hands? Have you any sufficiently decided means of preventing him from sucking your blood by speculations, commissions, and fees? Thus thousands of your people will be most shamefully robbed: our state sheriffs, those unfeeling blood-suckers have, under the watchful eye of our legislature, committed the most horrid and barbarous ravages on our people. It has required the most constant vigilance of the legislature to keep them from totally ruining the people; a repeated succession of laws has been made to suppress their iniquitous speculations and cruel extortions; and as often has their nefarious ingenuity devised methods of evading the force of those laws: in the struggle they have generally triumphed over the legislature....

> Henry was hardly taking an unbiased look at the new government, but like other Anti-Federalists, he was wary of institutions that he thought might be aristocratic in nature, particularly the presidency and the Senate. Other Anti-Federalists made similar accusations against the unelected members of the judicial branch.

Your President may easily become king. Your Senate is so imperfectly constructed that your dearest rights may be sacrificed by what may be a small minority; and a very small minority may continue forever unchangeably this government, although horridly defective. Where are your checks in this government? Your strongholds will be in the hands of your enemies. It is on a supposition that your American governors shall be honest, that all the good qualities of this government are founded; but its defective and imperfect construction puts it in their power to perpetrate the worst of mischiefs, should they be bad men; and, sir, would not all the world, from the eastern to the western hemisphere, blame our distracted folly in resting our rights upon the contingency of our rulers being good or bad? Show me that age and country where the rights and liberties of the people were placed on the sole chance of their rulers being good men, without a consequent loss of liberty! I say that the loss of that dearest privilege has ever followed, with absolute certainty, every such mad attempt.

Source: *The Debates in the Several State Conventions on the Adoption of the Federal Constitution.* 2nd ed. Vol 3. Edited by Jonathan Elliot. New York: Burt Franklin, 1888, pp. 44–64.

> *"It is on a supposition that your American governors shall be honest, that all the good qualities of this government are founded; but its defective and imperfect construction puts it in their power to perpetrate the worst of mischiefs, should they be bad men . . ."*

The Great National Dome
The Federal Pillars
1788

> **INTRODUCTION**
>
> The Constitution specified that it would go into effect when ratified by nine states. This editorial cartoon, initially published in the *Massachusetts Centinel* on August 2, 1788, visualizes each state as a pillar holding up the federal edifice.

Note that the last two states to ratify at the time the cartoon was published (Virginia and New York) were among the largest and most populous. As of its printing, North Carolina and Rhode Island had yet to ratify. One impetus for adopting the Bill of Rights was the hope that it would induce them to do so and thus underscore the unity of the new nation.

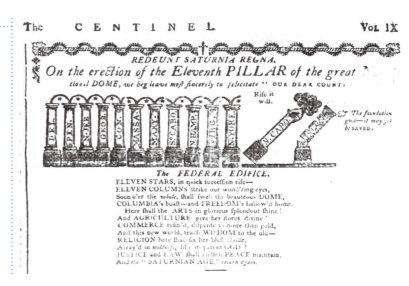

Source: Library of Congress.

Ratification and the Bill of Rights
Letters between Madison and Jefferson
1787–1789

> **INTRODUCTION**
>
> Although it is common to associate the call for a bill of rights with the Anti-Federalist opponents of the Constitution, there were some constitutional supporters who had their own reservations. None was more articulate than Thomas Jefferson, who was serving as an ambassador to France during the ratification drive. Few individuals have had a more productive political relationship than Jefferson and fellow Virginian James Madison—the former had proposed and the latter had largely secured the adoption of the Virginia Statute for Religious Freedom, and both would later found and lead the Democratic-Republican Party. Although Madison was bound by rules of secrecy during the Convention, he thereafter attempted to secure Jefferson's support for the document. In their correspondence, Jefferson frankly expressed his disappointment with the absence of a bill of rights. Madison would later use some of Jefferson's arguments in defending such a bill in the first Congress.

Jefferson to Madison (Paris, December 20, 1787)

The season admitting only of operations in the Cabinet, and these being in great measure secret, I have little to fill a letter. I will therefore make up the deficiency by adding a few words on the Constitution proposed by our Convention. **I like much the general idea of framing a government which should go on itself peaceably, without needing continual recurrence to the state legislatures. I like the organization of the government into Legislative, Judiciary and Executive. I like the power given the Legislature to levy taxes and for that reason solely approve of the greater house being chosen by the people directly. For though I think a house chosen by them will be very ill qualified to legislate for the Union, for foreign nations, etc. yet this evil does not weigh**

> These initial comments, although undoubtedly influenced by his friendship for Madison, clearly seem to put Jefferson in the Federalist camp. Jefferson was a clear proponent of separation of powers, of vesting Congress with the power of taxation, and of the compromise involving state representation within that body.

against the good of preserving inviolate the fundamental principle that the people are not to be taxed but by representatives chosen immediately by themselves. I am captivated by the compromise of the opposite claims of the great and little states, of the latter to equal, and the former to proportional influence. I am much pleased too with the substitution of the method of voting by persons, instead of that voting by states: and I like the negative given to the Executive with a third of either house, though I should have liked it better had the Judiciary been associated for that purpose, or invested with a similar and separate power. There are other good things of less moment.

I will now add what I do not like.

> It hardly seems coincidental that the first concerns Jefferson addressed (freedom of religion and the press) would both find their way into the First Amendment. In arguing for these and other rights against the arguments of James Wilson, Jefferson observed that the proposed Constitution did not contain a provision, similar to that in Article II of the Articles of Confederation and to today's Ninth and Tenth Amendments, reserving unenumerated powers for the states or for the people.

First the omission of a bill of rights providing clearly and without the aid of sophisms for freedom of religion, freedom of the press, protection against standing armies, restriction against monopolies, the eternal and unremitting force of the habeas corpus law, and trials by jury in all matter of fact triable by the laws of the land and not by the law of Nations. To say, as Mr. Wilson does that a bill of rights was not necessary because all is reserved in the case of the general government which is not given, while in the particular ones all is given which is not reserved might do for the Audience to whom it was addressed, but is surely gratis dictum, opposed by strong inferences from the body of the instrument, as well as from the omission of the clause of our present confederation which had declared that in express terms. It was a hard conclusion to say because there has been no uniformity among the states as to the cases triable by jury, because some have been so incautious as to abandon this mode of trial, therefore the more prudent states shall be

reduced to the same level of calamity. It would have been much more just and wise to have concluded the other way that as most of the states had judiciously preserved this palladium, those who had wandered should be brought back to it, and to have established general right instead of general wrong. Let me add that a bill of rights is what the people are entitled to against every government on earth, general or particular, and what no just government should refuse, or rest on inference.

The second feature I dislike, and greatly dislike, is the abandonment in every instance of the necessity of rotation in office, and most particularly in the case of the President. Experience concurs with reason in concluding that the first magistrate will always be re-elected if the constitution permits it. He is then an officer for life. This once observed it becomes of so much consequence to certain nations to have a friend or a foe at the head of our affairs that they will interfere with money and with arms.

> Recent years have witnessed numerous calls for legislative term limits, some of which have been enacted at the state level. Jefferson was more concerned about the need for presidential term limits, which were finally enacted with the adoption of the Twenty-Second Amendment in 1951.

A Gallo man or an Anglo man will be supported by the nation he befriends. If once elected, and at a second of third election outvoted by one or two votes, he will pretend false votes, foul play, hold possession of the reins of government, be supported by the states for voting for him, especially if they are the central ones lying in a compact body themselves and separating their opponents; and they will be aided by one nation of Europe than ever the election of a king of Poland was. Reflect on all the instances in history ancient and modern, of elective monarchies, and say if they do not give foundation for my fears, the Roman emperors, the popes, while they were of any importance, the German emperors till they became hereditary in practice, the kings of Poland, the Days of the Ottoman dependencies. It may be said that if elections are to be attended with these disorders, the seldomer they are renewed the better. But experience shows that the only way to prevent disorder is to render them uninteresting by frequent changes. An incapacity to be elected a second time would have been the only effectual preventative. The power of removing him every fourth year by the vote of the people is a power which will not be exercised. The king of Poland is removable every day by the Diet, yet he is never removed.

Smaller objections are the Appeal in fact as well as law, and the binding all persons Legislative, Executive and Judiciary by oath to maintain that constitution. I do not pretend to decide what would be the best method of procuring the establishment of the manifold good things in this constitution, and of getting rid of the bad. Whether by adopting it in hopes of future amendment, or, after it has been duly weighted and canvassed by the people, after seeing the parts they generally dislike, and those they generally approve, to say to them 'We see now what you wish. Send together your deputies again, let them frame a constitution for you omitting what you have condemned, and establishing the powers you approve. Even these will be a great addition to the energy of your government.

At all events I hope you will not be discouraged from other trials, if the present one should fail of it's full effect.

One of the key factors that encouraged states to send delegates to the Constitutional Convention was the outbreak of Shays' Rebellion in Massachusetts the prior winter. Perhaps in part because he was writing from a distance, Jefferson downplayed the event. In another letter, which he sent to William Stephens Smith on November 13, 1787, he would proclaim that "The tree of liberty must be refreshed from time to time with the blood of patriots and tyrants. It is its natural manure."

I have thus told you freely what I like and dislike: merely as a matter of curiosity for I know your own judgment has been formed on all these points after having heard every thing which could be urged on them. I own I am not a friend to a very energetic government. It is always oppressive. The late rebellion in has given me more alarm than I think it should have done. Calculate that one rebellion in 13 states in the course of 11 years is but one for each state in a century and a half. No country should be

so long without one. Nor will any degree of power in the hands of government prevent insurrections. France with all it's despotism, and two or three hundred thousand men always in arms has had three insurrections in the three years I have been here in every one of which greater numbers were engaged than in Massachusetts and a great deal more blood was split. . . .

After all, it is my principle that the will of the Majority should always prevail. If they approve the proposed Convention in all its parts, I shall concur in it cheerfully, in hopes that they will amend it whenever they shall find it work wrong. I think our governments will remain virtuous for many centuries; as long as they are chiefly agricultural; and this will be as long as there shall be vacant lands in any part of America. . . . Above all things I hope the education of the common people will be attended to; convinced that on their good sense we may rely with the most security for the preservation of a due degree of liberty. I have tried you by this time with my disquisitions and will therefore only add assurances of the sincerity of those sentiments of esteem and attachment with which I am Dear Sir your affectionate friend and servant,

> Whereas Alexander Hamilton envisioned an industrial and commercial nation, Jefferson saw agrarianism as the ideal, largely because—at a time when votes were cast publicly—he thought that farmers were less subject to outside influences. These different views would lead to significant conflict within George Washington's first cabinet, where Hamilton served as secretary of the treasury and Jefferson as secretary of state.

Jefferson to Madison (February 6, 1788)

I am glad to hear that the new constitution is received with favor. I sincerely wish that the 9 first conventions may receive, and the last 4 reject it. The former will secure it finally, while the latter will oblige them to offer a declaration of rights in order to complete the union. We shall thus have all that's good, and cure its principal defect.

Madison to Jefferson (New York, October 17, 1788)

> Madison's and Jefferson's correspondence continued throughout the ratification of the Constitution. In this letter, Madison supported a bill of rights in theory while raising some practical concerns.

> This hardly appears to be a ringing endorsement of the bill of rights by its central author, who appears to have worked on the bill as much to muster support for the document as because of his belief in its efficacy.

> *"[T]here is great reason to fear that a positive declaration of some of the most essential rights could not be obtained in the requisite latitude."*

... My own opinion has always been in favor of a bill of rights; provided it be so framed as not to imply powers not meant to be included in the enumeration. At the same time I have never thought the omission a material defect nor been anxious to supply it even by subsequent amendment, for any other reason than that it is anxiously desired by others. I have favored it because I supposed it might be of use, and if properly executed could not be of disservice.

I have not viewed it in an important light 1. Because I conceive that in a certain degree, though not in the extent argued by Mr. Wilson, the rights in question are reserved by the manner in which the federal powers are granted. 2. Because there is great reason to fear that a positive declaration of some of the most essential rights could not be obtained in the requisite latitude. I am sure that the rights of conscience in particular, if submitted to the public definition would be narrowed much more than they are likely ever to be by an assumed power. One of the objections in New England was that the Constitution by prohibiting religious tests opened a door for Jews, Turks and infidels. 3. Because the limited powers of the federal Government and the jealousy of the subordinate Governments, afford a security which has not existed in the case of the State Governments, and exists in no other. 4. Because experience proves the inefficacy of a bill of rights on those occasions when its control is most needed. Repeated violations of these parchment barriers have been committed by overbearing majorities in every State. In Virginia I have seen the bill of rights violated in every instance where it has been opposed to a popular current. Notwithstanding the explicit provision contained in that instrument for the rights of Conscience it is well known that a religious establishment would have taken place and on narrower ground than was then proposed, notwithstanding the additional obstacle which the law has since created. Wherever the real power in a Government lies, there is the danger of oppression.

In our Governments the real power lies in the majority of the Community, and the invasion of private rights is chiefly to be apprehended, not from acts of Government contrary to the sense of its constituents, but from acts in which the Government is the mere instrument of the majority of the constituents. This is a truth of great importance, but not yet sufficiently attended to: and is probably more strongly impressed on my mind by facts, and reflections suggested by them, than on yours which has contemplated abuses of power issuing from a very different quarter. Wherever there is an interest and power to do wrong, wrong will generally be done, and not less readily by a powerful and interested party than by a powerful and interested prince. The difference, so far as it relates to the superiority of republics over monarchies, lies in the less degree of probability that interest may prompt abuses of power in the former than in the latter; and in the security in the former against oppression of more than the smaller part of the Society, whereas in the former [latter] it may be extended in a manner to the whole. The difference so far as it relates to the point in question—the efficacy of a bull of rights in controlling abuses of power—lies in this: that in a monarchy the latent force of the nation is superior to that of the Sovereign, and a solemn charter of popular rights must have a great effect, as a standard for trying the charter of popular rights must have a great effect, as a standard for trying the validity of public acts, and a signal for rousing and uniting the superior force of the community; whereas in a popular Government, the political and physical power may be considered as vested in the same hands, that is in a majority of the people, and consequently the tyrannical will of the

"In our Governments the real power lies in the majority of the Community, and the invasion of private rights is chiefly to be apprehended, not from acts of Government contrary to the sense of its constituents, but from acts in which the Government is the mere instrument of the majority of the constituents."

Here, Madison focuses chiefly on the role of a bill of rights in educating the public.

sovereign is not to be controlled by the dread of an appeal to any other force within the community.

What use then it may be asked can a bill of rights serve in popular Governments? I answer the two following which though less essential than in other Governments, sufficiently recommend the precaution. 1. The political truths declared that in solemn manner acquire by degrees the character of fundamental maxims of free Government, and as they become incorporated with the national sentiment, counteract the impulses of interest and passion. 2. Although it be generally true as above stated that the danger of oppression lies in the interested majorities of the people rather than in usurped acts of the Government, yet there may be occasions on which the evil may spring from the latter sources; and on such, a bill of rights will be a good ground for an appeal to the sense of the community.

Jefferson to Madison (Paris, March 15, 1789)

In one of the great ironies of the Founding Period, Jefferson, who would later excoriate the Federalist-appointed judiciary for sapping democratic institutions, went on to argue that in addition to educating the public, a bill of rights would provide a mechanism for aggrieved individuals to bring cases to court. In so doing, he cited the reputation of a number of judges, including George Wythe, a delegate to the Constitutional Convention of 1787, under whom he had studied law. When adopted, the Bill of Rights was written in the form of prohibitions rather than aspirations, thus giving the judiciary this power. In the early years of the nation, however, the judiciary based relatively few cases on the Bill of Rights—a situation that has changed now that the judiciary has ruled that the due process clause of the Fourteenth Amendment applies the guarantees not only to the national government but also to the states. The term "civium ardor prava jubentium" is a reference to the "wayward ardor of the ruling citizens." Madison would later use this argument when defending the Bill of Rights in the first Congress.

Your thoughts on the subject of the declaration of rights in the letter of October the 17th, I have weighed with great satisfaction. Some of them had not occurred to me before, but were acknowledged just in the moment they were presented to my mind.

In the arguments in favor of a declaration of rights, you omit one which has great weight with me; the legal check which it puts into the hands of the judiciary. This is a body, which, if rendered independent, and kept strictly to their own department, merits great confidence for their learning and integrity. In fact, what degree of confidence would be too much, for a body composed of such men as Wythe, Blair, and Pendleton? On characters like these,

the "civium ardor prava jubentium" would make no impression. I am happy to find that on the whole you are a friend to this with some inconveniences, and not accomplishing fully its object.

But the short answers to the objections which your letter states to have been raised.

1. That the rights in question are reserved by the manner in which the federal powers are granted. Answer. A constitutive act may certainly be so formed as to need no declaration of rights. The act itself has the force of a declaration as far as it goes: and if it goes to all material points nothing more is wanting. In the draught of a constitution which I had once a thought of proposing in Virginia, and printed afterwards, I endeavored to reach all the great objects of public liberty and did not mean to add a declaration of rights. Probably the object was imperfectly executed: but the deficiencies would have been supplied by others in the course of discussion. But in a constitutive act which leave some precious articles unnoticed, and raises implications against others, a declaration of rights becomes necessary by way of supplement. This is the case of our new federal constitution. This instrument forms us into one state as to certain objects, and gives us a legislative and executive body for these objects. It should therefore guard us against their abuses of power within the field submitted to them.

2. A positive declaration of some essential rights could not be obtained in the requisite latitude. Answer. Half a loaf is better than no bread. If we cannot secure all our rights, let us secure what we can.

3. The limited powers of the federal government and jealousy of the subordinate governments afford a security which exists

"Half a loaf is better than no bread. If we cannot secure all our rights, let us secure what we can."

in no other instance. Answer. The first member of this seems resolvable into the 1st. objection before stated. The jealousy of the subordinate governments in a precious reliance. But observe that those governments are only agents. They must have principles furnished them whereon to found their opposition. The declaration of rights will be the next whereby they will try all the acts of the federal government. In this view it is necessary to the federal government also: as by the same text they may try the opposition of the subordinate governments.

> Although he acknowledged that a bill of rights would not provide a full security for rights, Jefferson believed that it would nonetheless be helpful. There is a certain belt-and-suspenders quality to this argument: While the structure of government might serve to preserve rights, it would not hurt to have additional precautions.

4. **Experience proves the inefficacy of a bill of rights. True. But though it is not absolutely efficacious under all circumstances, it is of great potency always, and rarely inefficacious. A brace the more will often keep up the building which would have fallen with that brace the less.**

There is a remarkable difference between the characters of the inconveniencies which attend a Declaration of rights, and those which attend the want of it. The inconveniences of the Declaration are that it may cramp government in it's useful exertions. But the evil of this is short lived, moderate, and reparable. The inconveniences of the want of a Declaration are permanent, afflicting and irreparable: they are in constant progression from bad to worse. The executive in our governments is not the sole, it is scarcely the principal object of my jealousy. The tyranny of the legislatures is the most formidable dread at present, and it will be for long years. That of the executive will come in it's turn, but it will be at a remote period. I know there are some among us who would now establish a monarchy. But they are inconsiderable in number and weight of character. The rising race are all republicans. We were educated in royalism: no wonder if some us retain that idolatry still. Our young people are educated in republicanism. An apostasy from that to royalism is unprecedented and impossible.

I am much pleased with the prospect that a declaration of rights will be added: and hope it will be done in that way which will not endanger the whole frame of the government, or any essential part of it.

Sources:

Jefferson to Madison, December 20, 1787. *The Writings of Thomas Jefferson: Being His Autobiography, Correspondence, Reports, Messages, Addresses, and Other Writings, Official and Private.* Vol. 2. Edited by H. A. Washington. New York: John C. Riker, 1853, pp. 327–333.

Jefferson to Madison, February 6, 1788. *The Thomas Jefferson Papers.* Series 1. Library of Congress.

Madison to Jefferson, October 17, 1788. *Letters and Other Writings of James Madison.* Vol. 1. Phildelphia, PA: J. B. Lippincott & Co., 1865, pp. 420–427.

Jefferson to Madison, March 15, 1789. *The Thomas Jefferson Papers.* Series 1. Library of Congress.

"I am much pleased with the prospect that a declaration of rights will be added: and hope it will be done in that way which will not endanger the whole frame of the government, or any essential part of it."

Summoned by My Country
George Washington's Inaugural Address
April 30, 1789

> **INTRODUCTION**
>
> Although the delegates to the Constitutional Convention signed the Constitution on September 17, 1787, it was not officially ratified until 1788, after which elections for the president and the Congress followed. Most delegates who attended the Constitutional Convention had anticipated that Washington would serve as the first president, and he was the only president ever to be selected unanimously by the electors casting votes. The president's inauguration, which took place in Federal Hall in New York City, where the nation's capital was then temporarily located, was a milestone in the establishment of the new government. The speech was largely composed by James Madison and was much shorter than one that had been proposed by David Humphreys, a former Washington aide.

Fellow Citizens of the Senate and the House of Representatives.

Among the vicissitudes incident to life, no event could have filled me with greater anxieties than that of which the notification was transmitted by your order, and received on the fourteenth day of the present month. On the one hand, I was summoned by my Country, whose voice I can never hear but with veneration and love, from a retreat which I had chosen with the fondest predilection, and, in my flattering hopes, with an immutable decision, as the asylum of my declining years: a retreat which was rendered every day more necessary as well as more dear to me, by the addition of habit to inclination, and of frequent interruptions in my health to the gradual waste committed on it by time. On the other hand, the

Whereas modern presidents often campaign for years for the office, Washington was a reluctant candidate who, in a letter to General Henry Knox, wrote that "My movements to the chair of government will be accompanied by feelings not unlike those of a culprit, who is going to the place of his execution; so unwilling am I, in the evening of a life nearly consumed in public cares, to quit a peaceful abode for an ocean of difficulties, without that competency of political skill, abilities, and inclination which are necessary to manage the helm." Washington reiterates such sentiments here, perhaps cognizant that the public will give him a greater benefit of the doubt if it thinks he is accepting the office out of a sense of duty rather than because of personal ambition.

magnitude and difficulty of the trust to which the voice of my Country called me, being sufficient to awaken in the wisest and most experienced of her citizens, a distrustful scrutiny into his qualifications, could not but overwhelm with dispondence, one, who, inheriting inferior endowments from nature and unpractised in the duties of civil administration, ought to be peculiarly conscious of his own deficiencies. In this conflict of emotions, all I dare aver, is, that it has been my faithful study to collect my duty from a just appreciation of every circumstance, by which it might be affected. All I dare hope, is, that, if in executing this task I have been too much swayed by a grateful remembrance of former instances, or by an affectionate sensibility to this transcendent proof, of the confidence of my fellow-citizens; and have thence too little consulted my incapacity as well as disinclination for the weighty and untried cares before me; my error will be palliated by the motives which misled me, and its consequences be judged by my Country, with some share of the partiality in which they originated.

Such being the impressions under which I have, in obedience to the public summons, repaired to the present station; it would be peculiarly improper to omit in this first official Act, my fervent supplications to that Almighty Being who rules over the Universe, who presides in the Councils of Nations, and whose providential aids can supply every human defect, that his benediction may consecrate to the liberties and happiness of the People of the United States, a Government instituted by themselves for these essential purposes: and may enable every instrument employed in its administration to execute with success, the functions allotted to his charge. In tendering this homage to the Great Author of every public and private good I assure myself that it expresses your sentiments not less than my own; nor those of my fellow-citizens

"[I]t has been my faithful study to collect my duty from a just appreciation of every circumstance, by which it might be affected."

George Washington's Inaugural Address

> Although the Constitution does not mention God, and the First Amendment prohibits the establishment of religion, elected officials constantly seek to invoke God's blessings upon the nation. Washington attributed the outcome of the Revolution, and the destiny of the nation, to God's special Providence.

"And in the important revolution just accomplished in the system of their United Government, the tranquil deliberations and voluntary consent of so many distinct communities, from which the event has resulted, cannot be compared with the means by which most Governments have been established, without some return of pious gratitude along with an humble anticipation of the future blessings which the past seem to presage."

at large, less than either. **No People can be bound to acknowledge and adore the invisible hand, which conducts the Affairs of men more than the People of the United States. Every step, by which they have advanced to the character of an independent nation, seems to have been distinguished by some token of providential agency.** And in the important revolution just accomplished in the system of their United Government, the tranquil deliberations and voluntary consent of so many distinct communities, from which the event has resulted, cannot be compared with the means by which most Governments have been established, without some return of pious gratitude along with an humble anticipation of the future blessings which the past seem to presage. These reflections, arising out of the present crisis, have forced themselves too strongly on my mind to be suppressed. You will join with me I trust in thinking, that there are none under the influence of which, the proceedings of a new and free Government can more auspiciously commence.

By the article establishing the Executive Department, it is made the duty of the President "to recommend to your consideration, such measures as he shall judge necessary and expedient." The circumstances under which I now meet you, will acquit me from entering into that subject, farther than to refer to the Great Constitutional Charter under which you are assembled; and which, in defining your powers, designates the objects to which your attention is to be given. It will be more consistent with those circumstances, and far more congenial with the feelings which actuate me, to substitute, in place of a recommendation of particular measures, the tribute that is due to the talents, the rectitude, and the patriotism which adorn the characters selected to devise and adopt them. In these honorable qualifications, I behold the surest pledges, that as on one side, no local prejudices, or attachments; no seperate views, nor party animosities, will misdirect the comprehensive and equal eye which ought to watch over this great assemblage of communities and interests: so, on another, that the foundations of our National policy will be laid in the pure and immutable principles of private morality; and the pre-eminence of a free Government, be exemplified by all the attributes which can win the affections of its Citizens, and command the respect of the world.

I dwell on this prospect with every satisfaction which an ardent love for my Country can inspire: since there is no truth more thoroughly established, than that there exists in the economy and course of nature, an indissoluble union between virtue and happiness, between duty and advantage, between the genuine maxims of an honest and magnanimous policy, and the solid rewards of public prosperity and felicity: Since we ought to be no less persuaded that the propitious smiles of Heaven, can never be expected on a nation that disregards the eternal rules of order and right, which Heaven itself has ordained: And since the preservation of the sacred fire of liberty, and the destiny of the Republican model of Government, are justly considered as deeply, perhaps as finally staked, on the experiment entrusted to the hands of the American people.

> Much as people today say that "honesty is the best policy," Washington links public virtue to public happiness. He further ties the new "Charter" (the Constitution), which he calls an "experiment," both to republicanism (representative government) and to the protection of liberty.

Besides the ordinary objects submitted to your care, it will remain with your judgment to decide, how far an exercise of the occasional power delegated by the Fifth article of the Constitution is rendered expedient at the present juncture by the nature of objections which have been urged against the System, or by the degree of inquietude which has given birth to them. Instead of undertaking particular recommendations on this subject, in which I could be guided by no lights derived from

> Leading Federalists had argued that those who questioned various provisions, or omissions, in the new Constitution should adopt it anyway, and afterward seek amendments through the pathways outlined in Article V of the document. Washington expressed the hope that proponents of change would seek appropriate protections for individual liberties while seeking to maintain "the benefits of an United and effective Government."

George Washington's Inaugural Address

official opportunities, I shall again give way to my entire confidence in your discernment and pursuit of the public good: For I assure myself that whilst you carefully avoid every alteration which might endanger the benefits of an United and effective Government, or which ought to await the future lessons of experience; a reverence for the characteristic rights of freemen, and a regard for the public harmony, will sufficiently influence your deliberations on the question how far the former can be more impregnably fortified, or the latter be safely and advantageously promoted.

Having thus imported to you my sentiments, as they have been awakened by the occasion which brings us together, I shall take my present leave; but not without resorting once more to the benign parent of the human race, in humble supplication that since he has been pleased to favour the American people, with opportunities for deliberating in perfect tranquility, and dispositions for deciding with unparellelled unanimity on a form of Government, for the security of their Union, and the advancement of their happiness; so his divine blessing may be equally *conspicuous* in the enlarged views, the temperate consultations, and the wise measures on which the success of this Government must depend.

Source: George Washington. Inaugural Address, April 30, 1789. Records of the U.S. Senate, Record Group 46, National Archives.

> "[S]ince he has been pleased to favour the American people, with opportunities for deliberating in perfect tranquility, and dispositions for deciding with unparellelled unanimity on a form of Government, for the security of their Union, and the advancement of their happiness; so his divine blessing may be equally conspicuous in the enlarged views, the temperate consultations, and the wise measures on which the success of this Government must depend."

To Administer Justice
Judiciary Act of 1789
September 24, 1789

INTRODUCTION

The U.S. Constitution devoted less attention to the federal judiciary than to either the legislative or executive branches; it did not even mandate the creation of any federal courts other than the U.S. Supreme Court. Fortunately, many of the same men who had attended the Constitutional Convention were also in the first Congress. The Judiciary Act of 1789 established an outline for federal courts that is still reflected in today's system, and thereby established a mechanism to assure that the Constitution was the supreme law of the land. Oliver Ellsworth of Connecticut, who had attended the Constitutional Convention and who would later serve as chief justice of the U.S. Supreme Court, was the primary author of this legislation.

CHAP. XX.–An Act to establish the Judicial Courts of the United States.

SECTION 1. Be it enacted by the Senate and House of Representatives of the United States of America in Congress assembled, That the supreme court of the United States shall consist of a chief justice and five associate justices, any four of whom shall be a quorum, and shall hold annually at the seat of government two sessions, the one commencing the first Monday of February, and the other the first Monday of August. That the associate justices shall have precedence according to the date of their commissions, or when the commissions of two or more of them bear date on the same day, according to their respective ages.

> Article III of the Constitution mentioned a Supreme Court but did not specify how many members it would have or how it would be organized. The initial Congress set the number of members at five. This was changed on a number of occasions until Congress established the present number of nine (a chief and eight associates) shortly after the Civil War.

Judiciary Act of 1789

> This section essentially created at least one federal court per state. Such district courts, of which there are currently 94 (including at least 1 for each state), continue as the entry points for the consideration of most federal cases.

SEC. 2. And be it further enacted, That the United States shall be, and they hereby are divided into thirteen districts . . .

SEC. 3. And be it further enacted, That there be a court called a District Court, in each of the afore mentioned districts, to consist of one judge, who shall reside in the district for which he is appointed, and shall be called a District Judge, and shall hold annually four sessions . . .

> Although U.S. Supreme Court justices technically each retain some supervisory jurisdiction over individual circuits, they are no longer expected to perform the onerous duty of "riding circuit" and sitting with district judges in order to staff U.S. circuit courts of appeal, which now have their own designated judges. This change further prevented judges and justices from sitting in judgment of their own earlier decisions, although it also made justices more remote than they were in the early republic.

SEC. 4. And be it further enacted, That the before mentioned districts, except those of Maine and Kentucky, shall be divided into three circuits, and be called the eastern, the middle, and the southern circuit. That the eastern circuit shall consist of the districts of New Hampshire, Massachusetts, Connecticut and New York; that the middle circuit shall consist of the districts of New Jersey, Pennsylvania, Delaware, Maryland and Virginia; and that the southern circuit shall consist of the districts of South Carolina and Georgia, and that there shall be held annually in each district of said circuits, two courts, which shall be called Circuit Courts, and shall consist of any two justices of the Supreme Court, and the district judge of such districts, any two of whom shall constitute a quorum: Provided, That no district judge shall give a vote in any case of appeal or error from his own decision; but may assign the reasons of such his decision.

> This oath makes for an informative comparison with the one the Constitution specifies for the president. Consistent with the supremacy clause in Article VI of the Constitution, both oaths are designed to emphasize the duty of federal officials to view the U.S. Constitution as the supreme law of the land.

SEC. 8. And be it further enacted, That the justices of the Supreme Court, and the district judges, before they proceed to execute the duties of their respective offices, shall take the following oath or affirmation, to wit: "I, A. B., do solemnly swear or affirm, that I will administer justice without respect to persons, and do equal right to the poor and to the rich, and that I will faithfully and impartially discharge and perform all the duties incumbent on me as, according to the best of my abilities and understanding, agreeably to the constitution, and laws of the United States. So help me God."

SEC. 25. And be it further enacted, That a final judgment or decree in any suit, in the highest court of law or equity of a State in which a decision in the suit could be had, where is drawn in question the validity of a treaty or statute of, or an authority exercised under the United States, and the decision is against their validity; or where is drawn in question the validity of a statute of, or an authority exercised under any State, on the ground of their being repugnant to the constitution, treaties or laws of the United States, and the decision is in favour of such their validity, or where is drawn in question the construction of any clause of the constitution, or of a treaty, or statute of, or commission held under the United States, and the decision is against the title, right, privilege or exemption specially set up or claimed by either party, under such clause of the said Constitution, treaty, statute or commission, may be re-examined and reversed or affirmed in the Supreme Court of the United States upon a writ of error, the citation being signed by the chief justice, or judge or chancellor of the court rendering or passing the judgment or decree complained of, or by a justice of the Supreme Court of the United States, in the same manner and under the same regulations, and the writ shall have the same effect, as if the judgment or decree complained of had been rendered or passed in a circuit court, and the proceeding upon the reversal shall also be the same, except that the Supreme Court, instead of remanding the cause for a final decision as before provided, may at their discretion, if the cause shall have been

This section is far and away the most important provision of this law. Although the U.S. Constitution did not specifically mention the power of judicial review, whereby courts have authority to invalidate laws that they consider to be unconstitutional, delegates to the Constitutional Convention were familiar with this mechanism, which had sometimes been exercised at the state level. Most delegates probably expected U.S. courts to exercise this power. It is certainly consistent with the idea of a written Constitution enforceable by a branch whose independence is furthered by presidential appointment and senatorial confirmation, by service "during good behavior," and by protections against Congress lowering judicial pay. U.S. courts exercise judicial review of both state and federal legislation. The first case involving the invalidation of a federal law by the U.S. Supreme Court (ironically, a section of the Judiciary Act that appeared to extend the Supreme Court's original jurisdiction beyond that of Article III of the Constitution) took place in the case of *Marbury v. Madison* (1803), one of the most important decisions that Chief Justice John Marshall authored during his tenure on that body.

once remanded before, proceed to a final decision of the same, and award execution. But no other error shall be assigned or regarded as a ground of reversal in any such case as aforesaid, than such as appears on the face of the record, and immediately respects the before mentioned questions of validity or construction of the said constitution, treaties, statutes, commissions, or authorities in dispute.

Source: An Act to Establish the Judicial Courts of the United States, September 24, 1789. Statutes at Large, 1st Cong., 1st sess., vol. 1, chap. 20: 73.

To Bigotry No Sanction

Correspondence between Moses Seixas and President George Washington

1790

INTRODUCTION

By the time of the American Revolution, there were established Jewish congregations in a number of American cities, but test oaths at the state level (subsequently declared unconstitutional) still sometimes required affirmation of the Trinity and other distinctly Christian doctrines. The following correspondence shows a Jewish congregation reaching out to the new president, and his liberal response.

Letter from Moses Seixas to President George Washington (August 17, 1790)

To the President of the United States of America.

Sir:

Permit the children of the stock of Abraham to approach you with the most cordial affection and esteem for your person and merits—and to join with our fellow citizens in welcoming you to NewPort.

Jews, Christians, and Muslims all identify Abraham as among the founders of their faith. The congregation used this common tie as a way to establish a connection to the chief executive.

With pleasure we reflect on those days—those days of difficulty, and danger, when the God of Israel, who delivered David from the peril of the sword,—shielded Your head in the day of battle:—and we rejoice to think, that the same Spirit, who rested in the Bosom of the greatly beloved Daniel enabling him to preside over the Provinces of the Babylonish Empire, rests and ever will rest, upon you, enabling you to

Correspondence between Moses Seixas and President George Washington

> This congregation, like Washington himself, associated the nation's destiny with divine Providence and sought to remind the president of the nation's commitment to liberty of conscience.

discharge the arduous duties of Chief Magistrate in these States.

Deprived as we heretofore have been of the invaluable rights of free Citizens, we now with a deep sense of gratitude to the Almighty disposer of all events behold a Government, erected by the Majesty of the People—a Government, which to bigotry gives no sanction, to persecution no assistance—but generously affording to all Liberty of conscience, and immunities of Citizenship:—deeming every one, of whatever Nation, tongue, or language equal parts of the great governmental Machine:—This so ample and extensive Federal Union whose basis is Philanthropy, Mutual confidence and Public Virtue, we cannot but acknowledge to be the work of the Great God, who ruleth in the Armies of Heaven, and among the Inhabitants of the Earth, doing whatever seemeth him good.

"For all these Blessings of civil and religious liberty which we enjoy under an equal and benign administration, we desire to send up our thanks to the Ancient of Days, the great preserver of Men . . ."

For all these Blessings of civil and religious liberty which we enjoy under an equal and benign administration, we desire to send up our thanks to the Ancient of Days, the great preserver of Men—beseeching him, that the Angel who conducted our forefathers through the wilderness into the promised Land, may graciously conduct you through all the difficulties and dangers of this mortal life:—And, when, like Joshua full of days and full of honour, you are gathered to your Fathers, may you be admitted into the Heavenly Paradise to partake of the water of life, and the tree of immortality.

Done and Signed by order of the Hebrew Congregation in NewPort, Rhode Island August 17th 1790.

Moses Seixas, Warden

Letter from George Washington to Moses Seixas (August 18, 1790)

To the Hebrew Congregation in Newport Rhode Island.

Gentlemen,

While I receive, with much satisfaction, your Address replete with expressions of affection and esteem; I rejoice in the opportunity of assuring you, that I shall always retain a grateful remembrance of the cordial welcome I experienced in my visit to Newport, from all classes of Citizens.

The reflection on the days of difficulty and danger which are past is rendered the more sweet, from a consciousness that they are succeeded by days of uncommon prosperity and security. If we have wisdom to make the best use of the advantages with which we are now favored, we cannot fail, under the just administration of a good Government, to become a great and happy people.

The Citizens of the United States of America have a right to applaud themselves for having given to mankind examples of an enlarged and liberal policy: a policy worthy of imitation. All possess alike liberty of conscience and immunities of citizenship. It is now no more that toleration is spoken of, as if it was by the indulgence of one class of people, that another enjoyed the exercise of their inherent natural rights. For happily the Government of the United States, which gives to bigotry no sanction, to persecution no assistance, requires only that they who live under its protection should demean themselves as good citizens, in giving it on all occasions their effectual support.

"If we have wisdom to make the best use of the advantages with which we are now favored, we cannot fail, under the just administration of a good Government, to become a great and happy people."

Correspondence between Moses Seixas and President George Washington

Although the necessary number of states would not ratify the Bill of Rights until the next year, Washington anticipated its adoption. He further interpreted the First Amendment as reaching beyond the mere toleration of rival opinions to a more positive affirmation of natural rights. One reason that Washington and other framers appear to have used generic, rather than specifically Christian, or denominational, references to God was their recognition that the nation embraced individuals of diverse religious beliefs. Washington used specific reference to Hebrew scriptures (what Christians call the Old Testament), like the reference to the vine and the fig tree, as a way of stressing a common spiritual heritage.

It would be inconsistent with the frankness of my character not to avow that I am pleased with your favorable opinion of my Administration, and fervent wishes for my felicity. May the children of the Stock of Abraham, who dwell in this land, continue to merit and enjoy the good will of the other Inhabitants; while every one shall sit in safety under his own vine and fig-tree, and there shall be none to make him afraid. May the father of all mercies scatter light and not darkness in our paths, and make us all in our several vocations useful here, and in his own due time and way everlastingly happy.

Source: Letters of Moses Seixas and George Washington, August 1790. American Treasures of the Library of Congress website. Accessed January 19, 2015. http://www.loc.gov/exhibits/treasures/trm006.html.

Amendments to the Constitution
The Bill of Rights
Proposed by Congress in 1789; ratified in 1791

> **INTRODUCTION**
>
> Although Federalists had initially claimed that a federal bill of rights was unnecessary because the Congress would be limited to the exercise of enumerated powers, key Federalists—most notably James Madison—agreed to work for such a bill once the Constitution was ratified. Madison took the lead in shepherding the Bill of Rights through the first Congress. He worked to ensure that the legislation would disable the new government from interfering with personal rights, but also guarded to make sure that it did not strip the new government of necessary powers over commerce, taxation, war-making, and the like. States adopted the majority of these amendments in relatively short order, a turn of events that seemed to vindicate the framers' argument that the new amending process would be responsive to public sentiments.

Transcription of the 1789 Joint Resolution of Congress Proposing 12 Amendments to the U.S. Constitution

The capitalization and punctuation in this version is from the enrolled original of the Joint Resolution of Congress proposing the Bill of Rights.

Congress of the United States begun and held at the City of New-York, on Wednesday the fourth of March, one thousand seven hundred and eighty nine.

THE Conventions of a number of the States, having at the time of their adopting the Constitution, expressed a desire, in order to prevent misconstruction or abuse of its powers, that further declaratory and restrictive clauses should be added: And as extending the ground of public confidence in the Government, will best ensure the beneficent ends of its institution.

RESOLVED by the Senate and House of Representatives of the United States of America, in Congress assembled, two thirds of both Houses concurring, that the following Articles

*"**THE** Conventions of a number of the States, having at the time of their adopting the Constitution, expressed a desire, in order to prevent misconstruction or abuse of its powers, that further declaratory and restrictive clauses should be added . . ."*

The Bill of Rights

be proposed to the Legislatures of the several States, as amendments to the Constitution of the United States, all, or any of which Articles, when ratified by three fourths of the said Legislatures, to be valid to all intents and purposes, as part of the said Constitution; viz.

ARTICLES in addition to, and Amendment of the Constitution of the United States of America, proposed by Congress, and ratified by the Legislatures of the several States, pursuant to the fifth Article of the original Constitution.

> This language seems designed to satisfy both the Anti-Federalists, who thought that it was essential to add additional guarantees to the Constitution, and the Federalists, who argued that the amendments were not so much changes to, as clarifications of, existing constitutional guarantees.

Article the first . . . After the first enumeration required by the first article of the Constitution, there shall be one Representative for every thirty thousand, until the number shall amount to one hundred, after which the proportion shall be so regulated by Congress, that there shall be not less than one hundred Representatives, nor less than one Representative for every forty thousand persons, until the number of Representatives shall amount to two hundred; after which the proportion shall be so regulated by Congress, that there shall not be less than two hundred Representatives, nor more than one Representative for every fifty thousand persons.

> These first two proposed amendments dealt with structural issues rather than individual rights and, perhaps as a consequence, were not initially ratified by sufficient majorities. None of the amendments had time limits, however, and states continued sporadically to ratify the second of these proposals. The second proposal was finally ratified as the Twenty-Seventh Amendment on May 7, 1992, more than 202 years after it was first submitted for consideration. Ratification was secured in no small part due to the efforts of Gregory Watson, an aide to a Texas legislator who campaigned for ratification throughout the 1980s.

Article the second . . . No law, varying the compensation for the services of the Senators and Representatives, shall take effect, until an election of Representatives shall have intervened.

> The reference to "Congress" is an indication that the original Bill of Rights was designed only to apply to the national government. The Supreme Court later interpreted the due process clause of the Fourteenth Amendment (1868) to apply those provisions of the Bill of Rights (now almost all), which were considered to be fundamental. No amendment is better known than this one, which is now known as the First Amendment. It provides for religious and political freedoms. Without the former, individuals would not be able to follow their own consciences. Without the latter, representative (Republican) government would be almost impossible.

Article the third . . . Congress shall make no law respecting an establishment of religion, or prohibiting the free exercise thereof; or abridging the freedom of speech, or of the press; or the right of the people peaceably to assemble, and to petition the Government for a redress of grievances.

Article the fourth ... A well regulated Militia, being necessary to the security of a free State, the right of the people to keep and bear Arms, shall not be infringed.

> One antidote to the possibility of a standing army was the presence of state militias, which this amendment protects. Recent Supreme Court decisions have also interpreted this provision to provide an individual (albeit not absolute) right to own weapons for self-defense.

Article the fifth ... No Soldier shall, in time of peace be quartered in any house, without the consent of the Owner, nor in time of war, but in a manner to be prescribed by law.

> Most provisions of the Bill of Rights can be traced to historical experience. During the events leading up to the Revolutionary War, the British had quartered troops in American homes in Boston and elsewhere. This provision sought to prevent the new government from acting in a similarly arbitrary way.

Article the sixth ... The right of the people to be secure in their persons, houses, papers, and effects, against unreasonable searches and seizures, shall not be violated, and no Warrants shall issue, but upon probable cause, supported by Oath or affirmation, and particularly describing the place to be searched, and the persons or things to be seized.

> Although this amendment originated in perceived British abuses (they had used general warrants, or so-called writs of assistance), it extends much wider. Modern courts have generally required particularized warrants in order for searches to pass the Fourth Amendment reasonableness requirement. Such warrants may not be based on mere suspicion but require "probable cause" to believe that they will produce evidence that a crime has been, or is about to be, committed.

Article the seventh ... No person shall be held to answer for a capital, or otherwise infamous crime, unless on a presentment or indictment of a Grand Jury, except in cases arising in the land or naval forces, or in the Militia, when in actual service in time of War or public danger; nor shall any person be subject for the same offence to be twice put in jeopardy of life or limb; nor shall be compelled in any criminal case to be a witness against himself, nor be deprived of life, liberty, or property, without due process of law; nor shall private property be taken for public use, without just compensation.

> This amendment, like others near it, was designed to protect the rights of individuals who were accused of crimes. The due process clause is thought to have been designed to mirror the provision in the Magna Carta of 1215 that referred to "the law of the land."

Article the eighth ... In all criminal prosecutions, the accused shall enjoy the right to a speedy and public trial, by an impartial jury of the State and district wherein the crime shall have been committed, which district shall have been previously ascertained by law, and to be informed of the

The Bill of Rights

nature and cause of the accusation; to be confronted with the witnesses against him; to have compulsory process for obtaining witnesses in his favor, and to have the Assistance of Counsel for his defence.

Article the ninth . . . In suits at common law, where the value in controversy shall exceed twenty dollars, the right of trial by jury shall be preserved, and no fact tried by a jury, shall be otherwise re-examined in any Court of the United States, than according to the rules of the common law.

Article the tenth . . . Excessive bail shall not be required, nor excessive fines imposed, nor cruel and unusual punishments inflicted.

Article the eleventh . . . The enumeration in the Constitution, of certain rights, shall not be construed to deny or disparage others retained by the people.

The last two amendments were designed to assure Anti-Federalist opponents of the new Constitution that the federal government would not usurp the role of the states, and that individuals would retain powers that the Constitution had not vested in the government.

Article the twelfth . . . The powers not delegated to the United States by the Constitution, nor prohibited by it to the States, are reserved to the States respectively, or to the people.

ATTEST,

Frederick Augustus Muhlenberg, Speaker of the House of Representatives

John Adams, Vice-President of the United States, and President of the Senate

John Beckley, Clerk of the House of Representatives.

Sam. A Otis Secretary of the Senate

Source: Bill of Rights. Library of Congress Charters of Freedom website. Accessed January 20, 2015. http://www.archives.gov/exhibits/charters/bill_of_rights_transcript.html.

Timeline of Events

1215
English noblemen convince King John of England to sign the Magna Carta, which will serve as the foundation of representative government and of expectations of due process.

1492
Christopher Columbus discovers the Americas and launches a period of European exploration and colonization that will result in the settlement of North, Central, and South America.

1517
Martin Luther nails 95 theses to the door of the Castle Church in Wittenberg, Germany, initiating the Reformation, which will split the church into Catholic and Protestant divisions that engender centuries of political conflict.

1534
King Henry VIII splits from the Roman Catholic Church and declares himself to be head of the English (Anglican) Church.

1588
The English prevail over an armada of invading ships from Spain.

1603
The first English settlers arrive in Virginia.

1610

Sir Edward Coke argues in the case of Dr. Bonham that even acts of parliament are subject to the dictates of right reason.

1619

Virginia establishes the House of Burgesses, a representative assembly. The first slaves arrive in Virginia.

1620

Puritans arriving on the *Mayflower* draft the Mayflower Compact, which they sign before debarking from their ship.

1630

John Winthrop delivers his "Model of Christian Charity" sermon, which outlines the idea that the colony will be a "city upon a hill" for all the world to see.

1639

The citizens of Connecticut draw up the Fundamental Orders of Connecticut.

1641

The colony of Massachusetts adopts the Body of Liberties.

1649

Charles I of England is beheaded and the nation is governed by a protectorate.

1651

Thomas Hobbes publishes *The Leviathan*, in which he argues for the virtues of a powerful state.

1689

James II flees England and is replaced by William of Orange and his wife, Mary, both Protestants.

1689

Parliament drafts the English Bill of Rights. John Locke publishes his *Second Treatise on Government*.

1692

The Salem Witch Trials result in the executions of those believed to be witches.

1701
William Penn drafts his Charter of Privileges for Pennsylvania.

1701
Judge Samuel Sewell drafts *The Selling of Joseph*, the first antislavery publication in America.

1706
Benjamin Franklin is born.

1729
The Pennsylvania Assembly authorizes the construction of the State House (today's Independence Hall).

1733
Andrew Hamilton defends Peter Zenger for publishing materials critical of the New York governor in a case that is now considered to be a landmark for liberty of the press.

1738
George III is born.

1743
Thomas Jefferson is born.

1751
The Liberty Bell is cast.

1751
James Madison is born.

1754
Representatives from the colonies meet and propose the formation of what is known as The Albany Plan of Union.

1754–1763
The French and Indian War pits Britain and France (and their colonies in America) against one another and results in the British acquisition of Canada.

1755
John Marshall is born.

1760
George III becomes king of Great Britain.

1761
James Otis argues against the British writs of assistance, a form of general warrant that the king had authorized in the colonies.

1763
The British ban settlements west of the Appalachian Mountains.

1763–64
British prosecutions of John Wilkes, a radical member of Parliament, for seditious libel in England stir support for liberty of the press in England and in the American colonies.

1764
The British impose a tax on American sugar.

1765
The British enact a stamp tax on colonial documents and publications.

1765
The Stamp Act Congress meets to protest British taxation of the colonies.

1770
British troops in Boston fire on citizens, killing five, in the Boston Massacre.

1773
Angry colonists throw British tea into the Boston Harbor in what comes to be known as the Boston Tea Party.

1774
The British enact a series of laws that the colonies call the "Intolerable Acts."

1774
The First Continental Congress meets in Philadelphia.

1774
Britain adopts the Quebec Act, which recognizes the rights of Catholics to practice their religion in Canada but stirs fears in other North American colonies, which are largely Protestant.

1774
Thomas Jefferson authors *A Summary View of the Rights of British America*.

1775
Patrick Henry delivers his famous "Give Me Liberty or Give Me Death" speech at St. John's Church in Richmond, Virginia.

1775
Fighting breaks out between the colonists and the British at Lexington and Concord, Massachusetts.

1775
Congress appoints George Washington of Virginia as commander in chief of colonial forces.

1775
Congress sends the Olive Branch Petition to King George III, which he refuses to read.

1776
Thomas Paine, a recent British immigrant, publishes *Common Sense*, advocating independence.

1776
Congress authorizes states to begin drawing up new constitutions.

1776
Virginia draws up its Declaration of Rights.

1776
Thomas Jefferson drafts, and Congress adopts, the Declaration of Independence.

1777
Congress completes its drafting of the Articles of Confederation.

1777
Congress authorizes a flag of 13 stars in a blue background and 13 alternating red and white stripes, recognizing the existing states.

1779
Thomas Jefferson drafts the Virginia Statute for Religious Freedom.

1780
John Adams helps draft a new constitution for Massachusetts.

1781
Maryland's ratification completes state approval of the Articles of Confederation.

1781
Lord Cornwallis surrenders about 8,000 British troops in Yorktown, Virginia, effectively bringing about an end to the Revolutionary War.

1782
Congress finally settles on the design of a Great Seal for the United States.

1783
The Treaty of Paris officially brings the Revolutionary War to an end.

1783
George Washington sends a circular letter to the states pointing to deficiencies in the government under the Articles of Confederation.

1783
George Washington resigns his military commission and returns to private life in Virginia.

1785
Thomas Jefferson publishes his *Notes on the State of Virginia*.

1785
Delegates from Virginia and Maryland meet at Mount Vernon to draw up an interstate compact relative to navigation and commerce.

1786
The Annapolis Convention meets to discuss commerce and issues a call for what will become the U.S. Constitutional Convention.

1786
Largely due to the efforts of James Madison, Virginia adopts its Statute for Religious Liberty, drafted primarily by Thomas Jefferson.

Timeline of Events

1786–1787
A taxpayer revolt known as Shays' Rebellion breaks out in Massachusetts and seems to demonstrate national weakness.

1787
The Constitutional Convention meets in the State House in Philadelphia.

1787
The Virginia delegation introduces a plan not simply to revise, but to replace, the existing Articles of Confederation.

1787
Congress adopts the Northwest Ordinance, specifying how the Northwest Territories will be governed.

1787
The Convention sends a proposed constitution to Congress, which in turn sends it to the states, nine of which must ratify (in special conventions called for this purpose) before it will go into effect.

1787
Federalist supporters of the new Constitution and their Anti-Federalist opponents vigorously debate the merits of the new document in print and in state conventions, which continue into the next year.

1788
The first elections are held under authority of the new Constitution.

1789
The first Congress under the new government meets in New York, and George Washington is inaugurated as first president. He recognizes that all his official acts are likely to set precedents for the future.

1789
Washington chooses Alexander Hamilton as his secretary of the treasury, Thomas Jefferson as his secretary of state, and Edmund Randolph as his attorney general. Conflicts between Jefferson and Hamilton will eventuate in the formation of the first two national political parties, the Democratic-Republicans and the Federalists.

1789

John Jay is named as the first chief justice of the United States.

1789

Congress proposes the Bill of Rights.

1789

Congress adopts the first Judiciary Act, providing for the organization of the federal judicial system.

1789

Congress decides that the president does not need the approval of the Senate to fire cabinet officers.

1789

North Carolina joins the new government.

1790

Rhode Island, which had refused to send delegates to the Constitutional Convention, joins the new government.

1791

The necessary number of states ratify 10 of 12 amendments that Congress proposes, seemingly vindicating Federalist arguments that the new amending process was adequate.

Further Reading

Constitutional Antecedents

Adams, Willi Paul. *The First American Constitutions: Republican Ideology and the Making of State Constitutions in the Revolutionary Era.* Lanham, MD: Rowman & Littlefield, 2001.

Colbourn, H. Trevor. *The Lamp of Experience: Whig History and the Intellectual Origins of the American Revolution.* Chapel Hill: University of North Carolina Press, 1965.

Conley, Patrick T., and John P. Kaminski, eds. *The Constitution and the States: The Role of the Original Thirteen in the Framing and Adoption of the Federal Constitution.* Madison, WI: Madison House, 1988.

Frohmen, Bruce, ed. *The American Republic: Primary Sources.* Indianapolis, IN: Liberty Fund, 2002.

Kendall, Wilmoore, and George W. Carey. *The Basic Symbols of the American Political Tradition.* Reprint, Washington, DC: Catholic University Press, 1995.

Kruman, Marc W. *Between Authority and Liberty: State Constitution Making in Revolutionary America.* Chapel Hill: University of North Carolina Press, 1997.

Kurland, Philip B., and Ralph Lerner. *The Founders' Constitution.* 5 vols. Chicago, IL: University of Chicago Press, 1987.

Lutz, Donald S. *Colonial Origins of the American Constitution: A Documentary History.* Indianapolis, IN: Liberty Fund, 1998.

Lutz, Donald S. *The Origins of American Constitutionalism.* Baton Rouge: Louisiana State University Press, 1988.

Matthews, L.L. "Benjamin Franklin's Plans for Colonial Union, 1750–1775." *American Political Science Review* 8 (August 1914): 393–412.

McIlwain, Charles H. *Constitutionalism: Ancient and Modern.* Ithaca, NY: Cornell University Press, 1947.

Miller, Perry. *The New England Mind: From Colony to Province.* Cambridge, MA: Harvard University Press, 1953.

Pangle, Thomas L. *The Spirit of Modern Republicanism: The Moral Vision of the American Founders and the Philosophy of Locke.* Chicago, IL: University of Chicago Press, 1988.

Pocock, J. G.A. *The Machiavellian Moment: Florentine Political Thought and the Atlantic Republican Tradition.* Princeton, NJ: Princeton University Press, 1975.

Richard, Carl J. *The Founders and the Classics: Greece, Rome, and the American Enlightenment.* Cambridge, MA: Harvard University Press, 1994.

Robbins, Caroline. *The Eighteenth-Century Commonwealthman: Studies in the Transmission, Development and Circumstances of English Liberal Thought from the Restoration of Charles II until the War with the Thirteen Colonies.* Cambridge, MA: Harvard University Press, 1959.

Sandoz, Ellis, ed. *Political Sermons of the American Founding Era, 1730–1805.* Indianapolis, IN: Liberty Fund, 1997.

Stoner, James R. *Common-Law Liberty: Rethinking American Constitutionalism.* Lawrence: University Press of Kansas, 2003.

Tansill, Charles C., compiler. *Documents Illustrative of the Formation of the Union of the American States.* Washington, DC: US Government Printing Office, 1927.

Thorpe, Francis N., ed. *The Federal and State Constitutions, Colonial Charters, and Other Organic Laws of the United States*, 7 vols. Washington, DC: U.S. Government Printing Office, 1907.

Vile, John R. *History of the American Legal System: An Interactive Encyclopedia* (software). Santa Barbara, CA: ABC-CLIO, 2000.

Vile, John R. "Three Kinds of Constitutional Founding and Change: The Convention Method and Its Alternatives." *Political Research Quarterly* 46 (December 1992): 881–895.

Revolutionary and Confederal Periods

Bailyn, Bernard. *The Ideological Origins of the American Revolution.* Cambridge, MA: Belknap Press of Harvard University Press, 1967.

Becker, Carl L. *The Declaration of Independence: A Study in the History of Political Ideas.* New York: Vintage Books, 1970.

Brown, Richard D. "The Founding Fathers of 1776 and 1787: A Collective View." *William and Mary Quarterly*, 34th ser., 33 (July, 1976): 465–480.

Corwin, Edward S. "The Progress of Constitutional Theory between the Declaration of Independence and the Meeting of the Philadelphia Convention." In *American Constitutional History: Essays by Edward S. Corwin*, edited by Alpheus T. Mason and Gerald Garvey. New York: Harper and Row, 1964.

Fiske, John. *The Critical Period of American History, 1783–1789*. Boston: Houghton Mifflin, 1888.

Fleming, Thomas. *Liberty! The American Revolution*. New York: Viking Press, 1997.

Jensen, Merrill. *The Articles of Confederation*. Madison: University of Wisconsin Press, 1966.

Maier, Pauline. *American Scripture: Making the Declaration of Independence*. New York: Alfred A. Knopf, 1997.

McDonald, Forrest, and Ellen Shapiro McDonald. *Confederation and Constitution, 1781–1789*. New York: Harper and Row Publishers, 1968.

Morgan, Edmund S. *The Birth of the Republic, 1763–89*. Rev. ed. Chicago, IL: University of Chicago Press, 1977.

Reid, John P. *Constitutional History of the American Revolution*. 3 vols. Madison: University of Wisconsin Press, 1987–1992.

Tucker, David. *Enlightened Republicanism: A Study of Jefferson's Notes on the State of Virginia*. Lanham, MD: Lexington Books, 2008.

Webking, Robert H. *The American Revolution and the Politics of Liberty*. Baton Rouge: Louisiana State University Press, 1988.

White, Morton, *The Philosophy of the American Revolution*. New York: Oxford University Press, 1978.

Wills, Garry. *Inventing America: Jefferson's Declaration of Independence*. Garden City, NY: Doubleday, 1978.

Wood, Gordon S. *The Creation of the American Republic, 1776–1787*. Chapel Hill: University of North Carolina Press, 1969.

Wood, Gordon S. *The Radicalism of the American Revolution*. New York: Alfred A. Knopf, 1992.

Calling and Convening the Constitutional Convention

Beeman, Richard. *Plain, Honest Men: The Making of the American Constitution*. New York: Random House, 2009.

Berkin, Carol. *A Brilliant Solution: Inventing the American Constitution*. New York: Harcourt, 2002.

Bernstein, Richard B., with Kym S. Rice. *Are We to Be a Nation? The Making of the Constitution*. Cambridge, MA: Harvard University Press, 1987.

Bowen, Catherine Drinker. *Miracle at Philadelphia: The Story of the Constitutional Convention, May to September 1787*. Boston: Little, Brown, 1966.

Bradford, M.E. *Founding Fathers: Brief Lives of the Framers of the United States Constitution*. 2nd ed. Lawrence: University Press of Kansas, 1994.

Collier, Christopher, and James Lincoln Collier. *Decision in Philadelphia: The Constitutional Convention of 1787*. New York: Random House, 1986.

Edling, Max M. *A Revolution in Favor of Government: Origins of the U.S. Constitution and the Making of the American State*. New York: Oxford University Press, 2003.

Farber, Daniel A. "The Constitution's Forgotten Cover Letter: An Essay on the New Federalism and the Original Understanding." *Michigan Law Review* 94 (December 1995): 615–650.

Farrand, Max. *The Framing of the Constitution of the United States*. New Haven, CT: Yale University Press, 1913.

Farrand, Max, ed. *The Records of the Federal Convention of 1787*. 4 vols. New Haven, CT: Yale University Press, 1966.

Finkelman, Paul. *Slavery and the Founders: Race and Liberty in the Age of Jefferson*. Armonk, NY: M. E. Sharpe, 1996.

Gibson, Alan. *Interpreting the Founding: Guide to the Enduring Debates over the Origin and Foundations of the American Republic*. Lawrence: University Press of Kansas, 2006.

Gibson, Alan. *Understanding the Founding: The Crucial Questions*. Lawrence: University Press of Kansas, 2007.

Hendrickson, David D. *Peace Pact: The Lost World of the American Founding*. Lawrence: University Press of Kansas, 2003.

Hobson, Charles F. "The Negative on State Laws: James Madison, the Constitution, and the Crisis of Republican Government." *William and Mary Quarterly*, 3rd ser., 36 (April 1979): 214–235.

Hutson, James H., ed. *Supplement to Max Farrand's The Records of the Federal Convention of 1787*. New Haven, CT: Yale University Press, 1987.

Jillson, Calvin C. *Constitution Making: Conflict and Consensus in the Federal Convention of 1787*. New York: Agathan Press, 1988.

Johnson, Calvin H. *Righteous Anger at the Wicked States: The Meaning of the Founders' Constitution*. New York: Cambridge University Press, 2005.

Ketcham, Ralph. *Framed for Posterity: The Enduring Philosophy of the Constitution*. Lawrence: University Press of Kansas, 1993.

Kiernan, Denise, and Joseph D'Agnese. *Signing Their Rights Away: The Fame and Misfortune of the Men Who Signed the United States Constitution*. Philadelphia: Quirk Books, 2011.

Larson, Edward. *The Return of George Washington: 1783–1789*. New York: William Morrow, 2014.

McDonald, Forrest. *Novus Ordo Seclorum: The Intellectual Origins of the Constitution*. Lawrence: University Press of Kansas, 1985.

Meyers, Marvin, ed. *The Mind of the Founder: Sources of the Political Thought of James Madison*. Indianapolis, IN: Bobbs-Merrill, 1973.

Miller, William L. *The Business of May Next: James Madison and the Founding*. Charlottesville: University Press of Virginia, 1992.

Nelson, Eric. *The Royalist Revolution: Monarchy and the American Founding*. Cambridge, MA: Belknap Press of Harvard University Press, 2014.

Onuf, Peter S. *Statehood and Union: A History of the Northwest Ordinance*. Bloomington: Indiana University Press, 1991.

Robertson, David Brian. *The Constitution and America's Destiny*. New York: Cambridge University Press, 2005.

Robertson, David Brian. *The Original Compromise: What the Constitution's Framers Were Really Thinking*. New York: Oxford University Press, 2013.

Roche, John P. "The Founding Fathers: A Reform Caucus in Action." *American Political Science Review* 55 (December 1961): 799–816.

Rossiter, Clinton. *1787: The Grand Convention*. New York: W. W. Norton, 1966.

Solberg, Winton, ed. *The Federal Convention and the Formation of the Union of American States*. Indianapolis: Bobbs-Merrill, 1958.

St. John, Jeffrey. *Constitutional Journal: A Correspondent's Report from the Convention of 1787*: Ottawa, IL: Jameson Books, 1987.

Stewart, David O. *The Summer of 1787: The Men Who Invented the Constitution*. New York: Simon & Schuster, 2007.

Vile, John R. *The Constitutional Convention of 1787: A Comprehensive Encyclopedia of America's Founding*. 2 vols. Santa Barbara, CA: ABC-CLIO, 2005.

Vile, John R. "The Critical Role of Committees at the Constitutional Convention of 1787." *The American Journal of Legal History* 41 (April 2006): 147–76.

Vile, John R. *The Men Who Made the Constitution: Lives of the Delegates to the Constitutional Convention*. Lanham, MD: Scarecrow Press, 2013.

Vile, John R. *The Wisest Council in the World: Restoring the Character Sketches by William Pierce of Georgia of the Delegates to the Constitutional Convention of 1787*. Athens, GA: University Press of Georgia, 2015.

Vile, John R. *The Writing and Ratification of the U.S. Constitution: Practical Virtue in Action*. Lanham, MD: Rowman & Littlefield, 2012.

Vile, M. J. C. *Constitutionalism and the Separation of Powers*. 2nd ed. Indianapolis: Liberty Fund, 1998.

Debating, Ratifying, Implementing, and Amending the New Constitution

Alexander, John K. *The Selling of the Constitutional Convention: A History of News Coverage*. Madison, WI: Madison House, 1990.

Amar, Akhil Reed. *The Bill of Rights: Creation and Reconstruction*. New Haven, CT: Yale University Press, 1998.

Anderson, Thornton. *Creating the Constitution: The Convention of 1787 and the First Congress*. University Park: Pennsylvania State University Press, 1993.

Bailyn, Bernard, ed. *The Debates on the Constitution: Federalist and Antifederalist Speeches, Articles, and Letters during the Struggle over Ratification*. 2 vols. New York: Library of America, 1993.

Berkin, Carol. *The Bill of Rights: The Fight to Save American Liberties*. New York: Simon & Schuster, 2015.

Boyd, Steven R. *The Politics of Opposition: Antifederalists and the Acceptance of the Constitution*. Millwood, NY: KTO Press, 1979.

Conley, Patrick T., and John P. Kaminski. *The Bill of Rights and the States: The Colonial and Revolutionary Origins of American Liberties*. Madison, WI: Madison House, 1992.

DeRose, Chris. *Founding Rivals: Madison vs. Monroe, The Bill of Rights, and the Election That Saved a Nation*. Washington, DC: Regnery, 2011.

Elkins, Stanley, and Eric McKitrick. "The Founding Fathers: Young Men of the Revolution." *Political Science Quarterly* 76 (June 1961): 181–216.

Elliott, Jonathan, ed. *The Debates in the Several State Conventions on the Adoption of the Federal Constitution*. 5 vols. New York: Burt Franklin, 1988.

Gillispie, Michael Allen, and Michael Lienesch. *Ratifying the Constitution*. Lawrence: University Press of Kansas, 1989.

Goldwin, Robert A. *From Parchment to Power: How James Madison Used the Bill of Rights to Save the Constitution*. Washington, DC: AEI Press, 1997.

Hamilton, Alexander, James Madison, and John Jay. *The Federalist Papers*. New York: New American Library, 1961.

Heideking, Jurgen. *The Constitution before the Judgment Seat: The Prehistory and Ratification of the American Constitution, 1787–1791*, edited by John P. Kaminski and Richard Leffler. Charlottesville: University of Virginia Press, 2012.

Jensen, Merrill et al., eds. *The Documentary History of the Ratification of the Constitution*. 26 vols (ongoing). Madison: State Historical Society of Wisconsin, 1976–.

Kenyon, Cecilia, ed. *The Antifederalists*. Boston: Northeastern University Press, 1984.

Koch, Adrienne. *Jefferson and Madison: The Great Collaboration*. New York: Oxford University Press, 1950.

Labunski, Richard. *James Madison and the Struggle for the Bill of Rights*. New York: Oxford University Press, 2008.

Levy, Leonard W. *Origins of the Bill of Rights*. New Haven, CT: Yale University Press, 2001.

Maier, Pauline. *Ratification: The People Debate the Constitution, 1787–1788*. New York: Simon & Schuster, 2010.

Further Reading

Main, Jackson T. *The Antifederalists: Critics of the Constitution, 1781–1788*. Chicago, IL: Quadrangle Books, 1961.

Morgan, Robert J. *James Madison and the Constitution and the Bill of Rights*. New York: Greenwood Press, 1988.

Morris, Richard B. *Witnesses at the Creation: Hamilton, Madison, Jay, and the Constitution*. New York: New American Library, 1985.

Morton, Joseph C. *Shapers of the Great Debate at the Constitutional Convention of 1787: A Biographical Dictionary*. Westport, CT: Greenwood, 2006.

Rutland, Robert A. *The Birth of the Bill of Rights, 1776–1791*. New York: Collier Books, 1962.

Schultz, Bernard. *The Bill of Rights: A Documentary History*. 2 vols. New York: Chelsea House, 1971.

Siemers, David J. *Antifederalists: Men of Great Faith and Forbearance*. Lanham, MD: Rowman & Littlefield, 2003.

Smith, Craig R. *To Form a More Perfect Union: The Ratification of the Constitution and the Bill of Rights, 1787–1791*. Lanham, MD: University Press of America, 1993.

Storing, Herbert J. *The Complete Anti-Federalist*. 7 vols. Chicago: University of Chicago Press, 1981.

Utley, Robert L., Jr. *Principles of the Constitutional Order: The Ratification Debates*. Lanham, MD: University Press of America, 1989.

Vile, John R. *A Companion to the United States Constitution and Its Amendments*. 6th ed. Santa Barbara, CA: Praeger, 2015.

Index

abolition of slavery, 207
Adams, Abigail, 89–91
Adams, John
   Declaration of Independence and, 100
   Great Seal of the U.S. and, 125
   Resolution of Second Continental Congress and, 89–93
   Treaty of Paris and, 134
   on women's liberty/rights, 89–93
admission of new states
   in Northwest Ordinance, 198–205
   in U.S. Constitution, 245
   in Virginia Plan, 185
advice and consent, 220–221, 241
agricultural society, Jefferson on, 306
Albany Plan of Union, 66–72
amendment process
   Articles of Confederation and, 152–153, 162
   in U.S. Constitution, 246, 296–298
   in Virginia Plan, 185
American independence
   Declaration of, 100–107
   Lee's Resolutions and, 95
   Paine on, 85–88
   See also Revolutionary War
Annapolis Convention Resolution, 157–161, 162–163
antecedents, constitutional, xiii–xiv
Anti-Federalists
   Brutus as spokesman for, 263–271
   Constitutional debate and, 257, 261
   fears of, 45, 224, 234, 329
   Henry as spokesman for, 290–300
   See also Federalists
armies. *See* quartering of troops; standing armies
arms, right to bear, 48, 328
Articles of Compact, Northwest Territory, 198–205
Articles of Confederation, xv, 112–124
   Albany Plan of Union and, 66–67, 112
   Henry on, 293
   Northwest Ordinance under, 190–205
   Treaty of Paris and, 134
   Washington's critique of, 127–132
   weaknesses/defects under, 152–153, 157–174, 181–182
assembly, freedom of, 327
attainder
   bills of, 237, 238, 269
   of treason, 244
authority. *See* executive authority; federal authority; judicial authority; legislative authority

bail, excessive, 329
Baldwin, Abraham, 211, 224
barons, twenty-five, 6–8
Barton, William, 125
Bible
   education and, 204
   Liberty Bell and, 64

Paine and, 83
slavery and, 52–57
bicameralism, 183
bigotry, Washington on, 322–325
Bill of Rights, xix, 326–329
   Anti-Federalists and, 263–271, 302
   common law and, 9
   Jefferson on, 303–304, 306, 309–312
   judiciary and, 309–310
   Madison on, 307–309
   ratification and, 301, 302
   viewed as unnecessary, 257–258, 307–309, 326
   See also English Bill of Rights
bills of attainder, 237, 238, 269
Blackstone, Sir William, 9
Bonham. *See* Dr. Bonham's Case
Boudinot, Elias, 125
boundaries of U.S., in Treaty of Paris, 135
Brearly, David, 218–221
Bricker Amendment, 271
Brutus (for Anti-Federalists), 263–271
Burke, Thomas, 112
Butler, Pierce, 214, 323

cabal and corruption, fear of, 218–225
Canada and Articles of Confederation, 123
charity, Christian, 19–22
Charter of Privileges (Pennsylvania), 58–63
charters
   colonial, 58, 77, 104
   Jefferson on Virginia, 145–146
   Paine and, 87
   See also Magna Carta
checks and balances, 236, 242, 282, 285
Christianity, 19–22, 127, 133
churches, established, 4, 25, 50–51
Cincinnatus, 140
Circuit Courts, 319
Circular to the States (Washington), 127–132
citizenship, defined, 244
"city upon a hill" concept, 21
civilian control of military, 241
civill body politick, 11–12
Coke, Sir Edward, 9–10
commander in chief, 199, 236, 241
commerce, interstate and foreign

   under Articles of Confederation, 152, 157–159, 166–167
   in U.S. Constitution, 235, 237
common law, 9–10, 78
Common Sense (Paine), 83–88
commonwealth, Puritans and, 23
confederal systems of government, 117, 164–174, 290–291
Congress, 229–238
Connecticut, Fundamental Orders of, 23–29
Connecticut Compromise, 218
conscience, liberty of
   in Pennsylvania, 58–60, 62–63
   See also religious freedom
consolidated (unitary) government, 290–291
Constitution, Virginia, 146–150
Constitutional Convention, xvi–xviii
   Annapolis Convention Resolution and, 157–163
   call for prayer in, 194–197
   call for unanimity in, 226–228
   committees of, 218
   Connecticut Compromise in, 218
   Great Compromise in, 192, 208, 215–217
   money bills and, 215–217
   New Jersey Plan and, 187–190
   presidency debate in, 218–225
   rules of, 175–179
   slavery debate in, 206–214
   state legislatures and, 151, 160
   state representation debate in, 191–197
   vices under Articles of Confederation and, 164–174
   Virginia Plan and, 180–186
constitutional debate on ratification, xviii–xix
   Brutus (Anti-Federalist) on, 263–271
   "Grand Constitution" song and, 260–262
   Wilson on, 257–259
   See also Federalist, The
Constitution of the United States, xvii–xviii, 229–249
   advice and consent in, 220–221, 241
   amendment process in, 246, 296–298
   amendments to, 326–329
   bicentennial celebration of, 3
   Bill of Rights in (*see* Bill of Rights)
   checks and balances in, 236, 242
   common law and, 9
   Congress in, 229–238

Index

contract clause in, 238
due process clause in, 328
enumerated powers in, 235–237
establishment clause in, 327
federal power in, 235–237, 246, 270–271
free exercise clause in, 327
fugitive slave clause in, 245
House of Representatives in, 215, 229–230, 232–234
Judiciary in, 242–244
necessary and proper (elastic) clause in, 236–237
"power of the purse" in, 235
Preamble of, 229, 264
President in, 239–242
ratification in, 247
Senate in, 231–234
separation of powers in, 229, 233
signers of, 247–249
states in, 238, 244, 246
supremacy clause in, 246
three-fifths clause in, 230
transmittal to Congress of, 250–252
transmittal to states of, 253
war powers in, 236, 238, 241
as written document, 11
Continental Congresses, xiv
Articles of Confederation and, 112
Declaration and Resolves of First, 73–80
Resolution of Second, 94
contract clause, 238
copyrights, 235
Cornwallis, Charles, 133
corruption, fear of, 218–225
Council of Revision, 184
counsel, right to, 32, 329
covenants, 11, 20
cruel and unusual punishment, 5, 48, 329
currency/money, 165–166, 235

Dayton, Jonathan, 192
death penalty, Puritans and, 35
debts, 136–137, 246
Declaration and Resolves (First Continental Congress), 73–80
Declaration of Independence, 100–107
natural rights and, 73, 77, 96
defense

Albany Plan of Union and, 66–72
Articles of Confederation and, 112–113, 115–118, 181
Washington on, 130–132
demagogues, 284
Democratic-Republican Party, 302
democratic systems of government, 277–281, 291, 298
destiny, Puritan sense of, 21
Dickinson, John, 112–124, 212, 215–216
disputes
under Articles of Confederation, 118–120
in U.S. Constitution, 235, 243, 246, 320–321
District Courts, 319
District of Columbia, 236
double jeopardy, 328
Dr. Bonham's Case, 9–10
Dred Scott decision, 205
due process
Fourteenth Amendment and, 327
Magna Carta basis for, 5
in Pennsylvania, 61–62
Petition of Right and, 17
Puritans and, 31–33
in state constitutions, 267–268
in U.S. Constitution, 328–329
Virginia Declaration of Rights and, 96, 98
Du Simitiere, Pierre Eugene, 125

education, 204, 306
Electoral College, 218–220, 222–223, 239–240
Ellsworth, Oliver, 210, 318
English Bill of Rights, 44–51, 266
enumerated powers, 187, 235–237
E Pluribus Unum, 125–126
equality
Hobbes and Locke on, 37–38
of opportunity vs. results, 19
establishment clause, 327
executive authority
Albany Plan of Union and, 67, 69–70
Locke on, 40
in U.S. Constitution, 220–221, 241–242, 246
Virginia Constitution and, 146
in Virginia Plan, 184
executive branch
Constitutional Convention debate over, 218–225
in New Jersey Plan, 188–189

in U.S. Constitution, 239–242
in Virginia Plan, 184
experience, Dickinson on political, 215–217
ex post facto laws, 237, 238, 269

factions
    under the Articles of Confederation, 171–174
    defined, 274
    Federalist 10 on, 272–282
    Federalist 51 on, 282–289
federal authority
    under Articles of Confederation, 164–170
    in New Jersey Plan, 190
    in Virginia Plan, 180–186
federalism
    in *The Federalist*, 286–288
    in U.S. Constitution, 235–237, 246, 270–271, 290
Federalist, The (Hamilton/Madison/Jay), 239, 257
    No. 10, 238, 272–282
    No. 51, 174, 282–289
    No. 78, 283
Federalists, 175, 234, 326
    Constitutional debate and, 257, 261
    Jefferson and, 302
    See also Anti-Federalists
Federal pillars cartoon, 301
federal systems of government, 244, 286–288, 290
First Amendment, 327
Fourteenth Amendment, 230, 244, 309, 327
Fourth Amendment, 328
Franklin, Benjamin
    Albany Plan of Union and, 66
    call for prayer by, 194–197
    call for unanimity by, 226–228
    Declaration of Independence and, 100
    Federalists and, 261
    Great Seal of the U.S. and, 125
    Join, or Die sketch and, 65
    Treaty of Paris and, 134
free exercise clause, 327
fugitive slave clause, 245
full faith and credit (states), 114, 244
Fundamental Orders of Connecticut, 23–29

George III, King, 101–104
Gerry, Elbridge, 212, 226

"good behavior," judiciary and, 242
Gorham, Nathaniel, 221
government
    confederal systems of, 117, 164–174, 290–291
    consolidated (unitary), 290–291
    democratic, 277–281, 291, 298
    federal systems of, 244, 286–288, 290
    representative (*see* representative government)
    republican form of, 245, 279–282
government, limits on
    Bill of Rights and, 329
    Jefferson on, 304–305
    Locke on, 42–43
government, philosophy of
    Brutus on, 264–266
    Declaration of Independence and, 101
    Hobbes on, 37, 40, 42
    Locke on, 37–43
    Paine on, 83–88
government, state models of, 94
"Grand Constitution" song, 260–262
Great Seal of the United States, 125–126
grievances
    in Declaration and Resolves of First Continental Congress, 73–77, 79–80
    in Declaration of Independence, 101–105
    in English Bill of Rights, 45–46
    Notes on the State of Virginia and, 145–146
    redress of, 327
Guy Fawkes Day celebration, 81

"habeas corpus," 237, 269
Hamilton, Alexander
    at Constitutional Convention, 175, 196
    The Federalist and, 239, 257, 283, 294
    Jefferson and, 306
Hancock, John, 107
Henry, Patrick, 108, 290–300
Hobbes, Thomas, 37–38, 40, 42
Hopkinson, Francis, 125
House of Burgesses, 60
House of Representatives, 215, 229–230, 233–234
Houston, William Churchill, 125
human nature, factions and, 275, 284

impeachment, 242

Index

import/export duties, 237, 238
Inaugural Address (Washington), 313–317
injustice of state laws under Articles of Confederation, 170
inquests, Magna Carta and, 5
insurrections, Jefferson on, 305–306
interest groups. *See* factions
internal (state) violence, 167

James II, King, 44
Jay, John, 134, 272
Jefferson, Thomas
    on Bill of Rights, 303–304, 306, 309–312
    Declaration of Independence by, 100–107
    Great Seal of the U.S. and, 125
    Hamilton and, 306
    on the judiciary, 309
    on liberty and violence, 305–306
    Madison and, 164, 302–306, 309–312
    Notes on the State of Virginia, 142–151
    Virginia Statute for Religious Freedom by, 108–111
John, King, 3
Johnson, Samuel, 52
Join, or Die sketch, 65
judicial authority
    Articles of Confederation and, 118–120
    Bill of Rights and, 309–310
    Locke on, 40
    in U.S. Constitution, 235, 243
    Virginia Constitution and, 146
judicial branch
    in *The Federalist,* 283–284
    Judiciary Act (1789) and, 318–321
    in New Jersey Plan, 189–190
    in U.S. Constitution, 242–244
    in Virginia Plan, 184–185
judicial review
    common law and, 10
    Judiciary Act (1789) and, 320–321
    supremacy clause and, 246
Judiciary Act (1789), 243, 318–321
juries
    Declaration and Resolves of the First Continental Congress and, 78
    English Bill of Rights and, 48
    Magna Carta and, 6–8
    U.S. Constitution and, 243, 328
jurisdiction
    court, in Magna Carta, 5
    federal, 243, 246, 320–321

King, Rufus, 175, 212–213

land disputes in Articles of Confederation, 118
Langdon, John, 213
law of the land, 3–8, 246, 270–271, 328
Leclerc, Georges Louis, 142
Lee, Richard Henry, 95, 100
legislative authority
    Albany Plan of Union and, 67–72
    Articles of Confederation and, 114–115, 115–123, 131–132
    Locke on, 40
    in New Jersey Plan, 187–188, 190
    in U.S. Constitution, 220–221, 235–237
    Virginia Constitution and, 146–150
    in Virginia Plan, 183–184
legislative branch
    Magna Carta and, 6–8
    in New Jersey Plan, 187
    in U.S. Constitution, 229–238
    in Virginia Plan, 183
Leviathan (Hobbes), 37
libertarians, Paine and, 83
liberty
    Anti-Federalists on destruction of, 263–271, 290–300
    English Bill of Rights and, 44–51
    factions and, 273–277, 287–288, 307–309
    of foreigners and strangers, 35
    Magna Carta and, 3–8
    Massachusetts Body of Liberties and, 30–36
    in Northwest Territory, 202–203
    Pennsylvania Charter of Privileges and, 58–63
    Petition of Right and, 13–18
    separation of powers and, 283–286
    symbols of, 64–65, 125–126
    See also rights
Liberty Bell, 64
license/licentiousness
    defined, 294
    vs. liberty, 30, 38

Livingston, Robert, 100
Locke, John, 37–43
Louisiana Territory, 198
Lovell, James, 125

Madison, James
   Bill of Rights and, 307–309, 326
   at the Constitutional Convention, 179, 180, 193, 215, 222, 227–228
   on factions, 171–174, 272–289, 307–309
   The Federalist and, 238, 272
   Jefferson and, 164, 302, 306–309
   on vices under the Articles of Confederation, 164–174
   Virginia Statute for Religious Freedom and, 108
   Washington's address by, 313
Magna Carta, 3–8, 15–16, 266
majority, overbearing, 273–277, 307–309
Mannahoacs (Native Americans), 142–143
Marbury v. Madison, 320
Marshall, John, 236, 320
Martin, Luther, 191–192
Marx, Karl, 275
Maryland, Articles of Confederation and, 112
Mason, George
   at Constitutional Convention, 209–210, 223, 226
   Virginia Declaration of Rights by, 96–99
Massachusetts Body of Liberties, 30–36
Mayflower Compact, 11–12
McCulloch v. Maryland, 236
Middleton, Arthur, 125
militias
   in U.S. Constitution and, 236, 241, 295
   Virginia Declaration of Rights and, 99
Mississippi River, Treaty of Paris and, 138
"Model of Christian Charity, A" (Winthrop), 19–22
Monacans (Native Americans), 142–143
monarchy
   Henry on, 291, 299–300
   Madison on, 308
   Paine on, 84–85, 88
money. *See* currency/money
money bills, 215, 233
Montesquieu, Baron of, 272
Morris, Gouverneur
   at Constitutional Convention, 206–208, 213, 222–223, 224

   Preamble and, 229
   transmittal letter to Congress, 250
multiplicity of state laws, 169–170
mutability of state laws, 170

Native Americans
   Jefferson in, 142–145
   in Northwest Ordinance, 204
naturalization
   in New Jersey Plan, 190
   in U.S. Constitution, 235
natural rights
   Brutus on, 264–265
   Declaration of Independence and, 73, 77, 101
   Paine on, 88
   religious freedom as, 108–110
   Sewall and, 53
   Virginia Declaration of Rights and, 96–99
nature. *See* human nature; state of nature
necessary and proper (elastic) clause, 236–237
New England Confederation, 66
New Jersey Plan, 187–190, 220
"noble savages" (Rousseau), 143
Northwest Ordinance, 198–205
"no taxation without representation"
   Declarations and Resolves of First Continental Congress and, 73, 78
   District of Columbia and, 236
   English Bill of Rights and, 47
   Magna Carta foundation of, 4
   Petition of Right and, 17
   U.S. Constitution and, 235
   Virginia Declaration of rights and, 97–98
Notes on the State of Virginia (Jefferson), 142–151

oaths of office, 241, 319–320
opportunity, equality of, 19

Paine, Thomas, *Common Sense*, 83–88
"Palladium of Columbia" song, 260–262
pardons, 241
Parliament
   colonial grievances against, 103–104
   composition of, 44
   Magna Carta and, 6–8

Index

Petition of Right and, 13
supremacy of, 9
Paterson, William, 187
Pendleton, Edmund, 96
Penn, William, 58
Pennsylvania, Charter of Privileges of, 58–63
Perot, Ross, 3
petition, right of
   English Bill of Rights and, 47
   in U.S. Constitution, 327
Petition of Right, 13–18
Philadelphia, Albany Plan of Union and, 68
Pinckney, Charles, 175, 210, 213, 222–223
Pinckney, Charles Cotesworth, 210–211
piracy, 235
post office and roads, 235
"power of the purse," 235
Powhatans (Native Americans), 142–143
prayer at Constitutional Convention, 194–197
Preamble to U.S. Constitution, 229, 264
precedent, Petition of Right and, 13
President
   Constitutional Convention debate over, 218–225
   impeachment and, 242
   powers of, 234, 241–242
   qualifications for, 240
   structure and elections of, 239–241
   succession of, 240
press, freedom of
   in U.S. Constitution, 327
   Virginia Declaration of Rights and, 99
privileges and immunities (states), 244
Privy Council, 14
probable cause, 328
property
   factions and, 275–276
   just compensation for, 328
   Locke on, 37, 40
   Native Americans and, 204
   slaves as, 206–207
   Treaty of Paris and confiscation of, 136–137
proportionate representation. *See* representation, proportionate
proprietary colonies, 58
Providence
   Franklin and, 194–197

invoked by officials, 314–315
   Seixas on, 323
   Washington on, 127–128
public good
   factions and, 273–277
   Locke on, 37–43
   republican government and, 279
   separation of powers and, 282
public virtue and public happiness, 316
Publius (for Federalists), 272
punishment
   cruel and unusual, 5, 48, 329
   Puritans and, 33
Puritans
   Christian charity and, 19–22
   Fundamental Orders of Connecticut and, 23–29
   liberty and, 30–36
   Mayflower Compact of, 11
purse, congressional power of, 235

Quakers, 58
quartering of troops
   English Bill of Rights and, 45
   Petition of Right and, 15–16
   in U.S. Constitution, 328
quorums at Constitutional Convention, 176

Randolph, Edmund
   in convention debates, 196–197, 214, 216–217, 222, 225
   ratification and, 226
   Virginia Plan and, 164, 180
ratification
   under Articles of Confederation, 169, 182
   Bill of Rights and, 301, 302
   in U.S. Constitution, 247
   see also constitutional debate on ratification, 247
Read, George, 214
Reagan Ronald, 21
recess appointments
   in Articles of Confederation, 120
   in U.S. Constitution, 242
religious freedom, establishment and
   Articles of Confederation and, 124
   Magna Carta and, 4
   Puritans and, 30, 35–36

in U.S. Constitution, 327
Virginia Statute for Religious Freedom and, 108–111
religious freedom, free exercise of
    in Northwest Territory, 202–203
    in Pennsylvania, 58–60, 62–63
    in U.S. Constitution, 247, 327
    in Virginia Declaration of Rights, 99
    Washington on, 81, 322–325
"Remember the Ladies" (Adams), 89–91
representation, proportionate, in Virginia Plan, 182
representation, state
    Constitutional Convention debate over, 191–197
    in New Jersey Plan, 187
representative government
    Albany Plan of Union and, 66–72
    under the Articles of Confederation, 171
    in the colonies, 60–61
    Congress as, 229–237
    Fundamental Orders of Connecticut and, 24, 27
    in the Northwest Territory, 200–202
    in Virginia, 145–151
    See also republican form of government
reprieves and pardons, 241
republican form of government
    factions and, 279–280
    federalism and, 286–288
    size and, 280–282, 286–288
    in U.S. Constitution, 245
    in Virginia Plan, 185
Republicanism, 261
Resolution of Second Continental Congress, 94
revenue bills, 233
revolution, right of, 42, 97, 100–101
revolutionary spirit, Henry on, 295–296
Revolutionary War, xv
    Common Sense and, 83–88
    Declaration and Resolves of the First Continental Congress and, 75–80
    Declaration of Independence and, 100–107
    Guy Fawkes Day and, 81–82
    Lee's Resolutions and, 95
    Resolution of Second Continental Congress and, 94
    sovereignty and, 11
"riding circuit," 319
rights
    English Bill of, 44–51
    English subjects and, 77–80
    Petition of, 13–18
    Virginia Declaration of, 96–99
    See also Bill of Rights; natural rights
Rousseau, Jean-Jacques, 143
royal colonies, 58
rule of law, Paine on, 88
Rutledge, John, 125, 213

Salem Witch Trials, 35
sanctions and coercion under Articles of Confederation, 167–168
Scott, John Morin, 125
scutage, 4
Seal of the United States, Great, 125
search and seizure, 328
security
    Albany Plan of Union and, 66–72
    Articles of Confederation and, 112–113, 115–118, 181
    Washington on, 130–132
Seixas, Moses, 322–324
self-government. *See* representative government
self-incrimination, 328
Selling of Joseph, The (Sewall), 52–57
Senate, 231–234
Seneca Falls Convention, 92
separation of church and state
    in Magna Carta, 4
    in Virginia Statute for Religious Freedom, 108–111
separation of powers
    common law and, 9
    Declaration and Resolves of the First Continental Congress and, 79
    in *The Federalist,* 272, 282–288
    Jefferson and, 302
    Madison on factions and, 174
    in the Northwest Territory, 199
    Puritans and, 23–24
    in U.S. Constitution, 220, 229, 233
    Virginia Constitution and, 148–149
    Virginia Declaration of Rights and, 97
    Virginia Plan and, 183–184
sermons
    "A Model of Christian Charity" (Winthrop), 19–22
servants, liberties/rights of, 34
Seventeenth Amendment, 231

Index

Sewall, Samuel, 52–57
Shays' Rebellion, 162, 167, 261, 305
Sherman, Roger, 100, 194, 196, 208, 214, 222
"shining city upon a hill" concept, 21
Sixteenth Amendment, 237
slavery
   colonial grievances and, 104
   compromise on, 214
   Constitutional Convention debate on, 206–214
   Northwest Ordinance and, 205
   Sewall's case against, 52–57
   trade and, 209–210
   in U.S. Constitution, 230, 237, 245
social contract, Locke on, 37–43
sovereignty, American Revolution and, 11
speech, freedom of
   for legislators, 28, 48, 115
   in U.S. Constitution, 327
standing armies
   Declaration and Resolves of the First Continental Congress and, 79
   English Bill of Rights and, 45, 47
   Henry on, 298–299
   in state constitutions, 268–269
   U.S. Constitution and, 328
   Virginia Declaration of Rights and, 99
state of nature
   Brutus on, 264–266
   Locke on, 37–39
   Washington and, 132
State of the Union, 242
states, obligations of
   Articles of Confederation and, 113–117
   in U.S. Constitution, 238, 244
states, restrictions on, 238, 246
states, rights of
   Albany Plan of Union and, 71
   Anti-Federalists and, 263
   Articles of Confederation and, 112–113, 117
   in Bill of Rights, 329
   debate over representation by state and, 191–197
   Henry on, 290–300
   Jefferson on compromise over, 303
suffrage
   John Adams on, 92–93
   Virginia Constitution and, 147
   Virginia Declaration of Rights and, 97
Sullivan, James, 89, 91
Summary View of the Rights of British America, A (Jefferson), 105
supermajority requirement in Articles of Confederation and, 122
supremacy clause, 246, 270–271, 313
Supreme Court, 242–243, 318–319
symbols of liberty, 64–65, 125–126

taxation
   Henry on, 299
   in U.S. Constitution, 235, 237
   See also "no taxation without representation"
term limits, 304–305
Territories in U.S. Constitution, 245
Thirteenth Amendment, 230, 245
Thomson, Charles, 125
three-fifths clause, 230
titles of nobility, 238, 269
treason, 244
Treaty of Paris, 133–139
trials
   Puritans and, 32–33
   in U.S. Constitution, 328–329
troops
   quartering of British, 15–16, 45, 328
   Treaty of Paris and British, 137–138
Twelfth Amendment, 239
Twenty-Fifth Amendment, 240
Twenty-First Amendment, 246
Twenty-Seventh Amendment, 327
Two Treatises of Government (Locke), 37–43
tyranny
   of the majority, 273–277, 307–308, 311
   of rulers, 290–300

unicameralism, 187
unitary government, 290–291

Veto power of President, 234
Vice President, 220–222, 240
Virginia
   Constitution of, 146–150
   Declaration of Rights, 96–99

Notes on the State of, 142–151
   ratifying convention of, 290–300
Virginia Plan, 180–186
   basis of, 164
   presidency in, 218, 220, 283
voting qualifications. *See* suffrage

Ward, Nathaniel, 30
war powers, 236, 238, 241
warrants, search, 328
Washington, George
   Circular to the States of, 127–132
   Constitutional Convention and, 157, 175
   Federalists and, 261
   Guy Fawkes Day and, 81
   Inaugural Address of, 313–317
   letter of, to Moses Seixas, 324–325
   resignation of commission by, 140–141
   transmittal of Constitution to Congress and, 250–251
Watson, Gregory, 327
"We the People," 229
William and Mary (king and queen), 44, 49–50
Williamson, Hugh, 192–193, 196, 212, 224
Wilson, James
   at Constitutional Convention, 193–194, 211–212, 224–225
   on U.S. Constitution, 257–259, 302–303
Winthrop, John, 19–22
witnesses, right to confront, 329
women, liberties/rights of
   Abigail and John Adams on, 89–93
   Puritans and, 34
Wythe, George, 175

Yates, Robert, 263

About the Author

John R. Vile, PhD, is professor of political science and dean of the University Honors College at Middle Tennessee State University. He has written and edited a variety of books on legal issues, the U.S. Constitution, and the American Founding Period, including *Conventional Wisdom: The Alternative Article V Mechanism for Proposing Amendments to the U.S. Constitution* (forthcoming); *The United States Constitution: One Document, Many Choices* (2015); *A Companion to the United States Constitution and Its Amendments*, 6th ed. (2015); *The Wisest Council in the World: Restoring the Character Sketches by William Pierce of Georgia of the Delegates to the Constitutional Convention of 1787* (2015*); Encyclopedia of Constitutional Amendments, Proposed Amendments, and Amending Issues, 1789–2015* (2015); *Re-Framers: 170 Eccentric, Visionary, and Patriotic Proposals to Rewrite the U.S. Constitution* (2014); *The United States Constitution: Questions and Answers*, 2nd ed. (2014); *Essential Supreme Court Decisions: Summaries of Leading Cases in U.S. Constitutional Law*, 16th ed. (2014); *The Men Who Made the Constitution: Lives of the Delegates to the Constitutional Convention* (2013); *Encyclopedia of the Fourth Amendment* (2013); *The Writing and Ratification of the U.S. Constitution: Practical Virtue in Action* (2012); *Encyclopedia of the First Amendment* (2009); *James Madison: Founder, Philosopher, Founder and Statesman* (2008); *The Encyclopedia of Civil Liberties in America* (2005); *The Constitutional Convention of 1787: A Comprehensive Encyclopedia of America's Founding* (2005); *Great American Judges: An Encyclopedia* (2003); *Great American Lawyers: An Encyclopedia* (2001); and *History of the American Legal System: Interactive Encyclopedia* (CD-ROM, 2000).